BETTING *on* FREEDOM

BETTING *on* FREEDOM

My Life in the Church

CARDINAL ANGELO SCOLA
With LUIGI GENINAZZI

TRANSLATED BY CARLO LANCELLOTTI

The Catholic University of America Press
Washington, DC

Originally published as *Ho scommesso sulla libertà: Autobiographia*
© 2018 RCS MediaGroup S.p.A., Milan

English translation copyright © 2021
The Catholic University of America Press
All rights reserved
The paper used in this publication meets the minimum requirements of American
National Standards for Information Science—Permanence of Paper for Printed Library
Materials, ANSI Z39.48–1984.
∞

Library of Congress Cataloging-in-Publication Data

Names: Scola, Angelo, interviewee. | Geninazzi, Luigi, 1947- interviewer. | Lancellotti,
    Carlo, 1965- translator.
Title: Betting on freedom : my life in the church / Cardinal Angelo Scola with Luigi
    Geninazzi ; translated by Carlo Lancellotti.
Other titles: Ho scommesso sulla libertà.
English Description: Washington, DC : The Catholic University of America Press,
    2021. | «Originally published as Ho scommesso sulla libertà: Autobiographia, 2018
    RCS MediaGroup S.p.A., Milan.» | Includes bibliographical references and index.
Identifiers: LCCN 2021029894 (print) | LCCN 2021029895 (ebook) |
    ISBN 9780813234274 (paperback) | ISBN 9780813234281 (ebook)
Subjects: LCSH: Scola, Angelo,--Interviews. | Cardinals--Italy--Biography.
Classification: LCC BX4705.S5145 A5 2021 (print) | LCC BX4705.S5145 (ebook) |
    DDC 282.092 [B]--dc23
LC record available at https://lccn.loc.gov/2021029894
LC ebook record available at https://lccn.loc.gov/2021029895

To the People of God that has been entrusted to me

and which confirmed my faith

Contents

Preface to the First Edition

Having kept hardly any written record of that which Providence has given me to live during my now-long existence, I felt the need to write one down now, first of all for my own sake. In the end, after speaking with some friends, I let myself be persuaded to make the result public. Hence this peculiar autobiography. I chose the form of a dialogue because it may be easier on the reader, and is a helpful way of communicating various stories and ideas that have characterized my years. The dialogue is with Luigi Geninazzi, my countryman from Lecco. Our long-standing professional relationship, marked by deep friendship, ensures the objectivity of the work. Geninazzi has worked as a reporter for *Avvenire*, especially in Eastern Europe. After covering the experience of Solidarity, he wrote about the significance and the consequences of the fall of the Iron Curtain, the collapse of the Soviet Union, and the wars and revolutions in the Middle East. Before becoming a journalist, he was a philosophy teacher. He took upon himself the writing of this interview.

This volume contains several episodes, from my childhood up to the present, and also some short digressions on certain important topics for the life of the Church and of society. Yet this work has a fragmentary character. Many topics, and also many names of people I met, are missing.

Here I want to say something about the two poles on which the book hinges. The first is freedom, a factor that has dramatically interested me since adolescence. Every man, for the duration of his life, dialogues with a great X that directs his journey, just as the banks of a raging river determine its flow, prevent it from overflowing, and lead it to the sea. This X is the inescapable question of the meaning [*senso*] of life. People use this expression a lot, but do not always appreciate its double meaning. The Italian word *senso* means both "meaning" and "direction." Why to live, in other words, and what roads to take in order to reach one's fulfillment.

The Gospels are filled with facts, stories, and reflections about freedom as the embrace that Christ constantly offers to man. In the Gospel of John, Jesus says, "Those who follow me will be free." As a Christian, I am convinced that the Christian proposal will be able to show its power to fulfill, to make happy, the whole human community only if it again begins to address the freedom of today's man, starting with children.

The second pole that underpins many of the considerations in this book is the desire to document the beauty and lovability of the Holy Church, in the wake of "Him who loved us first." Many saints and great authors have poured this peculiar love into their writings. Personally, when I was about twenty years old, I was moved by the reflections in the book *The Splendor of the Church* by the theologian Cardinal Henri de Lubac. Can we still talk about beauty and lovability if we look realistically at the current situation of this old boat rocked by stormy waves? I am not thinking only of the behavior of her "personnel" (including bishops and consecrated people), of the often-revolting mistakes and crimes before our eyes. . . . The interview includes some attempt to dig deeper and explain the roots of these evils.

Where does the Church stand, under the guidance today of an unconventional pope, who is a "sign of contradiction" for the people of God? In a context that quite a few people describe as post-Christian, do not the divisions among Catholics that have arisen especially in the last few years compromise the Church's ability to address man's freedom, which I mentioned earlier?

Here I must describe the ongoing dialectics in a few words. Two ways of conceiving the faith coexist, and often clash, in the Church. The first tends to reduce Christianity to a mere civil religion, demanding that it serves as glue for a fragmented society full of problems and contradictions. The second proposes that we go back to the purity of the Gospel by picking up the cross of Christ for the salvation of "every other." Period and full stop. From such a perspective, being concerned, for example, about the so-called new rights, about the way in which our pluralistic society acts and legislates about them, is a distraction from Christ's authentic message of mercy.

I am convinced that neither one of these two interpretations of faith expresses adequately the true nature of Christianity or its public dimension. The first position falls short because it reduces Christianity to its secular aspect, cutting it off from the original strength of the Christian subject. The second fails because it deprives the faith of its carnal reality.

Personally, I think that today the path of the Church is a narrow one. To use an image which is familiar to me, I would like to call it the path along the ridge, running between the two slopes I just described. I cannot forget my youthful climbs to the top of the Grigna along the Segantini ridge. Only a few people at a time can walk along it! The "path along the ridge" for us means proposing the event of Christ in its wholeness, irreducible to any human party. How can we do that? The ecclesial subject can make explicit all the implication of faith by living its mysteries integrally. Then one discovers how faith mingles with the human vicissitudes of every age, demonstrating the beauty and fruitfulness of life in the Church. For example, if I am convinced that the family is the union of a man and a woman—stable, faithful, and open to life—and I do not insert this conviction of mine into the public debate, first of all through witness, I deprive society of something. The common good is reached not by subtraction but only with the patient and untiring contribution of all and everybody.

Pope Francis never stops emphasizing gladness in his teaching. If today's European people, who often forget Christ, had the possibility of glimpsing even from afar the fullness of freedom that is at the heart of the Christian experience, they would come running back to the Church.

† Angelo Cardinal Scola
Imberido di Oggiono, May 10, 2018
Feast of the Ascension of the Lord

Acknowledgments

I must express my gratitude to all those who collaborated directly in this book's final writing.

To my interviewer, first of all, for doggedly challenging me and patiently indulging me.

To Micaela Pirola, for carefully assisting me in multiple revisions of the manuscript.

To Msgr. Gabriel Richi Alberti, my long-time theological collaborator, for precious suggestions and for reminding me of several facts mentioned in this book.

To Maria Laura Conte, my press secretary and spokeswoman when I was in Venice, for carefully reading the manuscript and making astute and pertinent comments.

To Carla Gianella, my secretary of over thirty years, for contacting all the necessary parties for fact-checking, and for managing the graphic design of the manuscript with her customary accuracy.

What Future for Christians?

Two Years Later

The decision by the publisher to release a new edition of this book, only two years after the original publication, will no doubt provoke a question from readers, which, in fact, I share. Since this is a book in which biography is intertwined with elements of Italian Church history from the last few decades, what happened over this time that is so relevant it deserves to be mentioned?

On the personal level, I am progressively adapting to this new stage of my life. Perhaps I am learning to grow old a bit, to come to terms with my increasing frailty, and to accept the inevitable struggle with death. This struggle looms more and more in my daily life, but it does not weaken my burning prayer that the struggle be won by the desire to see the face of God and to access the life of the Trinity, the House with so many open doors.

On the ecclesial level, I am more and more convinced of the lovability of the Church, for which I intend to spend what energies are left. Indeed, without the Church—which is the "person" par excellence, always to be distinguished from her "personnel," to use the words of Jacques Maritain—the imposing presence of Christ dissolves and human freedom is left prey to its limited possibilities.

Regarding my person and my actions, there is no need to add anything to what was said in the previous edition. However, the situation of the Church, which is undoubtedly convulsive, demands that we verify that adjective—"lovable"—of which I remain deeply convinced.

Is the Catholic Church in Decline?

So, how far is the Church through the storm that it seems to be crossing? From the numerical standpoint, the ongoing erosion of

Catholicism and, more generally, of religious belief in Europe and in America, is undeniable. The category of the "nones"—that is, those who answer "none" when asked about their religion—seems to be growing, so much so that some observers are starting to wonder whether agnosticism may end up becoming the "first religion" of the Western world. According to the predictions, ten years from now the "nones" may reach between 25 and 30 percent, which would make them the relative majority, surpassing both Catholics and Protestants, both at 22 percent.

However, sociological analyses always give ambivalent signals. We commonly talk about the collapse of the Church in Europe, but there are countries like Poland, and to some extent also Italy, were a significant percentage of religious practice endures. Moreover, even though it is true that the number of the baptized keeps growing in the developing countries, in Latin America many Catholics are migrating to evangelical sects. In Asia, adult catechumens are increasing in newly evangelized countries like Korea, but in the Philippines, religious practice is clearly declining.

The most common judgment is that the crisis is serious and deep, of a kind that, according to some observers, occurs in the history of the Church every five hundred years. For example, the scholar of religions Jean-François Colosimo argues, "The current earthquake resembles, because of its systemic character, the crisis of the heresies of the fourth century, that of the investitures of the eleventh century, that of indulgences in the fifteenth century. Every time there was moral disorder. Every time the catastrophe came not from the outside, but from the inside. Every time the crisis hit the institution hard, and this time it is concentrating more than ever on the Curia and the clergy."[1]

To me the idea that the crisis has a cyclical character, like geophysical movements, seems a stretch that ignores how different the events just mentioned are. The struggle over the investitures, which was clearly political, cannot be compared to the phenomenon of heresies. Perhaps it would be better to narrow down the historical consideration to the most recent "systemic crisis," that of the Protestant Reformation—which was not just about indulgences, though, but involved the interpretation of the sacred Scriptures, the structure of the sacraments, and the Petrine ministry, touching essential factors for the life of the Church. However, in the current situation, we are not dealing with a "Protestantization" of Catholicism, but more precisely with a falling into "worldliness." This term was defined already by the theologian Cardinal Henri de Lubac in his book *The Splendor of the Church,* as a gradual acceptance of the mentality of this world, "a crafty humanism that is the enemy of the living God (and in secret equally the enemy of man)."[2]

Here lies the deep root of what the news often put in front of our eyes—scandals, crimes, and aberrant behaviors, like child abuse, committed even by consecrated people. Indeed, if we stop relying on grace and live "as if God did not exist," slowly but surely personal morality will also crumble and fall apart.

The Discernment of Pope Francis

We are thus led to reflect on the meaning of the word "crisis." On this theme I found some very astute observations in the book *Brief Apology for a Catholic Moment* by French philosopher Jean-Luc Marion. According to Marion, the fact that by now the crisis seems to affect every aspect of society means that this society is no longer able to reform itself.[3] Therefore, we should speak of failure more than crisis. In fact, as the Greek etymology of the word suggests, a crisis is an occasion to judge and to discern, which implies the act of making a decision. From this perspective, today's society is characterized not by a crisis, but by the total absence of a crisis, that is, by the lack of a resolutive judgment. We are not in a crisis; we are in a state of decline.

Unlike other institutions that cannot admit their weakness, the Church finds itself by nature in a permanent state of "authentic crisis," because it does not draw its strength from itself but must constantly opt for Christ. Therefore, *Ecclesia semper est reformanda,* "the Church must always reform itself." As Pope Francis recalled in his *Address to the Roman Curia* in December 2019, changing is converting, because "Christian life is a journey . . . a summons to discover the movement of the heart, which, paradoxically, has to set out in order to remain, to change in order to be faithful." In this context, the pope has been talking again about discernment, a core theme of his magisterium, in order to face the challenges of the present time which *"is not simply an epoch of changes, but an epochal change.*"[4] However, discernment does not mean a more or less intelligent analysis capable of explaining the complexity of reality, and even less can it be reduced to various attempts at untying some of its complicated knots. Discernment aims at forming a judgment about reality that starts every time from a certainty, from a renewed decision for Christ, in order to illuminate circumstances and situations. As is written in *Evangelii Gaudium,* "each truth is better understood when related to the harmonious totality of the Christian message."

Pope Francis's goal is to jolt us out of complacency by calling into question established habits and behaviors, also inside the Church, raising the bar every time, so to speak. This can produce some bewilderment and even emotional turmoil. But the ever harsher and more insolent attacks against the pope's person, especially those that come from inside the Church, are wrong. From childhood, I learned that "the Pope is the Pope," to whom a Catholic believer owes affection, respect, and obedience, as the visible sign and secure guarantee of the unity of the Church following Christ. Communion with the successor of Peter is not a matter of cultural affinity, human sympathy, or sentimental feeling, but concerns the very nature of the Church.

I often say that each pope must be "learned" in his style and his deepest logic. Well, this learning process is even more necessary with respect to a Latin American pontiff, whose mindset and type of approach are different from those of us Europeans. In fact, something of this kind happened already with John Paul II, who showed himself from the first day to be an absolutely innovative, and I daresay unprecedented, personality in the history of the Church. I view as truly admirable and moving Pope Francis's extraordinary capacity to come close to everybody, in particular the marginalized, those who suffer most from the "throwaway culture," as he often reminds us in his zeal to communicate the Gospel to the world.

Threatened by Schism?

Some people foresee dark scenarios for a Church that is allegedly threatened by schism. Polemics and divisions—which grow ever sharper, even at the expense of truth and charity—concern me. I do not see the risk of a schism, but I fear that we are moving backward.

To those who think that the Church has fallen behind, I respond that we are rather going backwards, specifically back to the epoch of the debates between conservatives and progressives after the council. I am seeing a renewed opposition, with much overexcitement, between the guardians of tradition as rigidly understood and the proponents of conforming practices, but also doctrine, to worldly demands.

According to the former, post-conciliar innovations caused the loss of believers. According to the latter, an insufficient response to the expectations of society was, instead, the main reason why people left the Church. These two opposing visions, which are coming back in more radical terms, are largely responsible for the state of confusion in which many Catholics live today, and not just simple believers. This saddens me because during the years of my episcopal ministry, I had the impression that people were moving past that fruitless opposition, that they sincerely wanted to talk to each other, but above all, that there was a renewed ability to work together in the various spheres of the ecclesial community and social engagement, beyond partisan labels that by then seemed old and worn out. Today, unfortunately, I must recognize that not only has that progress been interrupted, but that it is quickly being reversed. The "synodal path" that has started in the German Church seems to me the most glaring and baffling example of this leap backward. It attempts to discuss, and approve in a binding way, local-level decisions, including those of a doctrinal nature, that can be made only on the level of the universal Church. But the Spirit does not let himself be reined in by a partisan mindset, as we have been able to observe also in the very recent post-synodal exhortation *Querida Amazonia*.

The Italian Situation

To focus on the Italian situation, but perhaps of the whole "northwestern" area, I am afraid that the two diametrically opposed cultural interpretations of the faith which I discuss in this book are becoming radicalized.

The first interpretation reduces Christianity to mere civil religion, a sort of ethical glue for a fragmented society, but also to a constitutive factor of the national and European tradition. For many people this goes hand in hand with a doctrinaire defense of the mysteries of the faith. It is a rigidly identitarian form of Catholicism which intends to reaffirm religious values in the secular sphere, even apart from the experience of faith of people and communities in the Church. As the historian of religions Olivier Roy has pointed out, this position "gives value to what is primarily cultural in Christianity, to the detriment of the element of faith, which is tantamount to secularizing what is left of the Catholic tradition in our society."[5]

It is not coincidental that such an interpretation is used on the cultural and political level as a form of defense against the Islamic "invasion." It is true that, from a historical standpoint, Europe's Catholic identity established itself in opposition to the advance of Islam in the Mediterranean and on the European continent. This means, however, that there is no sharp boundary between us and them: Europe and Islam have always been in relation. The relationship is complicated and often very conflictual, but we must not overlook the fact that whole chunks of Europe—ideas, buildings, institutions— have been transplanted in the Middle East and in North Africa and vice versa. We must find a new capacity for dialogue, as stated by the *Document on Human Fraternity* signed by Pope Francis and by the Great Imam of Al-Azhar. This document does not just talk about the need for dialogue but invites us to transform the relationship between Christians and Muslims into a paradigm of civic friendship valid for everyone. The challenge Christians must face today consists, then, in rediscovering forms of communal life that do not become self-referential aggregations, pathologically closed to dialogue with the other. Otherwise, if identity is not conceived dynamically, intelligently, and welcomingly, the proclaimed defense of the Christian identity risks being a mere abstract affirmation of values.

The second, subtler, interpretation tends instead to reduce Christianity to the announcement of the pure and naked Cross for the salvation of every other human being. What matters then is taking upon ourselves needs and problems whenever they surface (mass immigration, climate change, social exclusion, etc.), in the name of acceptance and openness to the other. Allegedly, this is the only distinctive public character of the action of believers, who otherwise act like everyone else. Faith as such has nothing to say about the questions and the solutions under debate in public opinion. As a result, a great attention to social themes is matched by an almost complete indifference to ethical questions, which supposedly divide and tear apart social co-existence. Such an attitude produces what we might call a "crypto-diaspora," meaning a dispersion of Christians within society which ends up hiding the human relevance of faith as such.

Against the reductionism of these interpretations (the first, reducing Christianity to its cultural and secular dimension, the second, depriving the faith of its carnal consistency), I believe that today, the Church must follow the path that I have called a narrow ridge between these two slopes. This is the path of proposing Christianity as an event that is relevant to the complexities of human life, the path of witness by an ecclesial community that lives the mysteries of faith, trying to make explicit all their anthropological, social, and cosmological implications. In this way, Christianity becomes an experience which, by mingling with the vicissitudes of every day and every age, demonstrates the beauty and fruitfulness of faith for everybody. For example, if I believe that man is created in the image and likeness of God and is saved by Christ, I will hold a certain conception of life and death, of marriage and family, of how to use things, and the like. Witnessing the practical implications of faith is an obligatory task of every believer, from the pope to the simplest believer. If this personal and communal witness fades away or grows weaker, the power of the Christian announcement is diminished and the image of the Church gets obfuscated, reduced to a social agency like countless others that exist in our world. It is not just the ecclesial community that suffers in this case, but all of society, which loses the unique contribution of Christians to the construction of the common good. This latter, in fact, is reached not by subtraction, but with the patient and untiring contribution of all religious, social, and civil actors, which must strive, as Paul Ricoeur used to say, for "mutual recognition."

An Organic Proposal of the Faith

We must admit that today, the Church as whole struggles to present itself as an organic proposal of faith, incarnated in a community capable of transmitting the encounter with Christ. An emblematic and dramatic manifestation of this is the Church's lack of appeal to young people. A study of youth religiosity in Europe shows that the "nones" (turning again to this definition of nonreligious people) are the absolute majority, 55 percent, although with strong variations between countries, from a record of 91 percent in the Czech Republic to a minimum of 17 percent in Poland. In Italy, the "nones" are less than one out of four among the young, of whom 52 percent declare themselves Catholic. However, 60 percent of the people interviewed answer "little or nothing" when asked about the importance of the religious dimension in their lives. The agnosticism of today's young people is very different from that of their parents, as the philosopher Massimo Borghesi has pointed out. Whereas the dominant attitude towards religion among the 1968 generation is skepticism, "for today's young people being agnostic means knowing nothing about God and Christianity. They are not opposed to faith, even though they are not exempt from the prejudices coming from the Enlightenment. They are rather alien, distant, removed."[6] Young Europeans are generally second- and third-generation agnostics who did not "lose the faith." They actually never knew it and, even less, experienced it. In Italy, since Catholicism still has popular roots, this phenomenon still affects a minority, even though it is growing. A large fraction of our kids attend catechism, participate in rituals, and learn to approach the sacraments. But after being confirmed, most of them fall off the radar of the parishes, and during adolescence, the separation from the Church becomes a done deal. All of this shows the inadequacy of a pastoral approach that comes from another age. Children are introduced to the Christian life through a sequence that mimics the school system, in which catechism is the learning stage and sacraments are the final exams. Once the obligation is fulfilled, one moves on. This creates a sharp break, which we try to remedy with youth ministry. The word already indicates that we address young people within an organizational scheme based of separation from what is being proposed to the adults. In my opinion, this separation does damage to both because on the one side, it confines the education of the young to a box, a separate sector, and on the other side, entrusts adults with responsibilities that tend to be lived as power. We must free youth ministry from schemes that are no longer effective. I am thinking, for example, of the WYDs, the World Youth Days. They were born from a genial intuition by Pope John Paul II, and they changed the life of many young people by making them rediscover the concrete meaning of the word "vocation." They carried the visible and exciting imprint of the strong personality of the Polish pope, and thus it is inevitable that without him, the WYDs have become less incisive, becoming a somewhat aged and repetitious format in today's context.

To understand the relationship between young people and faith, perhaps we can use an episode from Jack Kerouac's famous novel *On the Road*. Someone tries to offer a group of young drifters a job, addressing them as follows: "'You boys going to get somewhere, or just going?' We didn't understand his question and it was a damned good question."[7] According to the Scriptures, man has a path to walk because he is called by an Other. Hence the idea of vocation, which implies not only the existence of a destination but the fact that it not up to us to arbitrarily choose it. Today, the word "vocation" is considered obsolete. In the life of the Church also, even if "vocation" is commonly used, it seems worn out and deprived of its anthropological value. Pope Francis has reproposed it forcefully in the Apostolic Exhortation *Christus Vivit* at the conclusion of the synod on young people of October 2018. In it he reminds us that it is not "a new 'app' to be discovered, or a technique of mental self-improvement, [but] *an invitation to be part of a love story* interwoven with our personal stories."[8] It is an answer to Kerouac's "damned good" question, but the problem remains—why is it not understood and welcome?

For a Liberated Freedom

Today, even more than at the time of the Beat Generation, destinations are provisional and itineraries changeable. In the liquid and globalized society, young people change work, home, location, and social milieu with extreme facility. The idea of "forever," of a definitive bond, seems antiquated and ridiculous not only in the professional context but also in affective and sexual relationships. And yet, upon closer examination, everybody realizes more or less confusedly that his or her life—with its baggage of encounters and circumstances, of sudden accelerations and abrupt stops, of favorable coincidences and negative developments, in a word with the load of unpredicted and unpredictable events it carries with it—is evident proof that an Other leads us. The ancients felt its awful threat and called it Fate—in popular wisdom, it is a destiny to be accepted with resignation; for Christians, it is a good Father. Here we see that vocation is the greatest expression of freedom. Starting in 1968, a concept of freedom as self-affirmation against social conditioning and cultural prejudices has become prevalent. However, we have neglected the second pole of freedom, that of the inevitable exit towards the other. From this perspective, the question that must be posed to young people, starting from the circumstances and relationships they find themselves living, is not "why?" but "for whom?" We must not ask for an abstract motivation, but prompt them to indicate a person, a face, a community to which they can entrust themselves forever.

This is a question that no one can avoid. It is the question about the meaning of life, which is shared, even if the answers are radically different, by all religions and all worldviews, and which will never cease reemerging from the human heart. This is confirmed by an external and terrible factor, which affects not only the life of the Catholic Church but of all Christian churches. There is an immense persecuted people in our world, a people which is not distinguished by ethnicity or language but by faith in Christ. According to the Open Doors International, which monitors the situation worldwide, during 2019 at least 260 million Christians have been attacked, kidnapped, killed, raped, forced into hiding, or heavily marginalized because of their faith. Of those, three thousand have been killed, almost twice as many as in the previous year, adding to the great cohort of martyrs of our time.[9] We are left aghast by the widespread hatred and systematic violence confronting many Christians in their daily lives. We are dramatically reminded of this by the recently published book *Free at Last* in which Asia Bibi recounts her Calvary. She spent nine years in Pakistani prisons due to false accusations of blasphemy. The suffering and blood of persecuted Christians constitute the "martyrdom" that is the witness the Church has humbly and stubbornly offered to the world for 2,000 years, with unshakeable hope.

This is why, despite the almost complete domination of science and technology, religion will always have a future, whatever the numbers say. French psychiatrist Jacques Lacan used to say that "religion will triumph not only over psychoanalysis but over many other things. And even if science produces revolutionary changes in the life of each one of us, religion, especially the true religion, has resources that we cannot even imagine." He added, very significantly, "The Roman, i.e. Christian, religion is the only true one because the drama begins only when the Word comes into play, when it becomes incarnate."[10]

The Church as a community of believers is called to keep alive the question of "sense" for the life of every man and every nation. I am using the word "sense" as meaning, "for whom" do I live? and as direction, as choice of a path that fulfills my freedom in a companionship saved by Christ. In its elementary structure, in fact, Christianity is an event that takes place in an encounter that challenges the freedom of the person. I am convinced that if we Catholics, instead of going back to fruitless and anachronistic polarizations, were more united, more joyful, and more courageous in bearing witness to the richness and beauty of the message of Christ with all its implications, many men and women of our time would rediscover the fascination of being a Church.

Notes to Introduction

1.　Jean-François Colosimo interview with Jean-Pierre Denis, "L'Europe est-elle toujours chrétienne?" *Le Figaro Magazine,* nos. 23436 and 23437 (December 20–21, 2019).

2.　Henri de Lubac, *The Splendor of the Church* (San Francisco: Ignatius Press, 1986), 378.

3.　Jean-Luc Marion, *Brève apologie pour un moment catholique* (Paris: Grasset, 2017).

4.　Pope Francis, *Christmas Greetings of the Holy Father to the Roman Curia* (December 21, 2019). Italics in original. Official Vatican translation has "epochal change" rather than "change of epoch," but the original Italian has "*un cambiamento di epoca.*"

5.　Olivier Roy quoted by Jean-Marie Guénois, "Après une année noire, le catholicisme français en quête de crédibilité," *Le Figaro* (December 25, 2019).

6.　Massimo Borghesi, "I Nones della fede e il futuro del cristianesimo," *Vita e Pensiero* no. 6 (2019): 80–81.

7.   Jack Kerouac, *On the Road* (New York: Penguin, 1999), 18.

8.   Pope Francis, *Apostolic Journey to Panama: Vigil with Young People* (Campo San Juan Pablo II–Metro Park: January 26, 2019). Italics in original.

9.   "Christian Persecution," accessed November 28, 2020, www. opendoorsusa.org/christian-persecution.

10. Jacques Lacan, *Dei nomi del Padre: Il trionfo della religione* (Turin: Einaudi, 2006), 110.

CHAPTER 1

Faith of the Common People

Childhood and Adolescence in Post-War Italy

"I assimilated the faith from a very young age, naturally and without overthinking it. Faith is something rooted deep within our hearts thanks to our parents, who shared it with us mixed with milk and tenderness."[1] This is how your Eminence once responded when asked about your first encounter with the Christian fact. What memory do you have of those years?

Even now, I treasure that time as a period of joy and sweetness, even though there were also great difficulties. I was born in 1941 in Malgrate, close to Lecco, and my very first memories are tied to the war. We (my father, mother, older brother, and I) lived in a 35-square-meter apartment in an old building on the estate of a grand aristocratic villa. The building housed ten families with shared bathrooms. The villa was first occupied by the Germans, then by the Fascists, and finally by the Americans. I was very young, but there is a particular episode that left an impression on me. One day out of the blue, the Germans decided to change the password required to enter the complex, and there was a moment of panic because my father worked as a truck driver and often entered the complex quite late at night. We needed to let him know about the change before he came home, because the Germans never hesitated to shoot those who got close without saying the password. Anxiously, relatives and friends took positions at various points along the entrance to the town, hoping to spot him and warn him.

Along with the moments of fear that we experienced, there were also problems of poverty and even real insecurity, especially when we became refugees during the last months of the war. When we returned to Malgrate, I remember there was a group of American soldiers occupying the villa. That was the first time in my life I saw chocolate, because the Americans gave us kids a bar every week. My mother would take it and put it aside for my brother and me, saying, "We're keeping this for snack time, now don't eat it before." We were given one square every day over the course of the week, but I couldn't resist and often stole some before snack time. I was reprimanded for it regularly, but the stealing continued. In fact, it felt as if the prohibition made the chocolate taste even sweeter. One day, instead of the usual slap, mother struck me with these bitter words: "Why won't you just understand?" I was wounded by her pained and disappointed gaze. After that, I never dared to steal chocolate again. It was a good life lesson: What changes us is not punishment for a broken rule, but the sense of having fallen short of something we love.

Did hardship and poverty ever become an obstacle to your faith?

Absolutely not. Faith was for me a constitutive element of life; it marked its daily routine. There was no separation between one's private life and the public sphere, which at that time coincided mostly with the parish. It was no coincidence that the idea to dedicate myself to God and become a priest blossomed in me when I was only ten years old, in fourth grade. The idea had already taken root in me, even though it remained in the background for quite some time. The simple and solid faith that I had learned from my mother grew into something that penetrated every aspect of my life: friends, school, home, parish life. It was like this until middle school: I enrolled because my father Carlo (who considered it a point of pride that his sons be educated) wished it. I had to pass a highly selective entrance exam in order to attend middle school because at that time, most children opted to go to work after finishing elementary school; a few attended vocational schools and a very few enrolled into middle school. In that year, I was the only boy in my town to take and pass the entrance exam. It was quite rare for the son of a working-class father to pursue higher education; my luck was due to my father's stubbornness.

At middle school in Lecco, I discovered a world larger than the one I just described, a new reality in which I felt a bit lonely. Let's just say that, apart from the normal interactions with my classmates in school, the son of a truck driver was not regarded as equal to the other students, who were generally from richer families. I experienced a subtle marginalization. During those years, I discovered the shy and anxious side of my personality.

It's difficult to imagine a timid Angelo Scola. I always heard that you were an exuberant and undisciplined child. Is it true that you were suspended from school multiple times?

I was a very energetic little kid. Years later, I discovered that my elementary school teacher had made a sort of pact with my mother. "Dear Mrs. Regina," she wrote, "I am unable to keep your son in class all week. Let's arrange a schedule where you can keep him at home once in a while." It worked like this: I went to school every morning, but fairly often (around once a week) my teacher would suspend me from school at the beginning of class. She used to add that my grades were good anyway and that there was no need for me to remain in school.

Would it be correct to say that your restlessness did not detract from your sense of seriousness?

If you like, we could put it in those terms. What I want to emphasize is the fact that I never felt any conflict between the two essential elements of childhood—namely, wonder in front of reality and the effort to understand its meaning. The atmosphere of faith bore fruit in the simple and natural way we opened ourselves to the world.

It was another world compared to the one we see today, a world that has definitely disappeared.

Looking at Italian Catholicism, we must admit that the common mentality had already begun the process of separating from the Christian faith. I was always struck—as I recalled in my homily when I was installed as archbishop of Milan—by what Giovanni Battista Montini, the future Pope Paul VI, had written as a young priest, way back in 1934: "Christ is someone unknown, someone forgotten, someone absent in a large part of Italian culture."[2] Ever since unification, the intellectual elites of our country have been distant from and generally hostile to the Christian fact, even though it remained secure on the popular level. Their efforts never quite managed to undermine this *ethos* which served as the glue in daily life, permeating the customs, the values, and the ideas of the vast majority. It was a fact lived even by those who were not fully conscious of it.

This all began to change with the rise of the labor movement, with its twofold Socialist and Communist components. The social influence of the Church began to diminish when the Marxist idea of social justice became widespread, although it is interesting to note that within the sphere of moral norms, affectivity, and personal relations, the Christian principle still held value. Take for example the extremely critical reaction of the militants of the Italian Communist Party against the nonmarital union between Palmiro Togliatti and Nilde Iotti.[3] In the fifties, the family bond was unanimously recognized as something unquestionable, regardless of anyone's political opinions. At the same time, it was becoming increasingly evident that this was insufficient and that sooner or later, even moral norms would dwindle away without strong personal convictions to back them up. The economic boom was accompanied by a new way of thinking and living centered on personal gain and consumerism, while Christianity was increasingly reduced to little more than a collection of formal rituals and abstract principles. The catechism was whittled down to something to be memorized, an exercise in rote learning like the *Veritas* competitions,[4] in which the best memorizer won but doctrine had no longer anything to do with life.

Thus, the rock-solid faith of the people slowly started to crumble. It was a process that inexorably led to religious indifference, to a sharp decline in Catholic practice, and to the abandonment of the Church, all phenomena that we now know all too well.

How did the Church react to this new situation?

It tried to respond on multiple fronts. At the institutional level, the Church reacted by creating the Italian Episcopal Conference (CEI), a directing body which is partially autonomous from the Holy See.[5] Let me remind you that previously, the Church in Italy depended completely on the Vatican, even on an organizational level. For example, bishops were appointed directly from the relevant Congregation of the Holy See, without going through the Nunciature as was the case in many countries and as occurs in Italy today.

After a difficult initial period, marked by internal tensions, the CEI adopted its statutes in the midsixties. Later, at the level of content, it conceived of the so-called "tripod," namely liturgy, catechesis, and charity, the three elements that must characterize every ecclesial community. In practice it is a combination of morals and doctrine meant to give new momentum to Italian Catholicism.

Finally, there was a third level of response in which certain significant figures acted to relaunch the Christian presence in society. These were personalities with towering ecclesial, intellectual, and political profiles, like Giorgio La Pira, the mayor of Florence, or Giuseppe Dossetti, who was a politician and later a priest. There was Giuseppe Lazzati, the rector of the Catholic University of Milan, but there were also the "purebreds" of the Christian Democratic Party, Amintore Fanfani and Aldo Moro.[6] Having recognized that the mentality and customs anchored in Catholic tradition were fading away, the Italian Church increasingly relied on politics to influence society and to preserve what was once a spontaneous reality that sprang from the grassroots.

However, at that time there were also figures like Fr. Primo Mazzolari and Fr. Lorenzo Milani, whom the Italian Church marginalized and viewed with suspicion.[7] Today, they are being rediscovered. This rehabilitation is important because their proposal contained some prophetic elements. Yet, despite the dissemination of their works and their many followers, neither of them generated organic popular movements.

Is it fair to say that Vatican II was a shock for Italian Catholicism?

Since the midsixties, Vatican II has been continuously cited and brandished like a banner. Everyone refers to the council, but the most important documents (such as the dogmatic constitution *Dei Verbum*) are not adequately studied and assimilated. Of all the council's innovations, I would say only one reform has essentially been realized: that of the liturgy. There was a discussion about a new educational proposal, foundations were laid for new forms of catechesis, but overall, the Italian response to Vatican II remains partial, confined to specialists. Of course, the liturgy was reformed, more room was given to the Word of God, catechesis was renewed, *Caritas* was born[8]—all of these things are important. But among the people there was not a renewed awareness of faith. Doctrine and morality are not enough to reinvigorate the Christian fact.

Paul VI, a great and holy pope whose canonization will be celebrated on October 14, 2018,[9] understood this well. In the wake of his ministry as bishop of Milan, he became the promoter of a new idea of reform that "loves and does not hate, does not invent but develops, does not stop but continues," as he said in a 1958 homily.[10] Even today, I feel a sense of gratitude and great admiration when I reread the extraordinary talks and homilies from his time as the bishop of Milan. For Montini, the reformation of the church meant the restoration of its original splendor "in mindset and in customs." Paul VI proved himself brave indeed when faced with the protests that, as we know, marked the post-Council era. The case of the encyclical *Humanae Vitae* is emblematic. The heated polemics that exploded in the aftermath of its publication in 1968 all revolved around the problem of the birth control pill, while the main point of the encyclical, the affirmation that the two aspects of the spouses' sexual act —the unitive and the procreative—cannot be arbitrarily separated, went largely ignored. Paul VI also saw with great clarity that the use of chemical contraceptives would drastically alter the relationship between man and woman, both in conception and practice.

It is, however, a fact that the teachings of *Humanae Vitae* are largely ignored in the practical lives of believers.

In this regard, I recall a pertinent observation from Bishop Carlo Colombo. A celebrated Milanese theologian, he was one of Paul VI's principal collaborators in drafting this encyclical. Twenty years later, noting the extent to which the teachings of *Humanae Vitae* went unfollowed, he affirmed that he "understood how right St. Paul was when he warned the first Christians, and would warn the Christians of today, not to judge, leaving the final judgment to God."[11] Acknowledging human fragility and sin does not diminish the truth of a teaching, but instead reminds us of the necessity for mercy and conversion.

You have described a historical process that played out across the fifties and sixties. But what has your experience been on the personal level?

In my early high school years, I was lucky to meet a priest named Fr. Fausto Tuissi. He was a passionate teacher who introduced me to contemporary literature and the issues it posed, while at the same time making an essential connection with faith. It was an important relationship for a boy my age. Fr. Fausto was intellectually gifted. He would have liked to continue his studies, but the ecclesial authorities of the time generally had the strange idea that any priest showing a strong desire to do a particular thing must be destined to do something else entirely. So it was that Fr. Fausto found himself the assistant pastor of Malgrate, a parish of 1,500 souls, and began to teach the boys of the oratory there. His gaze, however, went beyond prayer, beyond catechesis and play, opening his students up to wider horizons.

In the afternoon, especially during summertime, he would call me over and read aloud writers like Dostoevsky, Camus, Faulkner, and Musil. He would tell me, "I can't give you this book, but listen to this passage. . ." Those passages, tackling the great themes of life and death, of good and evil, enchanted me and left an indelible impression.

I have also never forgotten my art history classes in high school. The teaching methods of Professor Balzaretti, who was herself a pupil of Longhi,[12] opened up my mind. A long-lasting bond formed between us, which in fact kept growing deeper until her recent death. I was also intellectually fascinated by my Latin and Greek professor, a brilliant and very anticlerical man. My interests in literature and philosophy extended to politics and social analysis, and I never missed an issue of Mario Pannunzio's magazine *Il Mondo*. I avidly read Ernesto Rossi's books on the formation of Italian capitalism, along with Giovanni Baldacci's editorials in *Il Giorno*, which were always critical of the Christian Democratic government.[13] In a certain sense, my political leanings began to resemble those of my father—a staunch socialist who worked himself to the bone to support my studies.

Besides these intellectual interests, did you have other hobbies? Did you play any sports?

I have always been very passionate about soccer, even though for a kid growing up in a provincial town, "playing soccer" essentially meant everybody chasing after a rag ball. Eventually we upgraded to a plastic one, while the oratory's only real leather ball was reserved for the main team. Since the elementary school classrooms were inside the oratory, I remember playing long matches during our midday recess. One side was "the team," made up of the six or seven best players, while the other side consisted of all the leftover reserve players. I was stuck with the reserves and this bothered me quite a bit. So, I made a deal with the captain of "the team," a certain Giulio, a really big kid who was still in elementary school at age thirteen because he had been held back so many times. "I'll let you copy my homework," I told him, "if you let me play on the main team." And so it happened, in spite of my classmates' protests.

As a child, I rooted for Torino, perhaps because of the tragedy of Superga,[14] which hit me hard even though I was only seven years old. Much later, in the eighties, I became a A.C. Milan fan. The team chaplain was my friend Fr. Massimo Camisasca. Thanks to him, I met the legendary coach Arrigo Sacchi and various players, including Donadoni.[15] I remember that Sacchi insisted that the whole team attend Mass . . . I always had the perception that sports were a central part of the educational proposal of the oratory—especially soccer, even if there was a risk that it would just be reduced to a ball game. Coaches and trainers remain important figures for today's teens, who will open up to them even more than to their parish priest or parents. This prompted me to propose an idea that has always been close to my heart, that of an "educational community."[16] By this I am not proposing yet another structure, but an informal cooperative among all those who educate our teens: parents, priests, teachers, catechists, and certainly soccer coaches, especially now that kids start playing at six or seven years old.

As a boy, did you always attend church?

Although I always felt closer to the worldview of my father, a committed Socialist, I remained attached to the Church thanks to the relationship with Fr. Tuissi and with my mother, a very religious woman. After I turned fifteen, I lived in a state of ambivalence, where the social and political aspects of life predominated, whereas Christianity remained merely a veneer, a façade. As far as I can recall, I never skipped Mass on Sunday, but it was as if it no longer mattered. Other things were those that mattered.

When you were the Patriarch of Venice, while reminiscing about your youth during a conversation with a group of teenagers, you said: "I had forgotten about the Church, which in some respects is more serious than abandoning her."[17] Isn't this judgment a little harsh?

I meant to say that indifference is worse than rejection. The latter implies a reflection, a criticism which is more or less motivated. On the other hand, reducing faith to a superficial belief with no real significance for life means emptying Christianity of its transformative power. I think it is a grave sin to live faith as a formality. It is a position that cannot endure and leads to practical atheism. I would have probably ended up like that, too, if I had not encountered someone who helped me to understand that Christ is not a theory, but a person who has to do with my life.

Notes to Chapter 1

1. Andrea Tornielli, *Il futuro e la speranza: vita e magistero del cardinale Angelo Scola* (Milano: Piemme, 2011), 21–22.
2. G. B. Montini, *Introduzione allo studio di Cristo - Schemi di lezioni di religione per studenti delle scuole superiori* (Rome: Studium, 1933), 23. Cited in Pope Benedict XVI, *Address to the Paul VI Institute - Concesio* (November 8, 2009).
3. Palmiro Togliatti (1893–1964) led the Italian Communist Party (PCI) from 1927 to 1964. Nilde Iotti (1920–1999) was a PCI member and president of the lower chamber of the Italian parliament from 1979 to 1992. Togliatti and Iotti were lovers from 1946 to his death. This created a scandal because Togliatti was married. He forced his wife, Rita Montagnana, to live in Moscow with their son Aldo, who was mentally ill.
4. The *Veritas* Competition was a contest in which high school students had to demonstrate their religious knowledge. It was very

popular in the fifties and sixties. It was organized by a department of the Catholic Action.

5. CEI is an abbreviation of *Conferenza Episcopale Italiana,*

6. Giorgio La Pira (1904–1977) was a politician, law professor, and member parliament for the Christian Democratic Party. He was mayor of Florence from 1951 to 1965 and was known as the "saintly mayor" for his fervid Catholicism and his commitment to promote peace and solidarity among peoples. He was declared Venerable by Pope Francis in 2013. Giuseppe Dossetti (1913–1996) was a member of parliament for the Christian Democratic Party after World War II who left politics and in 1959 became a priest. He participated in the Second Vatican Council as a collaborator of the Archbishop of Bologna, Cardinal Giacomo Lercaro. Giuseppe Lazzati (1909–1986) was a university professor and a politician in the Christian Democratic Party. He was rector of the Catholic University of Milan from 1968 to 1983. In 2013, he was declared a venerable by Pope Francis. Amintore Fanfani (1909–1999), academic, politician, and leader of the Christian Democratic Party, was prime minister of Italy several times between 1953 and 1987. Aldo Moro (1916–1978), an academic and politician, was one of the leaders of the Christian Democratic Party, in the sixties, in the first governments of *centro-sinistra* (center-left coalitions with the Socialists). In the seventies, he supported the idea of a *compromesso storico* ("historical compromise," i.e., a coalition of Christian Democrats and Communists). In 1978, he was kidnapped and then murdered by the Red Brigades.

7. Fr. Primo Mazzolari (1890–1959) was a priest and author; even though he served as pastor only in the small town of Bozzolo, in Northern Italy, he was a charismatic figure in Italian Catholicism and a precursor of the Second Vatican Council. Fr. Lorenzo Milani (1923–1967), priest, author, and educator, is remembered for having opened a school for poor children in Barbiana, a small town in Tuscany. He wrote *Letere a una professoressa* [Letters to a teacher], in which he denounced the scourge of illiteracy and criticized the Italian public school system.

8. *Caritas Italiana* is the CEI agency charged with humanitarian and charitable works. It was created in 1971 and is organized in 220 diocesan units. It is part of *Caritas Internationalis.*

9   Paul VI was indeed canonized after this interview on October 14, 2018, alongside Óscar Arnulfo Romero y Galdámez, Francesco Spinelli, Vincenzo Romana, Mother Maria Katharina Kasper, Mother Nazaria Ignazia March Mesa, Nunzio Sulprizio.

10. G. B. Montini, *Discorsi e scritti milanesi* (1954–1963) (Brescia: Studium, 1997), 1064.

11. C. Colombo, "L'insegnamento fondamentale di *Humanae Vitae*," in *Humanae Vitae: vent'anni dopo. Atti del II Congresso Internazionale di Teologia Morale, Roma 1988* (Milano: Ares, 1989), 412.

12. Roberto Longhi (1890–1970) was a distinguished art historian.

13. Mario Pannunzio (1910–1968) was a journalist and politician. In 1949, he founded the weekly *Il Mondo* to advance a secular-liberal position against both the Christian Democrats and the Communists. Ernesto Rossi (1897–1967) was a journalist and economist. He was one of the authors of the *Ventotene Manifesto* (1941) that promoted the idea of European unification along federal lines. Gaetano Baldacci (1911–1971) was a physician and journalist. He was the founding editor of daily newspaper *Il Giorno*.

14. Torino is one of the two soccer teams in the city of Turin (the other being Juventus). Superga is a locality on a hill overlooking Turin, which was the location of a tragic plane crash on May 4, 1949. The whole Torino soccer team died when a plane transporting the team hit the mountain due to low visibility.

15. Msgr. Massimo Camisasca (1946–) served as chaplain from 1987 to 1991 for the A.C. Milan soccer team. Since 2012, he has been bishop of Reggio Emilia. Arrigo Sacchi (1946–) coached A.C. Milan from 1987 to 1991, and then the Italian national team. Roberto Donadoni (1963–) played for A.C. Milan in the eighties and nineties.

16. On the concept of "educational community" and its link with the Church as communion, see *"La Comunità educante." Nota pastorale dell'arcivescovo cardinale Angelo Scola* (Milano: Centro Ambrosiano, 2014).

17. Angelo Scola, *Vogliamo vedere Gesù* (Venezia: Marcianum Press, 2007).

CHAPTER 2

A Surprising Encounter

The Experience of Gioventù Studentesca

You described the years of your adolescence as a period characterized by a passive and formalistic religious practice. How did the transition to a convinced and deep faith take place? What caused the rediscovery of Christianity as something, to use your own words, "that had to do with your life"?

The first time I perceived an element of novelty in the Christian proposal was near the end of high school, during the Easter Triduum that was held for Lecco's high school students. It was also the first time I saw Fr. Luigi Giussani.[1] I can still picture his figure standing upright in the Basilica of San Nicolò, his engaging eloquence as he discussed a theme that was itself unusual: "Youth as Tension." I expected the usual moralizing talk, maybe a few interesting insights at best, which then would inevitably leave no trace in daily life. Instead, I found myself confronted by a different way of speaking, which showed how faith can be a practical judgment on life. One could not remain indifferent because it did not call for a moral effort, but instead awakened a desire—if nothing else, the desire to understand and go more deeply. In short, it provoked my freedom.

That day, I felt a sort of shudder, a jolt that did not immediately change my way of life, focused as I was on socio-political interests. The decisive moment would come later, in a completely unexpected way.

How did it happen?

It was the summer of 1959. I was not yet eighteen and was just entering my last year of high school. There wasn't much money at home, so I had begun tutoring middle school kids. Over the summer, I had been teaching the students who had failed courses and had to take their remedial exams in October—sometimes working for as long as eight hours a day. One day, right after lunch, as I was lying down to rest at the hottest time of the day, I heard the doorbell ring and a person ask my mother to talk to one of her sons. The person wasn't quite sure which one of the two, he didn't even remember my name; his only indication was "the one with red hair." He was Fabio Baroncini,[2] a student of the Technical Institute Parini whom I had met while climbing the Grigna,[3] but we did not know each other well. He invited me to a *Gioventù Studentesca (GS)* summer camp. At that time, it was the high school branch of the Catholic Action (an experience that was developing in Italy after a French model, since it was now evident that the parish alone could no longer sustain an educational proposal for the students).[4] We would spend ten days at Falzarego Pass, Baroncini told me, explaining that the camp would cost very little—a thousand lire,[5] if I remember correctly. I had no real inclination to go, because the idea of sitting in conferences for ten days straight didn't sound terribly exciting. To convince me, he pointed out that we could take advantage of being in the Dolomites to go mountain hiking. And sure enough, that's exactly what we did.

After the first two—very boring—lessons, we decided to skip the rest and ended up spending most of our time in the mountains. On the last day, the camp leader, Attilio Nicora,[6] spoke to us about our lack of participation and urged us to at least attend the last meeting. There were testimonies from some GS boys from Milan. Over the same days they had had their own camp nearby, in Penìa di Canazei, with Fr. Giussani. One of them was Pigi Bernareggi.[7] Two hundred of us sat and listened to him in a big room at the house we were staying in. The building had belonged to the Gioventù Italiana del Littorio,[8] but after the war, it had passed into the hands of the Catholic Action. Though the house was in a beautiful spot, it had fallen into disrepair. The toilets were beaten up and the bathrooms were few, so we had to wash ourselves in the freezing water of a fountain in the courtyard. A curious episode has stayed with me: One morning at six (we woke up early), I was next to Attilio Nicora as we were heading to wash up. The spiritual assistant—a priest from South Tyrol, Fr. Sennen Corrà—stared at us intently and then uttered a prophecy, which at the time I found absolutely weird: "Here are two boys who will become priests!"[9]

And it was in that old, crumbling house that you discovered something new?

There, in that moment, my life was destined to change. There were bare light bulbs hanging from the ceiling, wrapped in yellow paper covered with flies. Not exactly a pretty picture! Well, Bernareggi began by saying: "If Jesus had nothing to do with that light bulb, I would not be a Christian." And from there, he went on to talk about how Christ had to do with how we went to school, with our passion for philosophy, or with the study of mathematics, and even (he said this very modestly) with falling in love, with affective life. In that moment I realized—with great surprise—that it was possible to live an experience of faith that did not leave out reality but that embraced and gave motive to everything.

In short, I intuited that faith is not something that can be added extrinsically and moralistically to what I do normally, it isn't a "supplement of soul," a slogan that would gain popularity starting in the seventies.[10] On the contrary: It is the sap that nourishes every twig of the tree of life. Starting from that encounter, I discovered a way to talk about Christianity that involved my person freely and spontaneously, not out of abstract duty. Christ manifested himself to me as a real, concrete figure who was a part of my everyday life. Faith was becoming something that I cared for, that was pertinent to all of my interests; it was the focal point through which I could judge reality. That summer night, the *encounter* that changed my life took place.

If I understand correctly, you put great emphasis on the encounter, not just in the sense of a mere occurrence, but as a fundamental category of the Christian fact.

What happened to me at summer camp, in the distant year 1959, was the encounter for me; that is to say, it marked a change of direction and opened the way to a true conversion. When speaking to young people in my pastoral mission, I often invite them to try a mental exercise that does not involve just memory, but is also authentically spiritual. I ask them to recall the moment when the encounter took place, which somehow made the sacrament of baptism they had received as babies effective. I like to quote a passage by Hans Urs von

Balthasar: "Even now, I could return to that grove in the Black Forest, pick out the big pine tree under which I clearly perceived that I was called to serve or, actually, that I had been taken into service."[11] For me, the encounter at camp had this same quality, reawakening what had struck me while listening to Giussani's lesson the year before. A second characteristic of the encounter is that it provokes a change in one's relationships, in everyday existence. I began to live the communal experience proposed by GS and found myself talking about Christ with my classmates, not to preach but as an ordinary subject of conversation. I stood up for it, so to speak, freely and naturally.

Does what happened to you have to happen to everyone? I mean, can't there be Christianity without personal encounter? Was Kierkegaard correct when he wrote in his diary, "This is the main thing in life, that one has seen something once, felt something so great, so matchless, that all else is nothing in comparison, that if one forgot everything one would never forget this?"[12]

I'd put it this way: The important thing in life is to have once seen something decisive. That is to say, I believe, as Benedict XVI so intelligently said in his encyclical *Deus Caritas Est*, that Christianity is not primarily a doctrine or an ethic but the personal encounter with Christ within the community of the Church.[13] In my opinion, the concealment of this fundamental truth is at the origin of the educational collapse within the European church, a collapse which not even the Second Vatican Council has been able to stop. The dynamism of the encounter is fundamental in the logic of Christianity. When talking with seminarians throughout my twenty-seven years of episcopacy, I've found that behind the decision to become a priest, there is always an encounter with a priest or, in any case, with a person who was significant to their faith experience. From this perspective, Pope Francis has added an invaluable element by insisting on the "culture of encounter." This means that Christianity must be cultivated in our communities as an event, as something that has happened to you and that you communicate to others. Picking up the famous expression of Romano Guardini that "the church must be reborn from souls,"[14] today we might say that the Church must be reborn from the person.

This is the task we face, and it has become ever more urgent after the crisis of the seventies. Up until that moment, the Christian proposal had not entirely lost this dimension, but it was overshadowed by an ethical concern to create a multiplying number of initiatives as defenses against the world. The oratory was implicitly expected to become a microcosm that would reproduce within itself all areas of life. Following the ideological inebriation which took hold even in the Italian church, initiatives were supplanted by the idea of service. Definitely, this emphasis on charity marked the beginning of an era of great generosity, but it often ran the risk of clouding the deeper nature of the Christian announcement. And so even today, an authentic culture of encounter is struggling to grow, because it is hard for us to live faith as an event.

Was it easier in the 1950s, when you were a young high school student?

Not at all, it was much more difficult. Just think of the general wariness with which Fr. Giussani's GS experiment was received, and the great resistance it met among the clergy. If I may cite my own case, I remember being given a stark choice by the local priests, including Fr. Tuissi: Either you come to the oratory or go with "those GS people." Keeping the two together was impossible.

It wasn't just a contrast between organizations. At the root was the idea that it was unnecessary and even inappropriate for a good believer to refer explicitly to Christ, as happened in GS. There were two reasons for this. First, there was an assumption that many non-Christians are better people than us believers and that, therefore, our faith should not be paraded around as if it were a universal remedy. This position relied on a misunderstanding, confusing the grace of salvation with the grace of faith. The second reason was psychological in nature: Talking about the "I," and the "I" changed by the encounter, and about how we live our relationship with God was considered a form of vanity which rubbed people the wrong way. As the poet Rainer Maria Rilke wrote, "All things *conspire to keep silent about us, half out of shame perhaps, half as unutterable hope.*"[15]

Even today, at the end of an encounter or assembly, I am always struck by the negative reaction that arises when you highlight what one person has said rather than someone else's intervention. The participants feel uneasy. This is a clear practical consequence of what happens when Christianity (in the sense of an event born from a personal encounter that we communicate by bearing witness to it) is mothballed.

Yet, when we were young, priests would often tell us about the importance of good examples.

Witness must not be reduced to good example. It's something else entirely. Don Giussani used to tell the story of one of his students at Berchet High School who had excellent grades and was held up as an example by the teachers. [16] "But what good is your success? You give glory to yourself, not to Christ," Giussani pointed out to him.

At best, good example can inspire a moral effort. The deep structure of witness is quite different. I had a direct experience of this during a pastoral visit in Venice. One day, as I was leaving the house of a sick person, the pastor pointed to a reserved-looking man about my age. His son, who had been severely disabled, unable to speak or walk, had died three weeks before. The man had taken loving care of him for more than thirty years, assisting him night and day and comforting him with his constant presence. The only times he'd ever left his side had been on Sunday mornings when he went to Mass. I felt a certain embarrassment in front of this person, but as often happens to us priests, I felt the need to say something. "The Lord will reward you," I stammered, a bit stunned. He responded with a big smile: "Patriarch, I have already received everything from the Lord because he has shown me what it means to love." Here is an authentic witness, which implies that the witness has known reality adequately and, consequently, has the capacity to communicate its truth in an adequate way.

You rediscovered the intensity of Christianity in GS. How did it operate and what did it ask of you?

The heart of the GS experience was the *raggio*, [17] the weekly meeting open to all high school students. The agenda was very simple; it consisted of two or three questions on existential issues, but also on the events that were emerging at school or being brought to the fore by the newspapers or TV. They were circulated on mimeographed sheets and distributed to all our classmates. The invitation was to a dialogue based on personal experience, and not to the usual clash of abstract opinions. Here lies the novelty of the method of the raggio. It goes beyond a purely intellectual participation, whereby even today, discussions follow a formula that has struck me since I was a boy, and that has not substantially changed: "What has been said so far is certainly important, but . . ." followed by a sequence of criticisms of what had been affirmed previously, ending inevitably in a sterile and repetitious back-and-forth. The true concept of criticism, of judgment, is instead a communication that starts from oneself, a narration of one's experience comparing it with what has been said, becoming involved with the other.

This was the dynamic that played out in the raggio, which constituted the center of GS life, where the link between the subject and Christ or the Christian community always reemerged. Life, then, developed along the three dimensions that became integral to the initial reality of GS: charity, culture, and mission. The gesture of "charitable work"—understood first of all as an education in gratuitousness, in giving some of one's free time to others—was very important. For example, my GS friends from Lecco and I would go every Sunday to Val Cavargna, on the mountains near the Swiss border. We would subject ourselves to two hours of travel each way on steep gravel roads in order to spend the afternoon playing with children and help the priest teach catechism. In Milan, those in GS would go serve in the Milanese "Bassa."[18]

Culture was another crucial aspect. We would write up critical reviews on various philosophical, historical, and literary topics that we were taught in class. The aim was not to make polemical attacks against our teachers, but to call into question certain statements that had been taken for granted in discussions about the relationship between the Church and power, or the Church and science, like in the debate over Brecht's famous play *Galileo*. Of course, some stances we took were off the mark and naive; we were adolescents. But what motivated us was a tension to face every aspect of our lives—beginning with our studies, which played such a big part—with a judgment in which faith was not an extrinsic element but the fundamental criterion for reading reality.

The third dimension of GS life was mission, which expressed itself concretely in saving a tenth of our (scarce) money to support Bernareggi and our other Milanese friends. They were the first of our members to leave for Brazil right after finishing high school—this was at the end of the fifties.[19] This was how words within GS, like event, encounter, and witness—which are crucial to Christianity— became for me a concrete life experience.

Do you believe that the Church today is more conscious of these fundamental elements than it was a few decades ago?

Let's say that these categories, especially after the clarifying power of John Paul II's magisterium, are sometimes mentioned, but they rarely become the method of Christian life, except among some minorities. I think I can say that we are still far away from an adequate comprehension of Christianity as an event that is born from an encounter, calls forth a witness, and generates belonging to the community.

Notes to Chapter 2

1. Msgr. Luigi Giussani (1922–2005), priest writer and educator. He founded the ecclesial movement Communion and Liberation (CL). For details about his life and works, see Alberto Savorana, *The Life of Luigi Giussani* (Montreal: McGill-Queen's University Press, 2017).
2. Fabio Baroncini (1942–2020) went on to become a priest, a leader of CL, and a pastor in Milan.
3. In the Italian system, an *Istituto Tecnico* is a type of high school focused on technical-vocational training. The Grigna is the highest mountain near Lecco (2,400 meters high) and a popular climbing destination.
4. Under Fr. Giussani's leadership, Gioventù Studentesca (GS) developed into a new and original form of Christian high school ministry. Eventually it parted ways with the Catholic Action and became the precursor of Communion and Liberation. The name GS is still used to indicate specifically CL's high school branch.
5. Roughly one dollar and sixty cents at that time.

6. Attilio Nicora (1937–2017), jurist, bishop, and later cardinal in the Roman curia.

7. Pigi Bernareggi (1939–2021) became a priest in the diocese of São Paulo in Brazil and then a pastor in Belo Horizonte.

8. The main Fascist youth organization during Mussolini's regime.

9. Sennen Corrà (1924–2005) became bishop of Chioggia (Veneto) and the Pordenone (Friuli).

10. The expression *supplément d'âme* was actually introduced by French philosopher Henri Bergson in his book *Les Deux Sources de la morale et de la religion* (Paris: Alcan, 1932).

11. Hans Urs von Balthasar, *Por que' me hice sacerdote* (Salamanca: Sigueme, 1982), 13–15.

12. Søren Kierkegaard, *Journals and Notebooks Vol. 1* (Princeton: Princeton University Press, 2007), 45.

13. Pope Benedict XVI, *Deus Caritas Est* (December 25, 2005), 1: "Being Christian is not the result of an ethical choice or a lofty idea, but the encounter with an event, a person, which gives life a new horizon and a decisive direction." Unless otherwise noted, all quotations of papal documents are from www.vatican.va.

14. Romano Guardini, *The Meaning of the Church* (Providence, R.I.: Cluny Media, 2018), 1.

15. Rainer Maria Rilke, *Duino Elegies,* ed. and trans. Stephen Mitchell (New York: Random House, 2009), 13.

16. Giovanni Berchet High School is a prestigious Milanese high school where Fr. Luigi Giussani taught religion and started Gioventù Studentesca.

17. Literally "radius."

18. In Milan, La Bassa is used to indicate the agricultural region south of the city, which in the fifties was still plagued by rural poverty.

19. Fr. Giussani encouraged some of the young people in GS to travel to Brazil as missionaries in order to learn the universal and missionary dimension of the Christian experience.

A Movement in the Church

The Involvement in Communion and Liberation

For many years you had leadership roles, first in Gioventù Studentesca and then in Communion and Liberation.[1] You experienced as a protagonist the tormented twists and turns and fiery polemics that marked the life of the Italian Church in the sixties and seventies. By now, there have been many accounts and interpretations of the period. Can I ask you for yours?

We have to start from an indisputable fact: Gioventù Studentesca grew explosively, and spread over a very short period of time, even beyond Lombardy and the Archdiocese of Milan where it was born. What's interesting is that there was never any plan to expand or to take over new areas. Everything came from the dynamism of a friendship, so much so that that Don Giussani was against the idea of founding a movement. In the meantime, the traditional associations like the Catholic Action, the backdrop from which Fr. Giussani's GS was born, were having great difficulties proposing themselves, particularly to young people. And when we *giessini* began to go to college, still trying to live naturally what we had experienced in high school, there were frictions between us and FUCI,[2] the association of university students linked with the Catholic Action.

This is why Cardinal Giovanni Colombo,[3] Montini's successor as the head of the Archdiocese of Milan, realized there was a serious imbalance among organizations responsible for educating the young and decided to intervene and put things back in order. He decreed that GS must remain an organization dedicated to the formation of high school students. GS could not be duplicated at the university level, where the only officially recognized entity would still be FUCI. At the same time, in order to guarantee educational continuity, FUCI had to welcome university students coming from GS. To this end, in 1965, Cardinal Colombo appointed as presidents Eugenia Scabini and myself, along with two members of FUCI.[4] This was undoubtedly an institutional compromise, typical of the ecclesiastical hierarchy of the time. Even considering this limitation, I believe it was an interesting experiment in how to introduce a new movement to a traditional association.

However, there remained profound differences, both in educational method and in how the relationship between faith and culture was conceived. According to the FUCI intellectuals around Professor Giuseppe Lazzati, who taught at the Catholic University of Milan and would later become rector there, our position failed to take into account the autonomy of social and political processes; in short, it was incapable of forming a correct analysis. Thus, they denounced as integralism the affirmation that Christ and the Christian identity are the unifying criteria with which reality can be judged—the focal point of GS's educational proposal. At the time, both GS and FUCI had their headquarters on Via Statuto in Milan and ours was on a higher floor. Don Giussani was walking down the stairs with two or three of us one day when we crossed paths with a group of *fucini*. An intense discussion broke out. Eventually, Don Giussani blurted out, "This is useless, we have different cultural interpretations of the faith." Cardinal Colombo's experiment was short-lived, swept away by the disputes of 1968. But the contrast reemerged in the seventies when the movement was reborn with the name Communion and Liberation. In 1971, together with others, I was appointed a leader of the university students of the movement, known as CLU.[5]

In that period, you were also busy directing a think tank. Was this your idea?

The research and cultural center called the Institute for the Study of Transition (ISTRA) was founded in 1972 in Milan. The initiative came from a group of young university professors. The strange-sounding name reflected our awareness of the massive cultural changes that had begun in 1968, whose future direction had to be inferred and, to whatever extent possible, influenced. Our work was meant to be interdisciplinary. The goal was to develop a common judgment articulated across various research areas: theological, philosophical, historical, political, economic, and artistic. I was joined by experts in these fields: Rocco Buttiglione, who at that time was a professor of political philosophy;[6] Fr. Pino Ruggieri, theologian; Santino Langè, professor of architecture; Massimo Guidetti, historian; Giuseppe Folloni, economist; and Rodolfo Balzarotti, art critic, along with around twenty young assistants and university researchers. After 1974, unfortunately, due to my illness, I was forced to take a step back from my involvement both with ISTRA and with Communion and Liberation.

1974 saw the referendum on divorce, a crucial test for the Italian Church.[7] Communion and Liberation was the only Catholic group that joined the fray in the referendum campaign to abolish divorce. How do you assess that choice now?

In the beginning, we planned to stay on the sidelines. Catholic Action seemed rather indifferent, while the so-called "democratic Catholics" launched an appeal against abolition. After that, the general secretary of CEI, Msgr. Enrico Bartoletti,[8] called us to Rome and told us that Pope Paul VI had been deeply disappointed by the behavior of the associations and many intellectuals of the Catholic world. He said that the pope was depending on Communion and Liberation to witness the Christian position on this fundamental issue, which demanded also a public effort. I remember a long discussion afterwards between the leaders of the movement in the ISTRA headquarters. Many questions were raised; it seemed useless to throw ourselves headfirst into what we all knew was a losing battle. Someone also pointed out that the speech by Sen. Fanfani, then secretary of the Christian Democratic Party, in favor of Gabrio Lombardi's "committee for yes" was going to be counterproductive.[9] As the discussion drew to a close, Fr. Giussani spoke up, "You all have plenty of reasons, but our criterion is different: In the Church we are called to obey the authority of the pope, and if the pope asks us to do something, we do it." This is why I still think our decision was not a mistake—because it was not made out of convenience, but was based on an understanding that Christianity as a communal event is ultimately ensured not by the intelligence of our reasoning but by discipleship exercised in obedience.

The referendum widened the rift within the Italian Church. The confrontation between Catholics of presence and Catholics of mediation, which you have mentioned, became a real clash.

The culminating moment of the story was the conference on "Human Evangelization and Promotion" held by the CEI in 1976. After the post-council turmoil and the defeat of the referendum, and finding itself in a political situation that was rapidly changing thanks to the electoral successes of the Communist Party, the Italian Church felt the need to speak to the country in a frank and open manner. Hence the idea of the conference. Its management was entrusted to Fr. Bartolomeo Sorge,[10] who gave preference to the "democratic Catholics" when choosing the speakers and setting the agenda.[11] CL as a movement was not given a voice, and those of us who participated did so as representatives of certain dioceses. For example, I was somehow slipped into the delegation of the Diocese of Civitavecchia!

The conference started with a bang, namely Bolgiani's keynote speech,[12] which included a strong attack against Pius XII and proposed the so-called culture of mediation as the road that the Italian Church had to take in order to keep up with the times. Paul VI—people said at the time—felt very bitter and immediately summoned Cardinal Antonio Poma, president of the CEI, and Msgr. Luigi Maverna, the new general secretary.[13] The next day they disavowed Bolgiani's speech and the conference went on, trying to strike a balance between the opposing factions, but the disagreements remained.

In retrospect, years later, it is clear that the mediation vs. presence clash, which was blown out of proportion by the press, was an oversimplification. It was not true that we in CL refused to analyze and seek compromises in the face of the problems of the day; consider all of ISTRA's work on Italian society and on the international situation. On the other hand, it wasn't true that the other side had lost sight of the Christian fact in their social and political engagement. Unnecessary mistakes, exaggerations, and accusations coming from both sides were not helpful when it came to what was later called the "recomposition" of the Catholic world. At any rate, Fr. Bartolomeo Sorge managed to bring the different Catholic groups to the same table at the Tra noi center in Rome.

You mentioned the work of ISTRA. Is it true that, as director of the Institute, you had a close relationship with Silvio Berlusconi, who was then a real estate developer?

The episode was inconsequential. When it was revealed years later after Berlusconi had become prime minister, it was given more attention than it deserved and was spun in a sinister way that had no basis in reality. Here is what happened: ISTRA financed itself through lectures and research projects commissioned by various public and private organizations. In this context, we were contacted by Fedele Confalonieri and asked to organize a series of lessons on anthropology, politics, and economics for some Edilnord managers.[14] The seminars took place in Silvio Berlusconi's house in Milan, on Via Rovani. If I recall correctly, they began in the winter of 1976 and ended the following spring. It was an interesting exercise for ISTRA, but not all that different from other things we had done, with well-defined content and duration. This was during the period when Berlusconi was trying to obtain authorization for his own TV channel. Once, I remember he took us to see the basement of his house in Via Rovani and proudly showed us the equipment for what would soon become Telemilano, his first private television channel. What happened after that is history, but obviously, neither ISTRA nor I played any role in it.

Eminence, let us talk about a story in which, instead, you participated. Referring to your long activism in CL, you once said that "it's like having two original sins." What is your current relationship with this movement?

That line about original sin was a joke at the expense of all those who insisted in reducing me to the "CL bishop," insinuating that I had kept close ties with past friends who had gone on to become political leaders. Needless to say, and needless to repeat, I saw them once or twice a year at institutional events, nothing like being in frequent contact. Since becoming a bishop in 1991, I have left all my CL posts and stopped taking part, in any way, in the guidance of the movement. This doesn't mean I am disowning the experience of Communion and Liberation, which for me has been decisive. I would not be who I am if I had not encountered the movement. It shaped me to the core of my being, making me discover the force and beauty of the Christian proposal.

What is your judgment on the current reality of Communion and Liberation?

It would be awfully presumptuous to express a judgment on a reality that I have not been part of for 27 years now. What I can say is that today I look upon CL, like other movements and new ecclesial communities, from the perspective of my episcopal mission. When Benedict XVI appointed me archbishop of Milan, he told me, "The new buds, that is to say the new groups, need to be grafted on the old trunk of the Church, lest the trunk die and the buds whither."

Today, some people are wondering whether ecclesial movements are hitting a wall. I think that we must be vigilant to make sure that the persuasive power of their charisms, and thus their transformative energy, do not weaken. That's the crucial question that Fr. Giussani kept raising even in the early years of the movement's history. From this point of view, I can say that the positive aspect of the CL method has never faded. The constant increase in conversions and vocations in many forms across ninety countries is a testament to this. In addition, from the beginning of the movement, we have learned to distinguish between the charism and its various forms of implementation. This is what has always given it a universal scope. Associations such as Nueva Tierra in Spain or a large part of Sem terra in Brazil have adhered to the movement.[15] And in my episcopal experience, especially in Milan, I have seen how many *ciellini* involved themselves in parishes and deaneries, with a particular involvement in catechesis and culture.

I remember an episode that illuminates this. It happened that a CL priest, just named the pastor of a Milanese parish, had the bocce field used by ACLI members destroyed overnight,[16] because "people would go to play without even setting foot in church." He was so proud of this that he told Fr. Giussani, who immediately corrected him: "You've done something very stupid. You shouldn't destroy anything, but respect all that exists, applying to it the method that educates people to faith." This idea is also fundamental for social and political action.

Here, we touch upon one of the sore points in the recent history of CL, which has been accused of acting as a political lobby.

Let's take a step back. With the birth of *Movimento Popolare* in the midseventies,[17] CL stopped involving itself directly in politics, but was able to give life to a pre-political entity that shared a common platform with the people from the Christian Democratic party, CISL, ACLI, Catholic Action, and other associations.[18] Even if some people disagree, I consider it a positive experience not only because it proved successful in electoral terms right from the start but also because it opened a new road for Catholics who wanted to engage in politics in a way that differed from the Christian Democratic party, which was starting to show signs of decay.

In my view, abandoning the model of *Movimento Popolare* had the effect of leaving to CL all the responsibility for party action. I am convinced that had a pre-political entity been preserved, the way forward would certainly have been more difficult, but the short circuit between CL and the political visibility of some of its members (who are personally responsible for it) would have been avoided. I believe that describing CL as a lobby is highly offensive and profoundly unjust for the tens of thousands of followers of the movement who have involved themselves in the life of the Church with creative liberty.

For some time now, we have observed diverging opinions within CL. In some cases, they go as far as being more or less openly critical of the movement's leadership. Is this the classic dilemma between authority and liberty?

In the Christian community, and so also in the Fraternity of Communion and Liberation, liberty is ultimately ruled, supported, and if necessary, corrected by the established authority, that is to say, by the authority recognized by the Church. On the other hand, obedience would not be obedience were it not the expression of freedom engaged "in the first person," which is constantly sticking its neck out. It is through these two factors that communion is lived and the mission of a Church movement unfolds. This is what I remember happened with "Gius"—our discussions were often frank and even testy, but they never reached a breaking point. And this was because we all prized the value of unity, which is ultimately guaranteed by authority. There is no true freedom unless it is expressed in a recognized and recognizable belonging to a guided ecclesial community; but at the same time, there is no true community if it does not cause individual freedom to fully flourish.

The impression, however, is that there is currently a conflict about how to interpret the texts and indications of Don Giussani, to the point of making the accusation that his spiritual heredity is being distorted, even betrayed. What do you think?

This is a serious risk that has presented itself in every great movement or religious order in the history of the Church; just think of the Franciscans. Conflicts of interpretation are a natural temptation when we find ourselves in front of a charism so rich and multifaceted, which lends itself easily to different readings, especially when applied to different situations. However, in the necessary attempt to identify with the experience and thought of the founder, one must not seek to confirm one's own interpretation as the only valid one. Such a position can only generate endless diatribes and paralyzing conflicts.

The charism of CL—which from the beginning was characterized by a desire to incarnate the faith in different worlds and environments—must constantly evolve in order to be ever more effective in front of changing historical circumstances. On this point, Pope Francis's speech to the movement of Communion and Liberation in St. Peter's Square in March 2015 is pertinent: Do not be "worshippers of ashes."[19] I must say, I consider it a formidable testimony to members' fidelity to the charism, I daresay a miracle, that an organization as international and complex as CL is still united thirteen years after the death of its founder. And I am certain that this will continue.

Notes to Chapter 3

1.   The name Communion and Liberation was first used in 1969 by a group of university students in Milan who intended to continue following Fr. Giussani after Gioventù Studentesca

disbanded because many of its leaders had joined the student movement of 1968. CL then because the official name of the entire movement. The Fraternity of Communion and Liberation was officially recognized by the Church as a lay association in 1982, with a decree of the Pontifical Council for the Laity. It is currently present in ninety countries.

2. *Federazione Universitari Cattolici Italiani*, Federation of Italian Catholic University students.

3. Cardinal Giovanni Colombo (1902–1992) was archbishop of Milan from 1963 to 1979.

4. Eugenia Scabini (1939–), psychologist and academic. She taught for many years at the University of Turin and then at the Catholic University of Milan, where she was Dean of the School of Psychology from 1999 to 2011.

5. Comunione e Liberazione – Universitari.

6. Rocco Buttiglione (1948–) later become a politician, a member of parliament, and a government minister.

7. The referendum, which was supported by the Italian bishops, was promoted to abolish the law that had introduced divorce in 1970. However, many Catholic associations refused to campaign in favor of abolishing the law, with the notable exception of CL. The referendum failed, with 59% of the votes in favor of keeping divorce legal.

8. Msgr. Enrico Bartoletti (1916–1976) was the general secretary of CEI from 1972 to 1976.

9. Gabrio Lombardi (1913–1976), jurist and academic, led the effort to abolish divorce.

10. Fr. Bartolomeo Sorge, SJ (1929–2020), Jesuit politologist and later editor of *La Civiltà Cattolica*.

11. These "democratic Catholics" were a group of Catholic intellectuals and politicians who took a stance in favor of the law on divorce and rejected the bishops' appeal to vote for abolition. The following year, 1975, they founded an organization called the Democratic League, aimed at steering Italian political Catholicism in a more "progressive" direction.

12. Franco Bolgiani (1922–2012), historian of Christianity and of religion.

13. Cardinal Antonio Poma (1910–1985) was archbishop of Bologna. He presided CEI from 1969 to 1979. Msgr. Luigi Maverna

(1920–1998), a bishop, was the general assistant of the Catholic Action from 1972 to 1976 and then secretary general of CEI from 1976 to 1982.

14. Silvio Berlusconi (1936–), entrepreneur and politician. He started his career as a real estate developer in 1963, then founded the first major private television network in Italy. He entered politics in 1992 and went on to serve several times as prime minister. Fedele Confalonieri (1937–) is a corporate manager and Berlusconi's long-time friend and most important collaborator. Edilnord is the real-estate branch of Berlusconi's business empire.

15. Nueva Tierra was a youth movement born in Spain in the seventies on the initiative of some priests, including the current president of the Fraternity of Communion and Liberation, Fr. Julian Carrón. Nueva Tierra merged with CL in 1985. The Sem Terra Association of workers was born in Brazil in 1984. Part of the movement joined Communion and Liberation in 2008.

16. ACLI is the acronym for the Associazioni Cristiane Lavoratori Italiani (Christian Associations of Italian Workers). It was founded by Achille Grandi in 1944, a Catholic politician and trade unionist. It was traditionally anti-Communist and close to the Christian Democratic Party, but in 1969 moved away from it toward a form of Democratic Socialism, while remaining linked to the Church.

17. Movimento Popolare (People's Movement) was founded in 1975 by some members of Communion and Liberation who wished to get involved in politics. The creation of a new organization answered the need to avoid misunderstandings about the involvement of an ecclesial movement like CL in political and electoral choices. Movimento Popolare was joined also by people coming from other Catholic associations who shared the vision of a social and political movement with a clear Catholic identity. Some members of Movimento Popolare ran for office under the banner of the Christian Democratic Party. In 1976, six of them were elected to parliament. However, the Italian press insisted on regarding Movimento Popolare as the political arm of CL. Movimento Popolare was disbanded in 1993.

18. The Confederazione Italiana Sindacati Lavoratori (Italian Confederation of Workers' Unions) is a large confederation of trade unions of Catholic inspiration, founded in 1950.

19. Pope Francis, *Address to the Movement of Communion and Liberation* (March 7, 2015).

CHAPTER 4

An Obstacle Course

Vocation and Priestly Ordination

You developed your vocation during your GS years. How did the idea of becoming a priest come about? Was there a precise moment when you made your decision?

When a missionary of the La Salle Brothers came to our school and spoke enthusiastically about his work in Africa. His testimony fascinated me. Returning home, I told my mother that I wanted to become a missionary priest. She brought me to the pastor, who cut me off. If I wanted to become a priest, he told me, there was no need to travel so far. I could do it perfectly well in Italy within my own diocese. And that was the end of that.

The idea reemerged during my first few years in the university. It became a serious prospect when a bout of tuberculosis forced me to interrupt my studies from May 1963 to June 1964. I was forced to spend long periods in the mountains, first at the Alpine House in Motta above Madesimo, then later at the Montanina House in Esino in Valsassina. Far from my friends and immersed in solitude, I had the opportunity to reflect on the Christian journey I had started with GS. I remember feeling a need to make my relationship with the Lord more personal. I began to recite the Liturgy of the Hours every day with an old priest. The rhythm of my daily life was set by the Mass, by prayer, and by the liturgical readings. I constantly questioned myself about the future.

Did you have any romantic ties at the time?

I had been engaged to a girl until May of 1963, but the affective dimension of my life remained unsettled. During the year of my illness, I realized that marriage would not satisfy my desire for fulfillment. Over those same months, the priestly vocation presented itself to me as a very distinct possibility. It was precisely at the end of that period, upon resuming my normal life and returning to the university, that I decided to consecrate my life to the Lord.

Did you discuss the matter with anybody before making your decision?

My choice matured through the experience I lived in GS. It was sustained by my conversations with Fr. Ambrogio Valsecchi, a professor of Moral Theology in Venegono.[1] In the Archdiocese of Milan, seminary professors traditionally have pastoral duties as well. They are assigned to a parish where they go each weekend to celebrate Masses, hear confessions, and preach. It is a good custom, an experience that enriches both the professors and the simple faithful. Fr. Ambrogio, who was from Lecco, had been assigned to the parish of St. Nicolò in his hometown. It was there that I came to know and appreciate his intelligence and his heart. He became my confessor and spiritual father very naturally. I made the explicit decision to become a priest during a discussion I had with him in Venegono. This was in the autumn of '64, if I remember correctly.

However, you did not enter the seminary for another three years. Why is that?

Life is never simple. In this case, many different factors played a part. I had already changed universities, leaving the Polytechnic in Milan, where I had started an engineering degree, to study philosophy at the Catholic University of the Sacred Heart. I had realized that I had little interest in pursuing an engineering career. I had made the choice subconsciously to please my father, who as a truck driver admired the engineers who were his bosses at SAE, a well-known manufacturer of trusses and electrical wires. Conversely, I was interested in philosophy. Just after my admission into the second year at the Catholic University, however, I fell ill and was only able to take up my studies again in the fall of '64. Finishing the university was very important for me, and I can say with some pride that I was able to do so in a little over two years. I graduated in February 1967. However, I never abandoned the idea of entering the seminary. I had discussed it also with Cardinal Giovanni Colombo when in 1965 he had called me to be the president of FUCI. He told me to be patient. "For now, get to the bottom of this new experience," he told me. "Later we shall see."

At a certain point, I considered becoming a missionary in Brazil, fascinated by the example of Pigi Bernareggi and my other GS friends who had entered the seminary in Belo Horizonte. I went to visit them in the summer of '66, but my initial enthusiasm quickly turned into concern. The whole group, with the sole exception of Pigi, emphasized political action and revolutionary plans—anticipating the split that GS would experience in Italy two years later. So, I left Belo Horizonte and went to São Paulo.

Fr. Ambrogio Valsecchi, who was also in Brazil at the time, introduced me to the archbishop, Cardinal Agnelo Rossi.[2] He was quite willing to accept me into his seminary. Upon my return to Italy, I relayed my impressions to Fr. Giussani, who was disturbed by the ongoing fight among the GS members in Brazil. He pointed out that it did not make sense for me to enter the São Paulo seminary in the midst of such a complicated situation. Meanwhile, I began to participate in the meetings of the "adult group," those people in CL who intended to choose permanent virginity and who would later take the name *Memores Domini*.[3] I was determined to consecrate my life to the Lord, but the way was still uncertain.

The turning point came in August 1967, during the spiritual exercises at Beato Lorenzo, a Benedictine retreat house near the Subiaco monastery. It was there that I decided to enter the seminary. Some friends of mine reached the same decision—Luigi Negri, Mario Peretti, Marco Martini, and Antonio Bellati.[4] At the end of a long discussion, Fr. Giussani hugged us and praised our decision with inspired words. "Your departure appears to leave the leadership of Gioventù Studentesca weaker. However, you are like Sputniks that, though they lift off and apparently leave the world behind, are really launching towards the future." That October, I began my preliminary year of Theology at the seminary of the Archdiocese of Milan in Saronno.

Shortly afterward, at the Catholic University of Milan, the student protests exploded. This would mark the beginning, also in Italy, of a massive youth rebellion. What is your judgment on what happened in 1968?

The seeds of rebellion had been germinating among students for some time, so the protests did not come entirely as a surprise. The year before, our Milanese FUCI group had organized a conference on the crisis in the universities with the participation of various professors and eight hundred students. We published a report that anticipated many of the themes of the protests of '68. When the protest exploded at the Catholic University in December 1967, Cardinal Colombo turned to Luigi Negri, Marco Barbetta, and myself. As leaders of GS, GIAC, and FUCI, we had a lot of experience in the student world. He asked us to help him understand what was happening. I remember he came to the seminary in Saronno one night after dinner to speak with us. At the end of the meeting, he requested that we write a report assessing the situation which we sent to him before Christmas.

I cannot give an exhaustive judgment on 1968 here. It was an international phenomenon with multiple roots which was born much earlier and then developed differently in various countries. To be concise, we can say that the events of 1968 initially represented a positive desire for change, an impulse of rebellion against a social system too often dominated by hypocrisy and authoritarianism. At first, the demand for authenticity and freedom was powerfully spotlighted. This original dynamic became overshadowed by two elements that radically changed its nature, especially in Italy. The first was the Marx-Leninist ideology that transformed the rebellious impulse into a revolutionary utopianism, presented as new and different from the "real Socialism" in Eastern Europe, which was deliberately ignored. My impression is that when people analyze 1968, they do not emphasize this transformation enough, which was already observable in Italy in the document *Tesi della Sapienza,* written during the occupation of the Scuola Normale di Pisa in 1967. Its theses define students as an intellectual workforce and configure the university protests as a class struggle closely aligned with the struggles of the factory workers. It was then, in my opinion, that the ideologization of the movement began. The result, as we know well now, was to fracture the movement into increasingly intolerant and violent groups that ultimately theorized about armed struggle and practiced terrorism. The second element was the sexual revolution, which loudly proclaimed what bourgeois respectability tended to hide away, namely sexual freedom, which is now flaunted as a form of social emancipation. The revolution they dreamt of (Marxist) and the revolution they practiced (sexual) simultaneously represent the endpoint of the demand for liberation that started the movement of 1968 and its betrayal.

You, with your group of friends, lived those events from the outside, living in the seminary. What was your reaction?

We were very curious and followed what was happening with interest and passion. We didn't just do so from the outside. We wanted to understand the roots and aspirations of the protest movement and for that reason, we traveled to Paris—the heart of the protests—during the summer break of '68. We joined marches in the Latin Quarter, especially the famous ones on boulevard Saint Michel, also known as "Boulmich." We requested and obtained (with some impudence) direct interviews with *maîtres à penser* of neo-Marxism like Althusser and Derrida, but also with religious thinkers such as the Jewish philosopher Emmanuel Lévinas and the Jesuits of the journal *Études*, including Michel de Certeau. We experienced firsthand the weakness and disintegration of Catholic organizations in France, which to us was the land of Péguy, Mounier, Claudel, Gilson, and Maritain; we saw that French Catholicism was floundering, slavishly repeating the slogans coming from the *rive gauche*. It didn't take much foresight to predict that soon this full-fledged hurricane would also hit the Italian Church. The vast majority of the young left the Catholic associations to join the student movement. To them, Christianity had become synonymous with generosity devoid of ideal motivations, which revolutionary utopianism forcefully provided. It was a mass exodus, the greatest crisis of the Church in the twentieth century.

Even worse than the Modernism of the early 1900s?

Certainly, Modernism was predominantly an intellectual phenomenon which developed, above all, among the clergy and that involved, at most, a few lay intellectual figures, but which did not touch the people. By contrast, 1968 burnt to the ground not only the Catholic youth associations, but also the Christian morality and *ethos*, which had been deeply rooted in the ordinary Italian people. The traditional model of Christianity was destined to disappear, as a way of looking at reality. Even in the best-case scenario, it could have endured only as a leftover and marginalized element. The movement of 1968 confirmed this.

Did the bewilderment and confusion that 1968 provoked also within the Church somehow influence your departure from the seminary of Venegono?

Let me start by pointing out that Cardinal Giovanni Colombo considered my entrance into the seminary, along with my other friends who had similarly developed their priestly vocations while in their 20's at the university, as a validation of the changes he had made at FUCI. Nicora had entered a few years before, after completing a law degree, so now there were five of us. Upon entering the seminary, we obviously did not renounce our GS history, our way of thinking. We respected the rules, but had our own opinions and openly expressed them. In short, we behaved with a spontaneity and a sense of freedom that concerned our superiors. I remember that the rector of the seminary in Saronno, Fr. Marco Ferrari,[5] once told me, "You're like an ocean liner in a canal!" It was a compliment, even overly flattering, which actually contained a warning—continue on your present course and you risk hitting a wall. In any case, Fr. Ferrari and I always had a good relationship, which grew even stronger during my episcopal ministry in Milan, when he was an auxiliary bishop and valued collaborator. I must say that there were no problems in the seminary of Saronno.

Things changed the following year when we moved on to the seminary of Venegono. A latent friction arose with the head rector, Msgr. Bernardo Citterio.[6] He was concerned about the influence we were having on other seminarians. There was also a nontrivial question about my military service. The draft was obligatory back then, but could be delayed for students until they turned 28. The obligation ceased for seminarians the moment they were ordained deacons, usually at the beginning of the last year of theology. I would turn 28 at the end of 1969, and if I did not reach the diaconate by that date, I would have to leave for a year and a half of military service. In fact, the dates aligned in such a way that I would have lost three academic years, an excessively long pause that would have endangered my whole seminary education. For this reason, I requested in the spring of 1969 to be ordained a deacon that fall, at the beginning of my second year of theology.

Msgr. Citterio's response was decidedly negative. "Ordaining a deacon two years early has never been done before. And, frankly, I don't think you're ready. Your style is still very secular—we're not there yet…" He advised me to speak to the archbishop, since he knew me personally. Cardinal Colombo said he was sorry for Msgr. Citterio's refusal, but he could not intervene against the rector's decision. And he invited me to be patient and accept this trial. That meant I would have to leave the seminary and come back at the age of thirty-one. Objectively, it seemed too long a wait. So, after discussions with Fr. Giussani and Fr. Francesco Ricci—who was regarded as CL's "foreign minister" for his extraordinary ability to form relations around the world (especially in Eastern Europe)[7]—I approached the bishop of Teramo, Msgr. Abele Conigli,[8] who greatly esteemed the movement. He agreed to ordain me, first a deacon and then, in July 1970, as a priest for his diocese.

How heavily did this break weigh on your life?

What caused me the most suffering, honestly, was not Msgr. Citterio's refusal, which was in some ways justified by the rules of the seminary of Milan. The most painful wound was inflicted after my priestly ordination, which was regarded as an all-out insult by the hierarchy of the Ambrosian diocese. Msgr. Conigli paid a heavy price for his openness towards me—he was expected to become bishop of an important diocese, possibly in his hometown of Modena, but from that moment on he was ostracized. As for me, I became persona non grata.

After receiving my license in theology at Fribourg, I was given the opportunity to become the assistant of Professor Langé in Milan. I would have been one of the few priests teaching at the State University of Milan. When I requested the archdiocese's permission, the reaction was harsh. Cardinal Colombo spoke to the Congregation of the Clergy to make sure I would be refused the authorization and my bishop, Msgr. Conigli, received a letter from the prefect. It explained that due to the opposition of the archbishop of Milan, I would have to find a teaching job at another university *pro bono pacis* (in order to keep peace). Msgr. Manfredini took me in and had me teach theology for a few hours a week in Piacenza.[9] I also commuted to Milan for my ISTRA research work. For a few years, I was not granted the faculty to celebrate Mass or to hold public meetings within the borders of the Ambrosian diocese.

My most bitter experience occurred in 1974, when I was forced to take a long stay in the Policlinico Hospital in Milan. The hospital chaplain did not come to visit me even once. He must have known there was a sick priest among the patients, but for him I never existed! Luckily, there was a good friar who brought me Communion and heard my confession, otherwise I would have been deprived of the sacraments. This inexplicable hostility hurt me deeply at the time. In 1991, when I became a bishop, a complete and even moving reconciliation with Cardinal Colombo took place. He sent me a card with the phrase *in osculo Christi una cum Petro pax tecum* (in the kiss of Christ in unity with Peter, peace be with you). I responded with a letter full of gratitude. We wrote to each other again before his death the following year.

As a bishop, did you get the chance to meet some of those who ran the Venegono Seminary at the time you left?

I remember the first time I participated in the national assembly of the CEI. As the youngest bishop, I decided to sit in the back of the synodal room. From the corner of my eye, I saw my old rector at Venegono, Msgr. Bernardo Citterio, as he approached and sat nearby. At that point, he noticed my presence with a start. "Oh, you're here too?" he asked. And I replied, "Well, yes, it happens sometimes."

Based on your personal experience, what is your assessment of the path of priestly formation in the Italian church, which has essentially remained the same for the last fifty years?

Let's just say that priestly formation is still shaped by the model created by St. Charles Borromeo. I consider this a very positive thing because it saved us from collapse. Where seminaries have been shut down, as often happened across Northern Europe, priests are disappearing. It's not easy to find an alternative to the Borromean type of seminary. Many attempts have been made, especially in Europe, but in the end the model proposed by St. Charles (adjusted over time) remains unbeaten still today. Over the years of my episcopacy, I've often reflected about how a new form of priestly formation might develop. In outline, I envision a three-stage process.

The first stage, once the call to the priesthood had been verified, would involve a decent period of time exclusively dedicated to community life, prayer, and study—in short, to knowing oneself and one's vocation. All of this would take place as an almost monastic experience of radical detachment from the world. At a second stage, after receiving his license in theology, each one would have to return, without any time limit, to a normal life in civil society—while staying in close contact with one's educators and spiritual father, and remaining securely within an ecclesial community. Finally, it would be the bishop's job to conduct the final, objective examination leading to priestly ordination. However, I'm well aware that there are many reasons a diocese might not choose to follow this approach.

"Sometimes I encounter laypeople who tell me that the priests feel discouraged."[10] You said this once speaking to the seminarians of Venegono. Isn't it paradoxical that this happens to the people who ought to bear witness to the faith and help people have hope? Is there a remedy to the current crisis in the priesthood?

As you well know, many competent people have weighed in on this question, but this obviously has not been enough. The life of a priest, in whatever situation he is called to work, be it in a large metropolis or a remote village, is very difficult. In most cases, he is no longer supported or accompanied by one or more "lay collaborators," as was normal up to a few decades ago. And in all parishes, whether in the city or the country, the solidarity and companionship that created a positive and stimulating atmosphere around the priest and that in some ways protected him, has been considerably weakened. Certainly, today's priest is surrounded by coworkers and deals with many people, but these relationships are often purely functional and are rarely based on ties of Christian friendship. This makes the priest increasingly fragile in this dizzying and, in many respects, indecipherable change of epoch, which also affects the Church.

In general, priests do not reach the point of questioning their vocations. It happens occasionally, but, based on my twenty-seven years as a bishop, I must say that it is rare. Typically, the priests I have met in the three dioceses where I served as bishop and at the Lateran University remain convinced of their vocations and have always shown great zeal. The danger, instead, is that the priest falls into depression, is "burned-out," as people say. It is not accidental that there is so much insistence now on the importance of rectory life and on exploring the synodal dimension of Church life—through "processes and exercises" of effective communion with other priests, with religious men and women, with families, and with young people. In the Archdiocese of Milan, the program for the permanent formation of priests is focusing on these aspects.

The priest of today risks living his mission as a role, without being able to communicate the beauty of the experience of faith. Instead, the "objective priesthood" of Christ—which the priest participates in through the sacrament of Holy Orders—must become one with the "subjective priesthood" of Christ, that is, with the complete gift of oneself. All of us must regain the awareness that life is a vocation. And the life that a priest is called to is the same life that the Apostles led with Jesus, witnessing to the beauty of a life spent in the service of the Other, and therefore of others.

Doesn't the crisis of the priesthood and of the steady drop in vocations also depend on the rule of celibacy, a Church law that applies only to the priests of the Latin rite?

No, I disagree, first of all because celibacy is not an extrinsic rule. Its roots can be found in the radical option of Christ's own virginity, which in the Latin Church has always been experienced as a powerful nourishment for the priesthood. Secondly, it's not as if Protestant communities, where ministers can marry, have more vocations, far from it. Regarding Eastern Rite Churches, we must not forget that, leaning on the monastic tradition, they require obligatory celibacy for bishops. Certainly, celibacy is not a dogma of the faith but an ecclesiastical law, and this explains why the issue keeps coming back.

In my opinion, I see no reason to call celibacy into question. In fact, we need to demonstrate its positive value and real fruitfulness.

Notes to Chapter 4

1. Ambrogio Valsecchi (1930–1983) was a priest and theologian. He taught moral theology at the seminary of Venegono, but found himself at odds with his superiors, who considered his views on sexual ethics heterodox. Eventually, he asked to be laicized and worked as a psychologist.
2. Cardinal Agnelo Rossi (1913–1995) was the archbishop of São Paulo from 1964 to 1974, and then prefect of the Congregation for the Evangelization of Peoples until 1984.
3. *Memores Domini* is an association of consecrated laypeople. It was born within Communion and Liberation and was approved by the Church with a Pontifical decree on December 8, 1988. Currently, it has roughly six thousand members all over the world.
4. All four became priests in the Archdiocese of Milan. Luigi Negri (1941–) went on to become bishop of San Marino from 2005 to 2013, and the archbishop of Ferrara until 2017.
5. Marco Ferrari (1932–2020) in the sixties was the rector of the archdiocesan seminary in Saronno. From 1987 to 2009, he was an auxiliary bishop in Milan.
6. Bernardo Citterio was major rector of the seminaries of the Archdiocese of Milan from 1963 to 1983 and then became auxiliary bishop.
7. Francesco Ricci (1930–1991) was a longtime collaborator of Fr. Giussani who traveled on behalf of CL to several foreign countries, especially to Eastern Europe under Communism. He established a wide network of contacts with Eastern European thinkers like Václav Havel, Józef Tischner, and Karol Wojtyła, and facilitated the knowledge of their works in the West.
8. Abele Conigli (1922–2005) was a bishop and teacher. When he was a young priest, he was involved in the resistance against Fascism. He was bishop of Teramo from 1967 to 1988.
9. Enrico Manfredini (1922–1983) was bishop of Piacenza from 1969 to 1983. In 1983, he was appointed archbishop of Bologna, but he died a few months later of a sudden heart attack.
10. Angelo Scola, *Dio ha bisogno degli uomini* (Milano: BUR, 2016), 12.

CHAPTER 5

An Educational Genius

By Fr. Luigi Giussani's Side

You had the opportunity to meet and come to know personally some extraordinary people in the worlds of faith and culture. Giants of the Church in the sixties and seventies were your teachers and companions. The first, undoubtedly, was Fr. Luigi Giussani. You always considered yourself his spiritual son, becoming one of his closest collaborators, his right-hand man, according to many people. How would you describe your relationship with "Gius"?

Quite often, small episodes hint at things that will later have great weight in a person's life, revealing the initiative of the Spirit in human history. The first time I met Fr. Giussani personally was in 1962, when I was the leader of GS in Lecco. The appointment was set up by Robi Ronza,[1] the driving force behind *Michelaccio*. It was a student-run newspaper, well produced, with contributions from groups in Varese, Busto Arsizio, Gallarate, Lecco, Como, and Sondrio, edited cooperatively. The paper managed to cover its costs through sales and advertisements. However, it failed to meet the high standards of the students in Milan, who thought that as an initiative *Michelaccio* was a bit too independent and provincial.

This is why Ronza organized some meetings between Gius and the people running the different editorial offices. He also scheduled one for me, as the editor for Lecco. When I showed up at the agreed time at the door of the Berchet High School, however, Fr. Giussani told me that there must have been some error, that he had no such appointment in his planner, that in fact he had to rush somewhere else to meet with an important person. He invited me to accompany him on the streetcar. We spoke for ten minutes and I could tell he had more pressing issues on his mind.

The meeting was so rushed and disappointing that it left me with a sour taste in my mouth. I would see him again on other occasions. But our real encounter was in 1965, when he conveyed Cardinal Colombo's desire that I take up the presidency of FUCI. I remember talking over lunch, in a trattoria on Via Statuto. It was there that my relationship with Fr. Giussani began.

This was the time when the "adult group" was born. Fr. Giussani paid particular attention to it, leading retreat days and spiritual exercises in the Benedictine retreat house of Subiaco. I also participated from time to time, in search of what God wanted from me. In those two years, from 1965 to 1967, I met with Gius more often, but it would take time before our encounters became more personal, in terms both of content and intensity.

When did this transition take place—after your ordination?

Yes, in a sense; the rapport grew stronger once I became a priest. Or, to be more precise, my connection with Fr. Luigi Giussani became decisive after the crisis of '68, which caused a mass exodus of GS and FUCI members, who were drawn to the extreme left in the wake of the student protests. However, there remained a small group of students who decided to maintain a connection with the original experience and with the charism of Fr. Giussani.

They included the so-called group of Mottarello, named after a house in a small town near Varese where they held their first meetings. It was a group I felt part of even though I was unable to attend regularly, since I was at the seminary in Venegono. In fact, Mottarello contributed to the birth of what would become a new movement, Communion and Liberation. When I became a priest, the relationship between Gius and me grew very close. I collaborated with him and became the leader of CLU, the university students of Communion and Liberation. In that period, I met him frequently. Almost every morning, at seven thirty, I would make my way to his home on Via Martinengo along with Sante Bagnoli, the founder of the publishing house Jaca Book.[2] We would speak to Fr. Giussani about ourselves and the life of the movement.

Is it true that Giussani thought of you as his successor at the helm of CL?

In those years, tales about "Scola, the heir of Giussani" began to circulate. Every once in a while, Giussani would say, "It's time for me to retire, and Angelo you can take my place." But I believe he said it as a joke. In reality, he had no intention of retiring, and neither I nor the other leaders ever believed him. In fact, to be completely sincere, I must admit that my rapport with Giussani was never easy or peaceful. Since our relationship was something very strong, intense, and significant, it was characterized by a certain tension. For example, during meetings, I would try to push my point of view even at the expense of contradicting and angering him. This never reduced my respect and affection for him, just the opposite.

Had I not encountered Fr. Giussani, I would not be who I am today. He helped, corrected, and supported me in my difficult moments as a father does his son. My friendship with him had nothing to do with the complicity, winking, or swagger of cheerful buddies. It was tremendously serious, challenging, and not without back-and-forths. With Giussani one never horsed around, and one was always glad. This is where his great strength as an educator emerged, the capacity to read the heart of whomever he was talking to and to accompany him on the walk of life, instigating a dynamic of freedom and creativity. This facilitated an atmosphere of joy and true gladness that found expression in Giussani's childlike spirit.

But his explosions are also memorable.

He had an irascible character, but it never prevented him from reopening a dialogue, with everybody, every time. Anger has nothing to do with spite; it is actually the opposite. A flash of anger does not ruin a relationship. It can sting at first, but it never prevents the embrace of reconciliation. An outburst, just like an invective, can simply express a style of evangelization (just think of all the invectives Jesus used against the scribes and Pharisees in the Gospel of John) that we are now giving up for the sake of being "religiously correct."

In your opinion, what was Fr. Giussani's defining characteristic? How would you describe him in few words?

An educational genius, that was Gius. He emerged from an atmosphere rich with cultural stimuli, such as prevailed at the seminary in Venegono. In the years of his training for the priesthood, Giussani gained a broad and critical vision of several fields of knowledge, which allowed him to integrate literature, art, philosophy, and theology—including American Protestant theology and Russian Orthodox theology. The neo-scholastic approach was prevalent in seminaries at that time. Instead, Giussani starts from experience, understood not individualistically but as the faith experience of a people. What matters to him is the relationship with Christ, who is contemporary with and relevant to my person, and who challenges my freedom. He senses that, as Kierkegaard wrote, the only relationship one can have with the grandeur of Christ is one of contemporaneity, otherwise it is like relating to a dead man. His life no longer provokes me. I can admire him and still go on living according to my own categories.

It is something exceptional when you really think about it. A young seminarian, isolated from the world, in the dark years of the war, assimilates what he is taught to the point of surpassing it and integrating it, so to speak, into an entirely new and original vision.

This is why I coined the word *sorgivo* to define Giussani's thought.[3] His reflections are nourished by many authors and philosophical and theological schools. However, what emerges is a surprising ability to go beyond schools and systems, and to affirm what he calls "the method" of Christian life, that is to say faith as a personal encounter with Christ, the Church as the fundamental modality for this encounter to happen, and the urgency to communicate the Church in one's environment. He had many valuable professors in the seminary. His true teacher was Gaetano Corti,[4] whose fundamental theology revolved around the key concept of the humanity of Christ as the "sacrament of his divinity," a definition that can now be found in the *Catechism of the Catholic Church*.[5] Hence the question Giussani asks: Why doesn't the event of Christ touch the hearts of people today, especially of young people, why doesn't it enter into the flesh and bowels of those who make history? His answer: because the "I" is the great missing factor in Catholic education. It is the "I" that needs to be reawakened in its freedom, in order for the conviction of faith to prevail over formal convention. At that time, formal convention was still dominant at the popular level, but Giussani perceived its fragility and predicted its rapidly approaching demise.

As he said to Robi Ronza in a book-length interview about Communion and Liberation, there was "a situation in which Christians politely excluded themselves from public life, from the culture, from grassroots organization, amid encouraging applause and the cordial consensus of the political and cultural forces that aimed to replace them in the public arena of our country."[6] Here we can see in all its genius and foresight Giussani's intuition that the Christian faith must be embraced and lived reasonably, that is to say in harmony with man's desire for fulfillment and his existential questions. Otherwise, faith desiccates to an abstract postulate or a sterile moralism. His educational genius led him to break all kinds of barriers, finding references and inspirations even in events and authors that are seemingly very distant from the Catholic tradition.

Are you saying that Giussani was not only a great educator but also a fine theologian?

Unlike many people, I believe that Giussani was a true thinker. However, he did not want his thought to remain just words on paper, beautiful but ineffective. Giussani was destined to be a professor, but he decided to leave the main highway, which would have been an easier and more prestigious course and might have led to a career, to take on the daily struggle of teaching young people about friendship with Christ. In the humility of this choice, he found his greatness.

Finally, there is another aspect that goes unremarked. Fr. Giussani always said that he learned a great deal from his encounters with figures of great faith and culture like Balthasar and Ratzinger. But I want to emphasize that those encounters were fruitful for them as well, inspiring them to bend, so to speak, their theological skills in a more pastoral and pedagogical direction. Balthasar admitted this in a card he sent to Giussani, expressing the wish that "my little shrub might be protected by the great tree you have grown." He was referring to the *Johannesgemeinschaft*, the community of consecrated adults that he and the mystic Adrienne von Speyr had founded.[7]

Fr. Giussani's relationships with Church authorities was often stormy and contentious. However, unlike the dissenting priests who were popular during those years, he always proclaimed the value of obedience. How did he live this interior conflict?

Here we can see another fundamental principle of his pedagogy. This principle was counter-cultural in those years, but even more so today—the value of authority. According to Giussani, there can be no education of any kind if one's freedom does not discover the convenience[8] of having an authoritative reference point in one's life. Authority, if rightly exercised, is not an obstacle or objection for my freedom; dependence is for my benefit, it is good for me! This is what he learned from an early age, on his mother's lap, and what he would go on to experience at the seminary and confirm through many, many trials in the course of his life.

It may seem paradoxical, but this unshakable acceptance of authority allowed him to express his opinion with immense freedom and even to openly criticize authority itself. He spoke clearly and without hesitating, expressing the truth that burnt inside him even to bishops and popes, at a personal and often heavy price. He suffered, but never moved away one bit from a position of docile and obedient fidelity to the authority of the Church. That was his position and he made it the position of the movement.

In this sense, CL has been and still is an authentically Catholic phenomenon, whereas many other groups that claimed to follow Church embraced a modern concept of the critical spirit—namely, an arrogant assertion of autonomy. And this attitude remains common today. You need only to hang around the Catholic world to see that for many people, participation is synonymous with criticism, plain and simple. Giussani witnessed to us that criticism can and in many cases must be raised, but by a personal and communal subject that recognizes in the authority of the Church the ultimate guarantor of the possibility of a Christian existence. As he loved to repeat, "Christ has founded the Church, not on the intelligence of human reasoning but on Peter and his successors," something we often forget.

You became a bishop, while Giussani remained a simple priest. How did your relationship change after your episcopal ordination in 1991? And when was the last time you saw him?

When I was told in July of 1991 of my appointment, I went to speak to Giussani. I met him in Val d'Aosta while he was leading some university students on a three-day retreat. We talked for a long time, and I couldn't tell you which one of us was more moved and emotional. However, when we parted, he told me, "Now you will walk down your own path, we as a movement will continue to walk down ours." And so it was, even if there are still many people who think otherwise. I no longer had any particular ties to CL, and from that day on, my encounters with Giussani took on a different cadence and always had a strictly personal character.

I remember that in the mid-1990s, someone proposed holding regular meetings between the bishops who came from CL and Giussani, which is common among other Catholic associations. We did it once, then never again. Only people who did not know Giussani could have thought that he would have tried to manipulate us. He seriously believed in the freedom of each person, and even more so in the freedom of bishops, and I can testify to that without fear of being contradicted.

I saw him for the last time the night before he died. He was already in a coma and hooked up to a respirator. I stayed alone in the room with him for five minutes, unable to stop looking at that face which seemed to have recaptured its usual appearance—no longer a mask deformed by the illness of those final years, but his expressive face, bursting with energy and happiness, which was typical of Gius. And I thought that was how he was presenting himself at the house of the Father.

In 2012, the canonical process began to open the cause for the beatification of Msgr. Luigi Giussani. Thirteen years have passed since his death, and six since the start of the procedures for his beatification. Some people are wondering—and not without a polemical edge—why things are taking so long. Can I turn the question to you, your Eminence?

All the necessary steps are being taken. They involve, among other things, assessments by a few historians about Fr. Giussani's life, and by theologians who must examine all his written works with any public relevance, down to even his mimeographs. I am not sure people understand how many tens of thousands of pages Don Giussani wrote, and as a result, the enormous amount of work that must be tackled. As far as I know, the experts are working tirelessly but in this, everyone involved is bound to absolute discretion. I will simply remark that the six-year period that has elapsed since the beginning of the process is not too long at all, if we consider the time the beatification cause has taken for many other candidates.

The important thing I really want to underscore is the veneration for the Servant of God Luigi Giussani, which has been spreading spontaneously from the day of his death, as is testified by the numerous visitors who come to pray at his grave and by the stories of many extraordinary events attributed to his intercession. It is the most comforting sign of the immense grace of his charism that many people have received and continue to receive.

Notes to Chapter 5

1. Robi Ronza (1941–) became a journalist and the author of several books.
2. Jaca Book is a publisher founded in 1966 by Sante Bagnoli, Maretta Campi, and Paolo Mangini. It originally focused on politics, macroeconomics, human sciences, Christianity, and theology. In subsequent years, its catalog expanded to art history, archeology, and architecture. Overall, it has published over 4,000 volumes by roughly 2,500 authors, including Jacques Derrida, Emmanuel Lévinas, Paul Ricœur, Luigi Giussani, John Henry Newman, Henri de Lubac, Hans Urs von Balthasar, and Mircea Eliade.
3. In Italian, *sorgente* is a natural spring of water, and *sorgivo* is the corresponding adjective. It indicates something that springs afresh, new and original. See also Angelo Scola, *Un pensiero sorgivo. Sugli scritti di Luigi Giussani* (Genova: Marietti, 2004).
4. Gaetano Corti (1910–1990) was a priest and theologian. He taught Dogmatic Theology and Patristics for many years at the seminary of Venegono.
5. *Catechism of the Catholic Church*, 515.
6. *Comunione e Liberazione, interviste a Luigi Giussani*, ed. Robi Ronza (Milano: Jaca Book, 1976), 25.

7. Hans Urs von Balthasar (1905–1988) was a prominent Swiss theologian. Adrienne von Speyr (1902–1967) was a Swiss mystic, physician, and author. In 1944, Balthasar and Speyr co-founded a secular institute called "Community of St. John" (*Johannesgemeinschaft*, in German). It is unrelated to the French Community of St. John founded by Fr. Marie-Dominique Philippe, which has admitted credible accusations of sexual, psychological, and spiritual abuse by its founder and other members.

8. In the original, the Italian word *convenienza* is hyphenated as *con-venienza* to emphasize its etymological meaning, "coming together."

CHAPTER 6

Great Teachers

In Contact with Balthasar, Ratzinger, and de Lubac

Let's talk about Hans Urs von Balthasar. You knew him personally, spent time with him, studied him, and made other people study him. What was the origin of this strong bond with the great Swiss theologian?

It all began one autumn day in 1970, in the cafeteria of the University of Fribourg.[1] I had been sent there by my bishop, Msgr. Conigli, to obtain my license in theology. Grabbing a copy of the newspaper *Le Monde*, I was struck by a brief article that gave the news that a conference in Paris had concluded in a stalemate. It had been organized by Marie-Joseph Le Guillou, along with other theologians such as Henri de Lubac,[2] Hans Urs von Balthasar, and Joseph Ratzinger, to found a new journal on theology and culture involving a few members of the International Theological Commission.[3] My immediate reaction was to talk to Eugenio Corecco,[4] a young university teacher and leader of a small community that had started in the student house where I was also living at the time. "We could start the journal in Italy," I told him. "Let's try to propose the idea to Balthasar. You know him personally. Let's go visit him." Balthasar agreed to meet us and then sent us to Ratzinger to discuss the project that would result in the birth of the journal *Communio*.

That first impromptu encounter marked the beginning of a relationship with Balthasar that grew ever closer. It developed in two directions: the first revolved around the work of preparing and editing *Communio* at the beginning of the seventies;[5] the second consisted of several personal meetings, which restarted after my return to Fribourg as a professor in 1979 and remained uninterrupted until the day of his death. It was a very intense exchange that allowed me to know him up close, to ask him questions on the various aspects of his research, to study him, and to make him studied.[6] But beyond scholarship, my relationship with Balthasar was filial and friendly, and one of the most valuable gifts life has given me.

I remember that in those years, when somebody wanted to invite Balthasar to Italy for a conference, they were always told the same thing: "You have to go through Scola, he never says no to him." What was this great personality like from up close?

Every time I called him up, fearful of disturbing him and convinced that he would gently refuse my invitation, I was myself astonished by his availability. Whether it was about holding retreats or exercises for priests, about a conference, about writing an article (not only for specialized journals but even for newspapers or magazines), or about giving his time to students and friends who wanted to meet him in Basel, he almost always agreed immediately without resistance—except when he had previous commitments—and actually with gladness in his voice. This availability was rooted in his profound conviction that Christian existence means allowing oneself to be made by God in the most complete *indiferencia*, as he had learned from St. Ignatius of Loyola. The term is not meant to be translated as "indifference," which implies a passivity or ignorance, but as absolute availability and poverty of spirit.

This was the man Balthasar I came to know up close, beyond his reserved character, which at times might seem surly. He was without a doubt a free spirit who always chose to remain outside the circles of official roles, prestige, and power. He had refused to go teach at the Gregorian in Rome and at the University of Munich in Bavaria, to fill the prestigious chair that had been Guardini's, preferring instead to be a chaplain ministering to students in his hometown of Basel. His theology was also very original and innovative. Being firmly anchored in Sacred Scripture and in Tradition mattered to him. The central idea of his thought was that we must begin from beauty (as a transcendental) to comprehend the Mystery in its attractive force. According to him, as he wrote in his second volume of *Herrlichkeit*, "Only beautiful theology, that is, only theology which, grasped by the Glory of God, is able itself to transmit its rays, has the chance of making any impact in human history."[7]

Another great theologian, Henri de Lubac, defined Balthasar as "perhaps the most learned man of our time" and a "novel Father of the Church." And yet for most of his life he did not gain much recognition on the ecclesiastical scene. He was sidelined and harshly criticized. How would you explain this?

That Balthasar was the most cultured man of the last century is plausible. His enormous body of work relies on a cultural background of immense learning and on an extraordinarily open point of view which had been nourished from a young age. Just think of his doctoral thesis, *The Apocalypse of the German Soul*, a three-volume review of Germanic thought written when he was just over thirty years old.[8] Philosophy, art, literature, and music were his daily bread, of course together with patristics and theology. His studies ranged from Mozart's *Magic Flute* to Hegel's idealism, from Claudel's poems to Dürer's prints. Above all, he had an impressive ability to produce mountains of work in very little time.

I remember a visit I paid to him in Basel. His house had a garden and he lived on the third floor, while the second was reserved for guests. He came to pick me up from the airport himself, in his old Volkswagen driven by his dedicated and intelligent secretary, Cornelia Capol. He had me sit down in his study. On his desk I saw a copy of the Old Testament in Hebrew, a copy the New Testament in Greek, and a pile of papers, nothing else. He told me, "From yesterday morning to last night, I've been scribbling down a few notes to help readers struggling to find their way through the fifteen volumes of the Trilogy." And so he'd written *Epilogue*, a synthesis of his thought which is a true masterpiece.[9] Most people would have needed months and months to produce such a book. It took him a day and a night! The fact that a thinker of this caliber, a theologian who in his writings had also been able to predict the turning point of the Church in the sixties, was not invited to the Second Vatican Council as an expert was truly incomprehensible and disconcerting. It was a grave error, which de Lubac openly denounced before the assembly of bishops. And all because of a few people's clerical narrow-mindedness!

A decisive part of the life and mission of Balthasar was marked by his encounter with the mystic Adrienne von Speyr, who died in 1967. Did you ever get the chance to talk about her with him?

Yes, certainly, and on more than a few occasions. Adrienne von Speyr had begun with him the experience of the *Johannesgemeinschaft*, a secular institute open to laypeople, both men and women, as well as to priests. Balthasar cannot be understood apart from his bond with von Speyr's extraordinary vocation, within that availability to the mystery that I mentioned earlier—so much so that he considered all of his work inseparable from that of Adrienne. He put himself at her service, gathering her mystical intuitions and assuming the difficult task of verifying their value in a fraught confrontation with the doctrine of the Church.

I particularly remember a lunch at a Roman restaurant in 1985 with Balthasar and Fr. Georges Chantraine,[10] one of the founders of the journal *Communio*. We had decided that ISTRA would organize a conference on "The ecclesial mission of Adrienne von Speyr," in homage to Balthasar's eightieth birthday. We discussed possible speakers; we mentioned several names, but he objected to one of them. "No, he won't do. I talked to Adrienne last night and she told me not to invite him." Chantraine and I exchanged a somewhat surprised look. Neither of us dared to ask for an explanation. We kept silent for a moment and then kept talking about the conference. But that was not the only time Balthasar told me about his conversations with von Speyr, who was already dead. He would do it very naturally, considering these conversations so normal that he had no problem telling others. He had abandoned everything to follow the mystical intuition of this woman, a decision that was disapproved of by his Jesuit superiors. This decision prompted him to leave the Society that he had joined in his youth with great conviction and passion.

Balthasar always remained profoundly a Jesuit and immediately recognized his encounter with Adrienne as continuous with the charism of St. Ignatius. The idea of a Christianity made up of "exercises" and not of "talks" is a key point of his theology. We can therefore imagine how much internal suffering he must have felt in having to leave his beloved Society, not to mention the problems and obstacles he was forced to face in his daily life. For a time, he had no home and was not incardinated in any diocese until he was taken in by the bishop of Basel. To be able to capture von Speyr's mystical experiences, he learned shorthand; this is how he was able to write dozens of massive volumes. It was a gargantuan task that Balthasar carried out alongside his own writing.

Many extraordinary phenomena occurred in the life of this woman. Take for example her commentary on the Gospel of St. John. Without holding the text, she used to recite it word for word and then comment on it. And yet neither of them gave much weight to these occurrences. What held importance for them was the objective mysticism to which all Christians are called, each according to his or her own vocation. Adrienne von Speyr was a practical woman, with her feet on the ground; she was one of the first women in Switzerland to be admitted into the medical profession, and volunteered at a hospital just outside of Basel for many years, caring for as many as sixty people a day. She was very ill, and near the end of her life, when her condition worsened and she became incapacitated, the great theologian cared for her personally.

I have always been struck by the simple humility of a man as intellectually and culturally superior as Balthasar. I remember his genuine wonder when we threw a party for his eightieth birthday. It was at Castel Sant'Angelo in Rome, on a beautiful moonlit night brightened by classical music. At some point he and Ratzinger played a duet on the piano. "If you, friends, are so happy, then I must be happy too," he told us with a little smile. Following Adrienne's advice, he had never wanted honors. He refused the first attempt to make him a cardinal. The second time, he gave in to the insistence of John Paul II who admired him very much, and who rehabilitated him after many years of slander and unjust criticism. He died three days before he received the red hat and, in this way—as his friend Ratzinger noted in the funeral homily held in Lucerne—he managed to obey both Adrienne and the pope at the same time, staying faithful to God's mysterious design to the end.

People still remember Balthasar's polemical exchange with Karl Rahner,[11] which gave him a reputation as a conservative and reactionary. In your opinion, what remains relevant today of his theology?

After the publication of *Theo-Drama*,[12] Rahner accused Balthasar of trying to rationally explain the entire mystery of the divine revelation, risking a slide towards Gnosticism. The theologian from Basel responded with *The Moment of Christian Witness*,[13] targeting Rahner's "demythologized" Christianity as too condescending towards the mentality of the world. However, in a later edition, Balthasar greatly softened his tone. In the years after the Council, his position was immediately criticized by the progressives, but later Balthasar would also be attacked by the conservatives for his ideas about hell being "empty." In truth, his thought was misinterpreted and banalized. He did not intend at all to negate hell's existence as a place of eternal damnation in any way, but to reiterate, in accordance with traditional doctrine, that it is permissible to hope in the salvation of all humanity. He talked about a possibility, not a certainty. In this sense, hell might be empty, but that didn't mean that I couldn't be the very first one to go!

All of these criticisms have by now faded into the past. What remains is the power of his thought which continues to be of great assistance to today's theology, which is plainly having trouble facing the new problems of the age, such as the debates over life, sexuality, and the techno-sciences. Balthasar's theology presents a clear alternative to the liberal one, but at the same time it is the opposite of a neo-scholastic and intellectualistic vision. He defended with conviction *Humanae Vitae*, the controversial encyclical of Paul VI, but did not agree with the way some people overemphasized the question of contraception. For him, the decisive issue was the spousal relationship between Christ and the Church, the foundation of the marital union. A humanity that no longer comprehends any of this, he said, will have a difficult time grasping the meaning of the moral indications in the encyclical.

The entire work of Balthasar is far from being a purely intellectual construction. In general, he always considered his activity as a writer and theologian as something secondary, *faute de mieux*, for lack of anything better, as he told John Paul II when he received the Paul VI Prize. His main interest, as testified by his enthusiastic commitment to *Communio*, was to work for the renewal of the Church from the grassroots. He witnessed to this by dedicating his energies above all to the care of priests and to the *Johannesgemeinschaft*. The fact that university people study Balthasar today is a consoling sign. Things are happening now that only recently seemed unthinkable.

Many young people are asking to write their theses on the works of the theologian from Basel, truly recognized as "a modern Father of the Church."

As you already recalled, you supported the *Communio* project from the start and personally participated in its foundation. Was it intended to be an initiative opposed to the theological magazine *Concilium,* which aimed to give expression to the more reform-oriented aspects of Vatican II?

No, not at all. This opinion, still common today, that our intent was to create an alternative journal to *Concilium* has absolutely no basis in reality. The idea had come from a few members of the International Theological Commission, which had been instituted by Paul VI in 1969. Our concern was not to oppose *Concilium,* but rather to *pose ourselves*, as Balthasar explained in the magnificent editorial of the first issue of *Communio.* In it, he proposes a theology of *poiesis,* meaning a theology that develops coherently by being the expression of a subject that poses itself with a dynamic ecclesial identity. At the same time— and this was the second fundamental element—it wasn't meant to be a strictly scientific journal for a circle of experts, but cultural in a larger sense. It had to be able to go beyond the limits of theology to respond to the challenges of today's world. Lastly, it had to be a truly international journal, not just one publication translated into different languages but a mix of common texts, selected at large annual meetings, along with contributions that every national office could add.

All this was clarified at a meeting at the Katholische Akademie in Munich in 1972 which set the practical foundations of *Communio.* As a young priest, I had the chance to get to know several exceptional personalities up close, such as de Lubac, Balthasar, and Ratzinger. I felt like a schoolboy who suddenly finds himself facing great teachers of Christian thought. But they were, more than anything, men of profound faith and intense prayer, who—as I learned with wonder when I was awakened in the middle of the night—got up at four thirty in the morning to go to chapel, well before Mass began. I learned then that as soon as you get up, you must let yourself be seen by the Lord, in order for your day to have meaning.

It was also fun to be together; they exchanged jokes and banter like little kids while drinking beer. Speaking with them, I felt the urgency to confront the questions and hopes of a world that seemed to be in great turmoil even then, swept up in the wave of protests that had touched even the Church. I remember that everyone, even Balthasar, looked to de Lubac, the grand old man, as the supreme point of reference.

How do you remember de Lubac?

It was the first time I had ever met him. I saw him again on later occasions, after he put me in contact with Lustiger,[14] at that time a pastor in Paris, and with Msgr. Charles, the rector of the Sacre Coeur in Montmartre, around whom had sprung a fine group of brilliant young intellectuals like Marion, Brague, Duchesne, and Armogathe, who would later become part of *Communio*.[15] My relationship with de Lubac was mainly carried out through letters, and therefore not comparable to my friendship with Balthasar. I remember how difficult it was to convince him to give me an interview on the twentieth anniversary of the Council in 1985. He refused repeatedly, only yielding in the end on the condition that I not record it on tape and that it last no more than an hour. However, when I went to the appointment with Alver Metalli from *30 Days* magazine,[16] a terrible thunderstorm broke over Paris and we were stuck in his home. We ended up talking for over four hours. The result was a book-length interview which de Lubac insisted on proofreading fastidiously before publication. At well over ninety years old, he had a very lucid awareness of the situation of the Church after the Council, and in that interview, he expressed himself without beating around the bush. For example, he said that much had been written on *Lumen Gentium* but few had read it and fewer had actually studied it in depth. Hence the many bizarre and preordained interpretations of a document that was supposed to embody the self-awareness of the Second Vatican Council.

Let's circle back to *Communio*. When was the name decided upon? Who came up with it?

The name came up during a meeting in Regensburg with Ratzinger. We had come on Balthasar's suggestion. At the time, the future pope, who was the vice rector of the University of Regensburg, was already a very well-known and esteemed professor. We were a small, four-man delegation: Fr. Eugenio Corecco, a young professor of canon law; Sante Bagnoli, a young publisher; and Fr. Pino Ruggieri and myself, two priests under the age of thirty. Ratzinger welcomed us with an availability which was all the more surprising because it was accompanied by his enormous kindness. He hosted us in his home, where we spoke all afternoon as his sister brought us strawberries she had picked from the garden. At the end of the discussion, he invited us to a nice restaurant, where he ate almost nothing while we stuffed ourselves shamelessly. This atmosphere of courtesy and attentiveness reinforced our consonance with Ratzinger, which until then had only existed at the level of ideas. We had read his book *Introduction to Christianity*.[17] This book, written fifty years ago and published all over the world, by now is a classic on which entire generations have been raised, and continues to be reprinted even today. We could fully recognize ourselves in that text even back then. Ratzinger reciprocated our intellectual and human sympathy, struck by our enthusiasm, as he openly admits in his autobiography.

During that first visit in early 1971, our idea of having an Italian edition of the journal was immediately approved. As I have remarked on many occasions, all of this would not have been possible without the energetic work of Corecco and the editing genius of Bagnoli. They were the first to propose the name *Communio*, which Ratzinger liked right away, even though initially the group of theologians surrounding Balthasar had wanted to name it *Internationale Katholische Zeitschrift* (International Catholic Journal). That name remained as the subheading of the German edition.

From there ensued a series of exchanges between American and European men of culture. Among the editors, a collaborative relationship was born that ran deeper and stronger than those at most journals. We were animated by a passion for the Church which was founded on the primacy of the experience of *Communio*, lived as the basis of an adequate philosophical and theological reflection. It was in this context that friendships developed with people like Christoph Schönborn, Marc Ouellet, Jorge Médina Estévez, André-Joseph Léonard, and Antonio Rouco Varela, who would go on to represent a sign of change in the Church.[18] It would later become visible also at the official level when they were named bishops, called by John Paul II to hold important positions and responsibilities.

We've talked about Giussani, Balthasar, de Lubac, and Ratzinger. Is there any other figure you'd like to add to this gallery of teachers that you encountered in the sixties and seventies?

Besides the great teachers, there were many fellow travelers, if I may define them as such, whom I found by my side and who helped me grow. There is one person in particular I must recall: Eugenio Corecco. We met at the beginning of the sixties during the Triduum of Holy Week at Varigotti. I was struck by a young Swiss priest who kept speaking up, subjecting Giussani to a barrage of questions and unnerving him quite a bit. He demonstrated the passion and curiosity of a frontiersman, not at all a "Ticinese" stuck inside Italian culture. He had studied in Rome, Monaco, and then in Fribourg, where he held the chair of canon law. And it was there that he welcomed me and helped me in two particularly difficult moments of my life—in 1969, after my departure from the Venegono seminary, and in 1979, at the darkest hour of my illness. Not only did he support me in my studies, but introduced me to his trailblazing community of young people in the student housing of rue Gambach.

I spent wonderful years with him. We got along well, despite our drastically different personalities. We would study, have discussions, and pray together with the same naturalness that we had preparing lunch or washing dishes. Corecco's personality was jovial and open, but severe and demanding at the same time. He was a theologian of law with great insight, held in great regard by John Paul II. It was no accident that he was called to Rome to be part of a special, very small commission that helped the pope in his personal work on the last revision of the *New Code of Canon Law*. In 1986, Corecco was appointed to lead the Diocese of Lugano. John Paul II would jokingly call him "the teenage bishop" because his wild hair gave him the appearance of eternal youth.

Many of his insights, developed over the course of his episcopal mission, are still extremely relevant. For example, his idea that the family is central to the life of the ecclesial community; Christianity, he used to say, cannot incarnate itself and become an effective reality in society if it does not pivot on the family. His premature death was a great loss for the universal Church, on which he might have had an even greater impact. What especially impressed me was Corecco's attitude towards the terrible illness that killed him. He publicly witnessed to the faithful his personal *via crucis*. Step by step, his gaze increasingly identified with the suffering Christ.

Your Eminence, we can say that you had the experience of a shared life based on friendship, on intellectual affinity, and on faith as a common judgment. Is this experience outdated by now, or is this still possible today? Are there examples of this in the current Church?

I have had the opportunity to live an experience that should be normal in Christianity, motivated by the desire to share the reasons for one's own faith with the world. There is no purely individualistic approach to Christianity, and there is no authentic community if it does not make the freedom of the person flourish. In *Communio*, I lived this experience which—I repeat—should be normal, but in an absolutely extraordinary and fascinating way. In order for this type of experience to reemerge, two factors are necessary: It must come from a culture of encounter, to quote Pope Francis, and it must critically abide history. It cannot, in short, re-propose itself abstractly.

In the world of theology there are undoubtedly notable personalities, but as far as I know it is harder to find examples of such a shared life, even if here and there, experiences can be found that seem interesting to me. I am thinking of the University of Saint Damaso in Madrid, founded by Cardinal Rouco Varela; of the Institut d'Etudes Théologiques in Brussels, born from Fr. Chapelle's initiative;[19] of the École Cathédrale and the College des Bernardins in Paris, founded by Cardinal Lustiger. These are all communities that seek to transcend the purely academic. Forty years ago, *Communio* was a journal with a European and Western vision. Today, we need a new *Communio* with a universal vision.

Notes to Chapter 6

1. Fribourg in Switzerland, not Freiburg in Breisgau in Germany.
2. Marie-Joseph Le Guillou (1920–1990) was a Dominican and theologian. He participated as an expert in the Second Vatican Council. Henri de Lubac (1896–1991) was a Jesuit and

theologian. He also participated in the Council. In 1983, he was appointed cardinal by John Paul II.

3. The International Theological Commission was instituted by Paul VI in 1969 as an advisory body for the major Vatican congregations. It has about thirty members from various backgrounds who are appointed by the pope.

4. Eugenio Corecco (1931–1995) was a bishop and jurist. He taught canon law at the University of Fribourg in Switzerland. In 1986, he was appointed bishop of Lugano.

5. *Communio* is an international theological journal. It was founded in 1972 and is published in seventeen national editions. The Italian edition has been published from the start by Jaca Book.

6. See Angelo Scola, *Hans Urs von Balthasar: Uno stile teologico* (Milano: Jaca Book, 1991).

7. Hans Urs von Balthasar, *The Glory of the Lord: A Theological Aesthetics*, vol. 2 (San Francisco: Ignatius Press, 1984), 13–14.

8. Hans Urs von Balthasar, *Apokalypse der deutschen Seele*, 3 vols. (Freiburg, Germany: Johannes Verlag, 1998).

9. Hans Urs von Balthasar, *Epilogue* (San Francisco: Ignatius Press, 2004).

10. Georges Chantraine (1932–2010), Belgian Jesuit and theologian.

11. Karl Rahner (1904–1984) was a German Jesuit and theologian. He participated in the Second Vatican Council and his thought was very influential in the Post-Conciliar period.

12. Hans Urs von Balthasar, *Theo-Drama*, 5 vols. (San Francisco: Ignatius Press, 1989–1998).

13. Hans Urs von Balthasar, *The Moment of Christian Witness* (San Francisco: Ignatius Press, 1994).

14. Jean-Marie Lustiger (1926–2007) was an archbishop of Paris and cardinal. He converted to Catholicism at the age of fourteen, coming from a Polish Jewish background. He was archbishop of Paris from 1981 to 2005, and a member of the Académie Française.

15. Maxime Charles (1908–1993) was a priest in Paris. He was the chaplain of the Sorbonne from 1944 to 1959, and then became rector of the Basilica of the Sacré-Cœur in Montmartre. Jean-Luc Marion (1946–) is a philosopher. He was a professor at the Sorbonne and at the University of Chicago. In 2008,

succeeded Cardinal Lustiger at the Académie Française. Remi Brague (1947–) is a historian of philosophy. He was on the faculty at the Sorbonne and at the University of Munich in Germany. Jean Duchesne (1944–) was the director of the French Catholic Academy and executor of Cardinal Lustiger's literary estate. Jean-Robert Armogathe (1947–) is a priest. He taught at the École pratique des hautes études and was given important responsibilities in the Archdiocese of Paris.

16. *30 Days* was an international monthly focused on international church news. It was started in 1989 and closed in 2012. Alver Metalli (1952–), a journalist and author who specializes on Latin America, was its editor from 1983 to 1989.

17. Joseph Ratzinger, *Introduction to Christianity* (San Francisco: Ignatius Press, 2004).

18. Christoph Schönborn (1945–) is an Austrian cardinal and theologian. He was a student of Joseph Ratzinger, and has been archbishop of Vienna since 1995. Marc Ouellet (1944–) is a Canadian cardinal and academic. Since 2010, he has been the prefect of the Congregation for Bishops. Jorge Médina Estévez (1926–) is a Chilean cardinal. He held several important positions in the Roman Curia. André-Joseph Léonard (1940–) is a Belgian archbishop. He was archbishop of Brussels from 2010 to 2015. Antonio Maria Rouco Varela (1936–) is a Spanish cardinal. He was archbishop of Madrid from 1994 to 2014.

19. Albert Chapelle (1929–2003) was a Jesuit philosopher and theologian. In 1968, he founded the Institut d'Études Théologiques, which was located first in Louvain and then in Brussels.

CHAPTER 7

Inside Suffering

The Experience of Illness

Your Eminence, in your youth you lived the experience of illness. I know that this is not an easy topic to discuss. In general, those who have been affected are justly and understandably reserved about it. May I ask you to make an exception and recount that difficult period?

I first experienced illness—and I mean a state of illness prolonged over time—when I was a little over twenty years of age. It was a tuberculosis infection, which at that time was rather common, and it forced me to interrupt my studies and live in the mountains for over a year. Physically, it was as if I had a permanent flu, but I had no particularly painful symptoms. When I recovered from the infection and returned to my normal life, I never thought of it again. It was nothing compared to the illness that would strike me ten years later, very painfully and traumatically.

It all began in the spring of 1974 with bouts of very high fever, strong stomach pains, nausea, and vomiting. In June, the decision was made to hospitalize me in the internal medicine ward at the Policlinico Hospital in Milan, where I remained almost without interruption until the end of the year. I was subjected to an infinite barrage of clinical tests, but they did not lead to a precise diagnosis. Meanwhile, my symptoms grew increasingly violent until they peaked on the night of the eighth of December when I fell into a coma. In that moment, two friends who were doctors, Leandro Aletti and Pieralberto Bertazzi, were there to help me. I will always remember what the former said, thinking that I was unconscious: "I am afraid that Angelo may not make it till tomorrow morning." The experience of a coma, which lasted three days, was completely different from sleep. It's something that disarticulates your perceptions and sense of time, and leaves a profound mark on you.

In the end, after six months, I was discharged from the hospital with the very generic diagnosis of an adrenal gland disorder. But the cause remained a mystery. In this situation, the idea of a psychoanalytic approach came up. The suggestion was given to me by Giacomo Contri, one of the best Italian representatives of Lacan's school.[1] In his opinion, my illness surely had a deep psychological component. Therefore, I decided to be analyzed by an early follower of Lacan, Louis Beirnaert, an Alsatian Jesuit,[2] and to travel to Paris twice a month for sessions at Lacan's seminar However, my physical condition continued to deteriorate. My bouts with vomiting and low blood pressure weren't diminishing. These were accompanied at times by strange, sudden incidents of paralysis. Once, as I was getting on a train, I was completely immobilized on the running board. It took a while before the travelers around me realized what was happening and intervened to help me.

I realized at one point that I could no longer keep up the intense routine I was used to. And so, on Corecco's invitation, in 1979 I returned to Fribourg and became the assistant of Otfried Höffe, a professor of political philosophy.[3] I carried out research on human rights financed by the Swiss Fund, while also resuming my studies of theology until I attained my doctorate. Despite the milder and more tranquil pace of life, however, my health did not improve.

The decisive turn for the better came by accident, as often happens. During my weekends in Fribourg, I would hang out with a few friends who worked in Bern. Among them was Dr. Carlo Felice Beretta Piccoli, who worked as a doctor at Inselspital, a world-class university hospital in the Swiss capital. When I happened to feel sick in his presence, he insisted that I retake all of my clinical tests, directing me to a famous endocrinologist in Bern. I went, subjecting myself to a thorough round of examinations that lasted three months. In May of 1980, I was diagnosed with Addison's disease, a rare illness characterized by chronic adrenal insufficiency. More importantly, I immediately began replacement therapy. Everything changed from that day forward, as if I had returned to a second youth after six years of suffering and uncertainty.

You mentioned using psychoanalytic treatment for your malady, which in the end turned out to be of a completely different nature and required a completely different therapy. Was this choice a mistake—a waste of time?

No, not at all. I have to say that it helped me; I learned a lot.

Isn't it a bit strange that a believer would entrust oneself to a psychoanalyst?

It might have seemed strange and bizarre in that era, because many prejudices about psychoanalysis still circulated. The crudest one was that seeking help from an analyst meant admitting to being a little crazy. In addition, there was the widespread idea that psychoanalysis and the Christian faith were in stark opposition. The professed atheism of Freud was considered to be more than enough of a reason to reject depth psychology, even though, by reading carefully, one can find interesting aspects in his thought. In particular, in a letter to the Protestant pastor Oskar Pfister, Freud affirms that "psycho-analysis is neither religious nor non-religious, but an impartial tool which both priest and layman can use in the service of the sufferer."[4]

The debate over psychoanalysis and religion has been extensive in the Lacanian school. My analyst, Louis Beirnaert, wrote the wonderful book, *Christian Experience and Psychology*,[5] and made very acute reflections on the psychology of St. Ignatius. His work was published in Italian in 1950, by Vita e Pensiero, the press of the Catholic University of Milan. Regarding Lacan, he held faith in high regard, to the point of affirming that the future belongs to religion. Unfortunately, for a long time the question of the relationship between religion and psychology has been set in the wrong terms, as if it were about finding a compromise or establishing a contrast between two doctrines, Christianity on one side and Freudian or Lacanian psychology on the other. However, psychoanalysis is by nature a clinical "practice" which obviously has theoretical implications, but is not a philosophical conception. It follows that the synthesis between faith and psychology takes place in the person of the analyst and not in the abstract confrontation between the two doctrines. It's a task that concerns the "I," a work that nobody else can do in his place.

True psychoanalytic practice has great respect for the freedom of the subject who undergoes it. This has been my experience, at least. A real psychoanalyst is one who listens a lot, limiting himself to a nod or two. He or she encourages you to keep talking, or insinuates that you are trying to wiggle out, but never tells you "this is what you have to do." If you stumble on an analyst who gives advice and suggests solutions, it is best to leave immediately! He or she must accompany you in reading into your symptoms, but then you must decide what to do. In this sense, I have gained enormous respect for the Lacanian school, even though back then there was great diffidence towards psychoanalysis in the Church.

Do you believe that things have changed in the last forty years?

Many prejudices have faded, but conversely a vulgarized form of depth psychology has taken hold and damaged the field. Psychoanalysis is being put to the test today in a radical way. The first reason is undoubtedly the progress in the research and production of targeted drugs. Secondly, depth psychology has been banalized. Psychoanalytic practice is a very delicate and serious process, which takes a lot of time and effort. However, new forms of psychotherapy have been invented as substitutes for psychoanalysis. Personally, I don't have much faith in them. I am particularly convinced that the combination of psychology and religion is a mess going nowhere fast. Lastly, there is a third element that explains today's low opinion of psychoanalysis, once so overly praised: the affirmation that sexual difference is insuperable. This concept is stressed by many of the great teachers of depth psychology, but it is not in harmony with today's dominant cultural climate. This may seem strange, but it is a fact that today certain statements about sexual difference are accepted only by the Church and by some psychoanalytic schools. As Louis Beirnaert wrote, the sexual difference is insurmountable.

A few years after your recovery, in 1983, you were affected by a particularly painful loss—the death of your brother Pietro in a car accident. How did you react to this tragedy that struck you and your family?

Obviously, it was a violent separation. My first thoughts were for my parents, both over eighty years old, for my forty-year-old sister-in-law and for my nieces, both teenagers at the time. It was the beginning of July, and I had just arrived in Fribourg to study there for a month as I always did. I returned to Malgrate that same day because I wanted to be the one to break the news to my parents. I remember finding them on their doorstep at six in the morning as they were heading to the shrine of the Madonna di San Martino above Valmadrera, to whom they were particularly devoted. They were going to pray for their granddaughter Cristina, who was taking her final senior exams that day.

As often happens, after such a sudden shock, many practical matters need to be taken care of. It fell to me to identify my brother in the morgue in Brescia and to organize the funeral. Paradoxically, all these preparations helped me process the blow. The certain faith that I would see him again someday in the House of the Father prompted me to recognize the deep truth of our affection for one another. On that sad occasion, I also had the opportunity to experience the solidarity of my large extended family and of the many people who had known and esteemed my brother because of his political activity. As the years went by after Pietro's premature death, and as I had to take on more responsibilities for my sister-in-law and nieces, Elena, Cristina, and Monica, my affection for them has grown as well. And the exchanges I have these days with my six grandnieces and nephews have become increasingly fascinating.

Knowledge comes through pain, as the ancients used to say. What have you learned from these trials?

The experience of pain and sickness prompted many reflections, which I have communicated in some of my writings and in my many encounters with health workers. I must confess I have been profoundly affected by a slightly angst-inducing sensation that I might express this way: lose the body, lose everything. The feeling has never left me since. I carry it inside as a sort of practical doubt about whether existence is truly possible beyond the corporeal dimension. However, this does not make me turn in on myself; rather, it spurs me toward the certain hope in the promise that Jesus made to us: that we will rise again in our true bodies and, as St. Paul says, we will be with the Lord forever.

The experience of illness makes clear the profound unity between body and soul. My faith makes me certain that there is another life beyond the decay of this body of mine, but it does not entirely erase my instinctive resistance. This is something that I strongly sensed when I had to identify my brother Pietro in the morgue. Looking at his disfigured face, his ruptured abdomen and the wounds left by the dreadfully violent impact of the accident, a question full of rebellion sprang from my anguish. How can a body like this rise again? Then the words of a "canon" of the Mass about Christ risen in his "real body" enlightened me—the resurrection of the flesh is not the reanimation of a corpse, but an experience of a different kind of corporeality, even if it is continuous with the previous one.[6]

You spoke of resistance and rebellion. But isn't suffering supposed to be a way for a believer to grow closer to God?

Yes, but it is not that easy or simple. I don't like the cheap mystique of suffering. When I was in the hospital, I read *The Imitation of Christ*, where the author writes that we must be very vigilant, because illness can lead us to lose our faith. Experiencing the fragility of one's own body is equivalent to the daily burden of death. It's what I call the "insurmountability of the corporeal dimension," most clearly perceived in the experience of sickness, which implies a daily struggle with the prospect of death. It is a dramatic struggle. In order to banish the fear of the disappearance and decay of the body, one yearns to feel and possess the body of another. Sexuality is where love and death meet.

Not to seem banal, but an old movie, *Moonstruck*, springs to mind. In it, a woman is tormented by the discovery of her husband's affair with a younger woman, searches for an explanation and finds it in the fact that "men are afraid to die…"

It is not a banality. Corporeal otherness is reassuring. But in our eroticized society, one's own body and those of others are reduced to a mechanism that must constantly rekindle the fire of pleasure. The disorder in sexual relationships is a signal of a deeper uneasiness. It must be condemned, but at the same time, great mercy is needed precisely because it is rooted in the fear of death.

The Church points to the path out of this impasse into which the society of pervasive eroticism has fallen. It is the path that Pope Benedict XVI, in the encyclical *Deus Caritas Est* calls surmounting the opposition between eros and agape. Eros is not in itself negative, but it must be purified by agape. This generates the dynamism of authentic love that accounts for all the factors, and in particular puts the factor of corporeality back in its rightful place.

There remains the question of individual suffering and of all the sorrows that afflict mankind. Addressing this, you once said that "man is tempted to demand that God justify himself for the existence of suffering in the world."[7] These words seem to echo those of Alessandro Manzoni, who wrote that when faced with the blindness of evil, "thought finds itself faltering in horror between two blasphemies—denying Providence or accusing it."[8] Is the question of pain destined to remain unsolved?

It is a question that many philosophers and theologians have tried to answer over the centuries–without ever arriving at convincing answers. The traditional doctrine from Augustine to Aquinas was summarized by Maritain as the *permission du mal*,[9] meaning that God permits evil as a means to good. The French thinker, however, added that this theory is insufficient and downright unacceptable in the face of, for example, the pain of an innocent child. When a child asked Pope Francis the reason for his grave illness, the pope admitted he didn't have an answer. Also, Benedict XVI answered the same during his visit to Japan when a little girl asked him why God had allowed the terrible catastrophe of the tsunami.

There is no "theory of suffering" in the Gospel, but only the upsetting affirmation we find in the Sermon on the Mount. "Blessed are those who suffer. . ." By effectively drawing his own self-portrait in the Beatitudes, Jesus offered us no explanations or justifications. He faced suffering by taking it upon himself. Thus, the only possible response to the mystery of suffering is a presence. In front of certain situations of extreme suffering there are no words; we must keep silent and look together at the crucifix. Pain must be shared more than understood. Staying near those who suffer is not a nice, consolatory gesture, but the way in which the believer bears witness to the love of Christ who saves us from evil, both physical and moral.

Personally, I find involuntary evil to be the most striking thing. It's not uncommon to hurt someone with your behavior or your judgment, but then you fail to notice and no one points it out to you. There is no direct responsibility in play, unlike intentional evil, but the effect is the same—or it may even be worse. I have reflected much on this aspect, and reached the conclusion that involuntary evil makes manifest the undeniable solidarity that binds us together. It is proof that the human family is truly one body—negatively so in terms of the original sin of Adam, but positively for the fact of having been created in Christ and redeemed by him who, by dying on the cross, atoned for all the sins of the world and thus revealed the fruitfulness of sorrow.

Suffering as atonement is a fundamental concept of Christian doctrine that is no longer acceptable to modern thought. Do you think that proposing it again today makes sense?

It is an outmoded term, not spoken of as much anymore because its power has dissipated in a world that has lost the sense of sin and therefore of guilt. But I am unconvinced that the concept of atonement no longer has a place in the conscience of modern man. I've been visiting prisoners for twenty-seven years now and have not met a single one who objected to the idea that his crime had to be atoned for. The heart demands it even before the law. There is always a punishment connected with any evil we do; this a universal experience connected with the concept of remorse. Like the title of a Paul Bourget novel I read as a boy says, *Our Actions Follow Us.*[10] Evil has an unnerving weight, and I mean the moral evil for which we are responsible. It found its most powerful description in Dostoevsky's narrative genius. Crime demands punishment.

Therefore, atonement is a matter of justice in the deepest sense. Catholic doctrine teaches this along with the concept that temporal punishment remains even after the sin has been confessed and the sinner has found forgiveness in the sacrament of reconciliation. This is not an abstruseness of faith; it is an evident reality that emerges from the experience of every person in every age. If one commits adultery, one cannot expect that his relationship with his wife will immediately become again calm and smooth like it was before, even if she forgives him. Time is needed for the wound to heal, a time of difficulty and penance, precisely. Suffering as atonement is always tied to the personal dimension, because it is humanly unthinkable that one might be called to atone for something he or she did not commit. But for the Christian, the meaning of atonement goes beyond what is required by justice. Suffering can be consciously offered as the "completion in us of the sufferings of Christ," as St. Paul writes in the letter to the Colossians. Fulfillment not in the sense that the passion of Christ was not enough. What's missing "is missing in my own flesh," the apostle says.

The suffering of Christ is inclusive, that is to say it contains all other sufferings, generating an atonement that is commonly shared. As much as this idea may seem foreign to our sensibilities, we see it realized in many examples of sainthood that rise in the life of the Church. One example is the suffering and prayer for the reparation of sins by Sister Faustina Kowalska, the Polish saint whose name is tied to the message of Divine Mercy. Yet another is the blessed Fr. Carlo Gnocchi, the priest who shared the sufferings of children who were crippled in World War II, teaching them to make themselves one with the suffering of Christ. In one of his writings, Fr. Gnocchi recounts that those children, once given this perspective, found an almost superhuman ability to deal with pain. Here, that familiar saying is inverted, the saying which is often spontaneously expressed even by many suffering believers: "What did I do wrong to deserve this?" But suffering as atonement for the sins of the world is not a scheme that one can apply mechanically. It involves the freedom of the person called to collaborate in the work of redemption in a most sublime and mysterious way. This is a dizzying perspective that makes one say—as I heard myself from the lips of a father whose twelve-year-old son had died in a car accident—"It's not true that God gives and takes away; God always gives."

In Italy, after Eluana Englaro and other similar cases that reso-nated in the media, we have been forced to speak about death in a different way than before.[11] Do you think that society is more aware of this problem, or is there still a lot of confusion?

I believe that the debate over the end of life has shed light on a pro-cess of deterioration that characterizes not only our country but all of Western culture. This process has brought us to embrace narcissism as the extreme consequence of individualism. A narcissist finds his sole enjoyment in contemplating himself and in satisfying his own changing desires through a potentially infinite gallery of pleasures. In this process of constant distraction in the etymological sense— that is, of pulling away from reality—our postmodern culture has come to the point of trying to break down even the last barrier, death, in front of which even traditional atheistic thought would stop.

Unlike birth, which is an event independent of the will of the newborn, death takes place in the course of life. Therefore, if I think that this course is always and entirely up to me, up to my own choice, even the action of dying can, and in some cases, must, be the result of my own decision. When considered in these terms, the problem of the end of life is falsified at its very root by such a mentality.

At the beginning of 2018, Italy introduced a law on living wills, which authorizes the so-called Anticipated Directives for Treat-ment.[12] What is your assessment?

Once, there was the unanimous recognition of a few fundamen-tal rights sanctioned in the constitution, including the right to life. In today's society there is the tendency to transform every subjec-tive desire into a right, and single citizens or a group of citizens expect the state to legislate and allow a determined behavior that suits their wishes. We have reached the paradox that the greater the request for liberty, the more stringent and suffocating the law becomes. To respond directly to your question, I don't think it was necessary to make a law in regard to the end of life. It would have been enough to forcefully reaffirm, at the level of social custom, that while there remains one breath of life, we must do all we can to defend it, without falling into futile care. Beyond that, let us just trust in the three freedoms at play when death approaches—the freedom of the dying person, that of family members, and lastly, that of the doctor.

In Italy, however, the judiciary has effectively taken over the role of the legislature with a few court decisions, and so it became opportune to make a law on living wills. Beyond the good intentions of those who wanted this measure, I find unacceptable its possible "euthanasic" interpretation based on the idea that hydration and alimentation constitute a therapy that can be interrupted. Moreover, it is a serious problem that conscientious objection by doctors is not allowed. In this regard, we must emphasize that no law can sanction the breakup of the therapeutic alliance between patient, family, and health care providers. In conclusion, I believe that there are still too many misunderstandings about the end of life.

What are you referring to?

First of all, I'm referring to the great confusion around the meaning of "vegetative state." The term is too generic and fails to take into account the latest scientific advancements. Besides, it has been confirmed that it is not an illness, but a serious state of disability that does not require a particular therapy, but simply what we all need to live—water, food, hygiene, and above all, an environment that can sustain the fragility of the person. Those who are "terminally" ill are a different case. Here, questions arise concerning the line between futile care and euthanasia, and above all on the line between deep palliative sedation and euthanasia. If, for example, a terminally ill patient contracts pneumonia, it is up to the doctor and the family to decide whether to cure him or not. We must be careful not to confuse our desires, even legitimate ones, with the good of the patient. When visiting the sick, I have often asked myself the question: Isn't "a dignified death" an invention of us healthy people, while the sick ask for a dignified life up to the last instant? Namely, a life marked by what characterizes an authentic human experience, the capacity to love and be loved?

Death has become our society's new taboo, removed from collective consciousness. And yet, as Balthasar said, "the folly of Christianity consists in making death not a limit, not a boundary, but the center."[13] Is it possible to live and act in a fully engaged way while thinking that we shall die?

I don't believe that death has been removed. Certainly, our society tries to remove it, but it cannot do so entirely. This is because, as the cynical and provoking French novelist Michel Houellebecq wrote, death is a background noise that accompanies us in every moment of our lives. I believe that the "preparation for a good death," a prayer familiar to our elders,[14] was very wise. It fits the evangelical exhortation "Be prepared!" Unlike most people today who hope for a sudden death, as if to exorcise every possible suffering, Christian tradition has always held that it is better to die knowingly in one's own bed.

I have always been struck by the German poet Rilke's famous prayer: "Give, oh God, to each of us our own personal death."[15] I think he's expressing the truest and most profound invocation of our hearts, unlike Adorno, who considered Rilke's prayer only a miserable lie to hide the fact that "human beings still only croak."[16] To the contrary, deep down each of us desires that even death, like life, will come with a personal mark. "My" death must be "my" completion, not an anonymous ending. But death can only be personal if it ties itself in some way to my freedom. This is the point, given that the experience of dying coincides with the absolute impossibility of choosing. How is it possible to affirm the contrary? The answer lies in recognizing that my freedom is not just my capacity to choose. In the act of dying, we leave behind the imperfect freedom of choice to set out toward its fulfillment. In Christ, death and freedom no longer mutually exclude each other. If I adhere to his death that won over our death, I become a participant in this freedom. No one can take it away from me, not even a suicide bomber catching me completely unprepared as I sit in a bar. All of this obviously does not eliminate the fear of death that I carry inside me. But it allows the prospect of death to become a challenge to freedom to give itself, because only in love is the experience of being limited and transient not an obstacle but the road to fulfillment.

I remember discussing this topic with Eugenio Scalfari during a public conversation in Cortina one summer.[17] He raised a rather ironic objection. "You Christians are afraid," said the founder of *La Repubblica*. "The prospect of death terrifies you and so you invented a tall tale about the afterlife." I responded that all men desire immortality. According to him, it is a desire born of fear, but for me it is founded on my hope and faith in Christ. Therefore, his objection does not hold. We are even. Each one has a 50% chance of being right!

Your Eminence, do you often think of death?

Yes, every day. And I pray to God that my desire to see his face be stronger than my fear of dying. Jesus forbade us from speculating too much on what eternal life will be like. What he did say is that we will always be with him, and that through him we will be able to see the face of the Father in the communion of saints. This idea that we will see each other again is a mystery that fascinates me. I reflect upon it often. I remember when I celebrated my dear friend Msgr. Gianni Danzi's last Mass at his deathbed.[18] His niece was there to hold his hand. At the moment of Elevation, he shuddered and tried to lift his head off of his pillow. In that instant I glimpsed the image of God's hand imperceptibly replacing that of his niece's. As Balthasar said, death is a slipping from the hands of men to the hands of God.

Notes to Chapter 7

1. Giacomo Contri (1941–) is a physician and psychoanalyst. He was a student of Jacques Lacan and a member of the École freudienne de Paris. Jacques Lacan (1901–1981) was a psychoanalyst and philosopher, one of the most famous and controversial figures in twentieth-century French culture.
2. Louis Beirnaert (1906–1985) was a Jesuit and psychoanalyst. He was a friend and long-time colleague of Jacques Lacan. In 1953, he cofounded the Association Internationale d'Études Médico-Psychologiques et Religieuses (International Association of Medico-Psychological and Religious Studies) to promote the understanding of psychoanalysis within the Church.
3. Otfried Höffe (1943–) is a German philosopher. He taught political philosophy first at the University of Fribourg in Switzerland, and then at the University of Tübingen in Germany.

4. Sigmund Freud, *Psychoanalysis and Faith: The Letters of Sigmund Freud and Oskar Pfister* (New York: Basic Books, 1964), 10.

5. L. Beirnaert, *Expérience chrétienne et psychologie* (Paris: Éd. de l'Épi, 1964).

6. The reference is to the Eucharistic Canon for Easter Sunday in the Ambrosian Rite.

7. Angelo Scola, *Address for the Feast of the Redeemer* (Venice: July 19, 2009).

8. Alessandro Manzoni, *Storia della colonna infame* (Rome: Newton Compton, 1993), 16.

9. Jacques Maritain, *Dieu et la Permission du Mal* (Paris: Desclée de Brouwer, 1963).

10. Paul Bourget, *Nos actes nous suivent* (Paris: Plon, 1927).

11. Eluana Englaro (1970–2009) was a young woman from Lecco who was left in a persistent vegetative state by a car accident in 1992. Her case led to a long legal battle and political battle, which ended in her death when the courts finally accepted her father's request to take her off life support.

12. The reference is to a new law signed into law in January 2018 which states that no one can receive medical care against his or her will. The law allows patients to refuse in advance artificial feeding and hydration.

13. From Balthasar's intervention at the *Meeting for Friendship among Peoples* in Rimini on August 26, 1984.

14. The prayer in question was originally part of St. Alphonsus Maria de Liguori's booklet *L'apparecchio alla buona morte.*

15. Rainer Maria Rilke, *Das Buch von der Armut und vom Tode* (Leipzig: Insel Verlag, 1905).

16. Theodor W. Adorno, *Minima Moralia*, Theodoro Ardono Archive, trans. Dennis Redmond (2005), no. 148. www.marxists.org

17. Eugenio Scalfari (1924–) is a journalist and author. He is a well-known representative of Italian secular culture. In 1976, he founded *La Repubblica,* one of the major Italian newspapers. He was the editor until 1996.

18. Gianni Danzi (1940–2007) was a bishop. Originally a priest from the diocese of Lugano (Switzerland), he worked many years in the Vatican. In 2005, he became bishop of Loreto, the location of a famous Marian shrine.

CHAPTER 8

The Pope of Freedom

Collaboration with St. John Paul II

Your Eminence, you knew St. John Paul II personally from the beginning of his papacy. What was your first impression of him?

I had already met Karol Wojtyła when he was the cardinal of Kraków, in the context of the international network of *Communio* editors. He had wanted to start a Polish edition of the magazine and had planned to set up a small group of people who would be the local editors, but the Communist regime stopped him. Balthasar decided to involve him in the German edition and in that context, I met him briefly.

I first met Pope John Paul II in January of 1979, when I and two other priests of the movement accompanied Fr. Giussani to a private audience with the pope. After the two finished their long conversation, he asked to greet us and we had a brief exchange. I then had the privilege to concelebrate Mass with the pontiff a few weeks later. The occasion left me deeply impressed. I perceived his intense and uninterrupted dialogue with the Lord in the way he celebrated Mass, a dialogue that continued even after the celebration was over. He was immersed in thanksgiving prayer as if the world around him did not exist. There I realized that I was in front of a mystic personality, who was totally seized by Christ.

At that time, I could not imagine how my relationship with John Paul II would develop. At first, everything happened in the context of Communion and Liberation and of movements in general. I was involved in the organization of the first conference on ecclesial movements held in September of 1981. It was during that occasion that the pope, greeting the participants at Castel Gandolfo, said something illuminating: "The Church itself is a movement that penetrates hearts and consciences."[1] He said it in a tired voice, his body was greatly weakened due to the attempted assassination in May and the complications that followed.

I must say that in those years, there was a very special relationship between the pope and CL. In 1982, he decided to visit the Meeting for Friendship among Peoples,[2] which was still not well known back then. It had been founded a few years before by some friends in Rimini, and it would go on to play an extraordinary role in the cultural, social, and political life of this country and beyond. Like every creative man, he was extremely curious, wanting to understand, to explore. Between 1979 and 1982, I think I met John Paul II at least ten times with Fr. Giussani and other leaders of CL. He loved to talk with us; he wanted to understand the situation of the Church in Italy and the West more deeply, so he constantly asked us questions. With each encounter, our wonder grew as we faced the extraordinary, innovative figure of a pope who never stopped surprising us.

I remember that at the time there was a great curiosity but an even greater puzzlement about a pope who was considered such an unknown quantity.

We must not forget what the atmosphere of the seventies was like, with the Church rocked by the post-conciliar convulsions and with Italian society tragically scarred by terrorism. The papacy of Paul VI ended with the dramatic and disturbing image of the funeral *absente cadavere* of Aldo Moro, presided over by the head of the Church who turned to God in anguish in his funeral homily, "for not having listened to our cry and not having answered our prayers" to save the life of the politician who had been kidnapped and subsequently murdered by the Red Brigades.[3] We lived under a dark cloud; there was such a collective depression that nobody could imagine a way out.

Some hope had been rekindled already by the appointment of John Paul I and his brief 33-day pontificate. But a new and unexpected gust of fresh air came with the Polish pope, who commanded the attention of the Church and the world with a different style from the very first day of his pontificate. He was different in the way he intervened, in the direct and spontaneous relationships he had with people, in his energetic and at the same time cordial way of speaking. These are all things we know well by now, but at the time they were a real surprise.

Karol Wojtyła was a man who did not hide his personal history—his family losses, the war, factory work, the difficulties stemming from the totalitarian regimes of Nazism and Communism. Rather, he brought this history to bear on his way of being pope, opening absolutely new and fruitful prospects for the life of the Church and the world, which drew significant opposition even from Catholics.

In 1982, you were called to be part of the Pontifical Institute for Studies on Marriage and Family, a new academic institution started a few months earlier at the explicit direction of the Holy Father. How did your appointment come about?

The call came from Msgr. Carlo Caffarra,[4] the head of the institute, who told me that after a one-year pilot program, he had spoken to the pope about a possible group of teachers, and I was one of them. It came as a genuine surprise to me, especially because I barely knew Caffarra. I had met him once at a conference, but had never had a chance to work with him. And so, I moved to Rome in September of 1982 to begin teaching theological anthropology at the institute that John Paul II had desired so much. He really cared about being recognized as its founder. He would have announced its creation, along with the Pontifical Council for the Family, at the end of the general audience in St. Peter's Square on May 13, 1981, the day of the attempted assassination.

The origin of the institute remains tied to that tragic event. John Paul II highlighted the fact that it coincided with the anniversary of the first Marian apparition at Fatima. This is why we decided to dedicate the institute to the Madonna of Fatima and asked to have an authentic and authorized reproduction of that statue at our headquarters. It was as if a blood tie was established between Wojtyła and the institute, an affective connection that manifested itself in the very particular attention he bestowed on his creation. I remember that he was always present at the first faculty meetings; and it was not a formal participation either. He would intervene with proposals and suggestions. During one of these meetings, while I was describing the syllabus I wanted to follow in my teaching, he told me that I would have to rethink the classic treatment of theological anthropology in the context of a reflection on the man-woman relationship directed towards marriage and family.

Another very valuable suggestion came from Professor Stratford Caldecott,[5] the editor of the *Second Spring* magazine and founder of the Oxford Center for Faith and Culture, where I had been invited to give a lecture. He had been reflecting on these themes for some time, and he encouraged me to continue my research. All this was a stimulus for my work on the nuptial mystery, which I later developed in various books,[6] but which began from my relationship with John Paul II. He had a great influence not only on me as a person, but on the nature of my research and on my teaching.

John Paul II suggested a change in perspective regarding the anthropological issue. Why did he feel it was necessary?

The change has to do with the profound and absolutely free way with which John Paul II dedicated an ample part of his Wednesday Catechesis to the theology of the body and more generally to the theme of sexuality. It came as a surprise to many that a pope would face this problem in such a direct way, without any false modesty, answering a question which was in the hearts of all the men and women of his time even if they did not know it. That catechesis not only formed a fundamental pillar for the reflection and the research at the Institute on Marriage and Family, but also had a vast resonance. Suffice to say that when it appeared in book form, it was reprinted twelve times—in Italian alone—and later was published in a critical edition.[7] Those texts were followed, not by chance, by the apostolic letter to women *Mulieris dignitatem* and the *Letter to Families* along with many other important contributions on this topic.

Your Eminence, can we say that the year 1982 marked the decisive turn in your life?

Yes, certainly. Cardinal Ratzinger was called to Rome and named prefect of the Congregation for the Doctrine of the Faith in November 1981. I began working with him and became a consultor for the Congregation, that is to say one of its experts. This meant regular meetings with the prefect, but I also met with the pope on more than one occasion because he wanted to be directly informed about the most delicate matters. We would come together in the morning in his private library. The experts would present their observations and he would take notes. Then we ate lunch together, continuing our work at the table and the Holy Father would intervene with directions on how to proceed.

I participated in the preparation of various documents of the Congregation for the Doctrine of the Faith, in particular the Instruction *Donum vitae* in 1987 concerning respect for unborn life and the dignity of procreation. It was the first document of the Holy See on in vitro fertilization, a theme destined to become very important in the following years. I helped revise the text along with Msgrs. Carlo Caffarra and Livio Melina, working in fairly regular contact with then Msgr. Giovanni Battista Re, the assessor of General Affairs of the Secretariat of State, along with Cardinal Ratzinger and John Paul II.[8] The same went for the apostolic letter *Mulieris dignitatem* in 1988. And again, in the early nineties, after my appointment as bishop of Grosseto, I worked as a consultor for the Congregation and I had the opportunity to meet the Holy Father in meetings with the experts, of which I was one, to prepare the encyclical *Fides et Ratio,* published in 1998.

My relationship with John Paul II became even more intense after my appointment to be the rector of the Pontifical Lateran University in 1995, and dean of the Institute for Studies on Marriage and Family. Besides the regular meetings in which I reported to the Holy Father the problems and prospects of the Lateran University, there were many other informal encounters. At times, John Paul II would have lunch with me, and we would converse in a very familiar way. I remember those years as a particularly happy time, full of grace, in close contact with the successor of Peter who guided and sustained me up close.

In addition to great intellectual harmony, you had an intense personal relationship with St. John Paul II. How did he impact your life? What remained with you from so many meetings with this extraordinary figure?

St. John Paul II changed my life—concretely, not just metaphorically. My relationship with him was always characterized by a great confidence and a delicate affection, without a shadow of incomprehension. Many beautiful and moving memories spring to mind.

I cannot help going back to the image I will always cherish of the pope in prayer. We habitually stopped at the chapel to recite the Angelus together before heading to lunch. This usually only takes a few minutes. Instead, the Holy Father remained there for so long that the rest of us could no longer remain kneeling on the floor. He was so immersed in prayer that for him it seemed as if neither time nor space existed. It was striking. In those moments, I could see firsthand that Christ was the emotional center of his person, as well as the deep root of his humanity. Cardinal Stanisław Dziwisz,[9] his faithful secretary with whom I have a close friendship, once told me that in the last years of John Paul's life, when he struggled to walk, he would spend most of the night in prayer before the tabernacle of the chapel, flat on the ground with his arms stretched out to form a cross. He would remain there for hours, immobile, to the point that Dziwisz and Sister Tobiana would have to regularly get up in the middle of the night to lift him up and invite him to go back to bed.

Pope John Paul II loved to crack jokes. It came to him as naturally as prayer. He listened a lot and was eager to answer. Once, when speaking of the Second Vatican Council, he confided to me that he, as a young bishop, had prepared an alternative outline for a section of *Gaudium et Spes*. We were on such good terms that I asked if I could take a look at the notes he had saved. He said yes, but the secretary of state intervened and the papers never came my way.

His personality struck me: He was a man who lived with great interior serenity, and this showed in his sincere cordiality. However, when something bothered him greatly, he did not hide his indignation. I remember one meeting where the pope became very angry. We were a group of experts who had been given the task of preparing the second Instruction on the theology of liberation, which the Congregation for the Doctrine of the Faith would publish in 1986. Someone, perhaps quoting Maritain, observed that Marxism could be considered a heresy of Christianity. John Paul II grew enraged, threw his fist down on the table and said, "This is nonsense that could have only come from someone who did not live under Communism!" There I saw from up close the pope who uttered invectives which by now have become history—against the mafia, war, social injustice, but also against laws allowing abortion.

I remember an extended meeting of the Institute for Studies on Marriage and Family presided over by the pope. There were members of the faculty from all the continents, a sort of general convention which was called together every ten years. It was 1997, and there were 170 of us in Castel Gandolfo. We spoke about abortion and UN policies that claimed it as a woman's right.

John Paul II already appeared very frail, he walked slowly and leaned on his cane. After the meeting, I was sent to walk him to the elevator. He was frowning, brooding over the discussions he had heard and was shaking his head. Then he spat out in anger, "Abortion is an abominable crime!" citing *Gaudium et Spes*. "How can people not understand this? How can the UN promote it?" I realized that he spoke in public the same way he spoke in private. That was his strength.

John Paul II has been defined in many ways: globe-trotting pope, geopolitical pope, anti-communist pope. How would you define him?

St. John Paul II was, above all, a mystic who lived a relationship of extraordinary immediacy with God. That was his fundamental characteristic, along with what I'd call being a metaphysical poet. Those two aspects were tightly intertwined: metaphysical poetry was the most natural way for him to express his own mystical experiences. Some splendid verses come to mind: "My place is in You, your place is in me. Yet it is the place of all men. And I am not diminished by them"; and "Where you are not, there are only people without a home."[10] This was the root of his extraordinary personality.

Mystical experience, communicated through poetry and more generally through artistic expressions like the "Rhapsodic Theater,"[11] is the source of the two major lines in the activity of Karol Wojtyła. First, there were his philosophical reflections born from the need to give a theoretical foundation to his mystical experience. Secondly, there was his pastoral engagement which led to the practical translation of his system of thought. I have had the opportunity, as a teacher at the Institute that bears his name, to study John Paul II's thought and to analyze his writings.[12] I must say that Wojtyła was an original thinker, gifted with a strong intellectual fiber that manifested itself in his papal magisterium.

And here we get to the most public and best-known aspect of his personality, his pastoral service to the Church. Karol Wojtyła was able to testify to the beauty of the Christian message within a great passion for humanity. He challenged the freedom of the person, he urged it, he lovingly drew it out. Whoever listened to him was forced to react, in one way or another. In this sense, John Paul II was truly the pope of freedom. He never acted with a project in mind, but instead interpreted circumstances and events as providential. He lived everything that happened to him as the way through which the Lord called him to salvation. I have known few men as free as Karol Wojtyła. He was also free from any narcissistic or self-gratifying temptation, and had a great sense of self-irony.

I remember when in 1983, we held an international conference, organized by ISTRA, on "Karol Wojtyła, philosopher, theologian, and poet." For the occasion we asked for an audience with the pope, but he did not want us to talk about this topic. In the end, we reached a compromise. We would go and have a drink with him at the end of the conference, but it had to remain private. When he met us, he said, "Now, you can openly admit it. If I had not become pope, you would have never organized a conference on my poetry and my writings in philosophy and theology!"

He changed the way the Petrine ministry is exercised, manifesting this in all its breadth from the very first day of his pontificate through his gestures, his travels, and his absolutely original initiatives. And he exalted that ministry even in the final years, marked by sickness and serious suffering, because he showed that in the Church, the faculty of government is not in the hands of whoever possesses it, but comes always and only from God.

John Paul II was able to create a special bond with the young, beginning with the invention of the WYDs, the World Youth Days. Why did he fascinate young people so much?

I remember very well that in 1983, during the extraordinary Jubilee of Redemption, John Paul II asked then Msgr. Cordes, vice president of the Pontifical Counsel for the Laity,[13] to organize a global encounter of young people. It was held the following year at the end of the Jubilee. The gathering was so massive that it exceeded all expectations. From there, the idea of having World Youth Days was born. The images of these rallies have become iconic of the pope's exceptional ability to speak directly to millions of young men and women, always eliciting an exceptional response and creating a style of approach that continued with Benedict XVI and Francis. "To stay young, one must stay with the young," he said, citing a Polish proverb during the 2000 WYD in Rome. It was clear that he participated in that relationship with all his heart.

Prior to being a great pope, Karol Wojtyła was a great man, gifted with artistic and philosophical sensibility magnified by his granitic faith, and marked by his direct experience of unimaginable tragedies and sociopolitical contradictions. All this allowed him to have such a deep knowledge of the world and of the human soul that he could immediately identify with the typical questions of young people. In this sense, John Paul II was a great educator who knew how to speak to the young about the most delicate aspect of their maturation, namely the affective dimension, exalting the beauty of virginity as well as that of married life. People could tell that, unlike many other clerical figures, Wojtyła had not bypassed the affective problem but had faced it directly. This is why he was able to talk about it in a new language. Every time he addressed young people, he invited them to connect the choice of a state of life and of a profession not only with their own desires, but also and above all with the good of the Church and of society.

John Paul II's pontificate is almost unanimously viewed as a political one. Do you agree?

If we're referring to the effect he had on an international level, certainly. But, as I have tried to explain, John Paul II didn't have a political project in mind that he intended to implement. Even regarding the fall of Communism, he never set himself such a goal, but instead followed and interpreted the circumstances as they came up. Just think of his first trip to Poland in 1979. He did not propose political solutions, he did not attack the powers that be, but spoke to his countrymen as a shepherd of the Church, as a witness of a faith that changes life and mobilizes the freedom of the person.

He did not found a movement like Solidarity—the Polish workers did. Their hearts were moved and their dignity reawakened by the words of the pope. They took an unthinkable and amazing initiative in the gridlocked circumstances of Europe split by the iron curtain: They created a union independent from the regime. Then, in front of this new situation, John Paul II took a position, said that it was a just thing, and defended it vehemently even when many people thought it was a lost cause. This was how he acted—which was as far as could be from ideological behavior.

From this point of view, the political aspect of John Paul II's papacy is an extraordinary gift that Poland has given to the universal Church. It affected not only his native country and Eastern Europe, but the entire world. John Paul II was a father of the nation for his countrymen and an authoritative point of reference for the whole world. The revival of the Church's social doctrine, the invocation of the identity and the role of Europe and of the right and duty of humanitarian intervention, the sharp condemnation of the Iraq war and the prophetic vision of the disaster that would ensue from it in the Middle East—all these and more would become a precious inheritance that John Paul II left not just to believers, but to all people of good will.

John Paul II was an interventionist pope, in the sense that on many occasions, he openly joined the fray against decisions made by governments, leaders, and international organizations. His criticisms of the Preamble to the European constitution because it did not contain any reference to the Christian roots of Europe are still memorable. His interventions against the legalization of abortion in Italy and Poland were even harsher. However, the Church of today, with Pope Francis, seems to have adopted an entirely different approach. What is your judgment?

St. John Paul II cared very much about the public role of the Christian faith and its capacity to impact society. And this had a decisive effect—particularly upon the Italian church because it was dominated by the so-called culture of mediation, which implied the danger of giving up on social and political action "as believers."

The pope's change of strategy had its culminating and paradigmatic moment at the ecclesial convention of Loreto in 1985. The atmosphere of the assembly was more or less the same as during the convention on "Evangelization and human promotion" nine years earlier, which I mentioned. The intervention of John Paul II tore down that way of thinking in one blow and opened a new era for our country. "Even in a partially de-Christianized society," said the pope, "the Church is called to make sure that the Christian faith has, or recovers, a guiding role and a driving effectiveness." In doing so, the Church "is not intruding into roles that do not belong to her, but acts by virtue of what originally belongs to her."[14] The conclusion was a vigorous appeal to not be afraid of the public role that Christianity can have for the good of the country. However, today that speech certainly cannot be reproposed in the same terms, because the situation has greatly changed and demands a different approach.

What has changed since then?

We must keep in mind the great principle of freedom that always inspired John Paul II in his actions. Pastoral engagement is not the fruit of an abstract project, but rather responds to the circumstances, following and interpreting whatever reality one faces at a given time. In a situation like that of Italy, where the process of secularization was not yet complete, where a popular Christianity still endured despite everything, the pope's invitation in the speech of Loreto had validity. It rallied believers to make an impact on society and to defend the fundamental values of life and family with cultural and, if necessary, political engagement.

Today, that context does not exist anymore. Pluralistic society is not only a factual reality but an idea rooted in the collective conscience and codified on all levels. Pope Francis is right to say that we are not facing "an era of change, but a change of era." We all have the perception that a historical era has ended, but we cannot imagine what humanity in the third millennium will be like. The problem is that Catholicism in general, and Italian Catholicism in particular, has not yet figured out how to witness the faith in a pluralistic society. There are two current interpretations. The first reduces the Christian tradition into a store of values, a sort of ethical cement capable of functioning as the social glue of democracy. The second identifies Christianity with the announcement of the pure and naked cross for the salvation of every "other." This is the only thing that matters; there is no need for all the other aspects to adopt a specifically Christian physiognomy. Such an attitude produces a dispersion of Christians in society and ends up hiding the human relevance of faith itself. We could call this the "crypto-diaspora."

Is this Pope Francis's approach?

The crypto-diaspora claims to represent the current pontificate. I do not think that it is a precise approach adopted by Pope Francis, because it is also a distinctly European approach. Following his speeches attentively, including those he gives every morning at Santa Marta, one notes that while on the one side the pope is very careful to avoid any kind of statement that might seem to interfere with the political decisions of a country or a government (such as the referendum on homosexual marriage in Ireland, or the US Supreme Court decision on the same issue), on the other side he also expresses very sharp judgments, in which a clear and determined proposal of the teachings of Christ and of the Church is evident. For example, his insistent teaching on the paramount importance of sexual difference, on marriage, on the family, and on the education of children. Personally, just as I do not share the doctrinaire type of opposition coming from many conservative groups, I am also convinced that many supporters of the crypto-diaspora risk abusing Pope Francis's position, interpreting it as a form of liberal Christianity.

Is there an alternative to what you call crypto-diaspora but also to the option of a civil religion?

I am firmly convinced that there is a third path between these two interpretations, which are both reductive of Christianity. It is the recognition that faith has an irreconcilable anthropological, social, and cosmological value, whose implications must be deepened on the personal and communal level and proposed to everyone. This means that the believer completely accepts the logic of dialogue among different subjects which should characterize a pluralistic society.

That is what emerged during the debate held at Munich in 2004 between then-Cardinal Ratzinger and the philosopher Jürgen

Habermas on Christianity and post-secular society.[15] Both agreed in recognizing that religion can no longer be considered the binding foundation of the state, but it has every right to be admitted to the public debate as a component of civilization capable of affirming principles and values, exercising an influence on the configuration of the civil order. This means that the religious vision enters fully into the process of forming consensus. In my opinion, it is vital that believers make this dynamic their own with the aim of gaining wider recognition, not through a comparison of abstract principles, but through the personal and public witness of lived values.

Notes to Chapter 8

1. Pope John Paul II, *Mass for the Participants in the Convention "Movements in the Church"* (Castel Gandolfo: September 27, 1981), 2. Available at www.vatican.va in Italian, Portuguese, and Spanish.

2. The "Meeting," as is colloquially known in Italy, is a week-long festival of talks, panels, exhibits, and artistic events. It is organized by a foundation tied to Communion and Liberation. It takes place every summer in August in Rimini, a seaside resort on the Adriatic coast of Italy.

3. From Paul VI's homily at the funeral of Aldo Moro in the Basilica of Saint John Lateran, May 13, 1978.

4. Carlo Caffarra (1938–2017) was a cardinal and moral theologian. After leading the John Paul II Institute in Rome, he was archbishop of Bologna from 2003 to 2015.

5. Stratford Caldecott (1953–2014), British writer and journalist.

6. See Angelo Scola, *Il mistero nuziale, Vol. 1: Uomo-donna* (Venezia: Marcianum Press, 2005) and *Vol. 2: Matrimonio e famiglia* (Venezia: Marcianum Press, 2007).

7. John Paul II, *Man and Woman He Created Them: A Theology of the Body* (Boston: Pauline Books, 2006).

8. Livio Melina (1952–) is a priest and theologian. He taught moral theology at the John Paul II Institute in Rome, of which he was dean from 2006 to 2016, until he was not reappointed in 2019 following its refounding. Giovanni Battista Re (1934–) is an archbishop and cardinal. He held various positions in the

Roman Curia and was prefect of the Congregation for bishops from 2000 to 2010.

9. Stanisław Dziwisz (1939–) is a cardinal. He was Karol Wojtyła's secretary for forty years, from 1966 to 2005. From 2005 to 2016, he served as archbishop of Kraków.

10. Karol Wojtyła, *The Place Within*, trans. Jerzy Peterkiewicz (New York: Random House, 1994), 117 and 118. The published English translation has for the latter, "Outside you, they [all men] are homeless."

11. Rhapsodic Theatre is a type of theatrical performance that emphasizes the text, spoken aloud with clarity, with only a minimum of stage movement. It was invented by Mieczysław Kotlarczyk in Kraków under the Nazi occupation. Young Karol Wojtyła was an enthusiastic actor in this clandestine theater.

12. Angelo Scola, *L'esperienza elementare. La vena profonda del magistero di Giovanni Paolo II* (Genova: Marietti, 2003).

13. Paul Josef Cordes (1937–) is an archbishop and cardinal. He presided over the Pontifical Council for the Laity from 1980 to 1995.

14. John Paul II, *To the Participants in the Convention of the Italian Catholic Church in Loreto* (April 11, 1985), 7. Available at www.vatican.va only in Italian.

15. Jürgen Habermas and Joseph Ratzinger, *The Dialectics of Secularization: On Reason and Religion* (San Francisco: Ignatius Press, 2007).

CHAPTER 9

To Be Truly Free

Bishop in Grosseto

On July 20, 1991, the Vatican Press Office announced your appointment as bishop of Grosseto.[1] You chose a phrase from the Second Letter to the Corinthians, *Sufficit Gratia Tua* (Your grace is sufficient), as your episcopal motto. Was there a particular reason for this choice?

I chose a well-known phrase of St. Paul, which expresses the Christian vision of life in its most essential aspect—namely, the fact that as creatures we find ourselves given to ourselves, and there is nothing in our being that ultimately does not have God as its origin. I have always loved a beautiful prayer which I have continued to use at the beginning of every meeting I had to preside over as bishop: "Inspire our actions, Lord, and come to our aid, so that every word we speak and action we take will always begin from you and be fulfilled in you." This prayer overturns our instinctive attitude that what we do comes from us and its outcome ultimately depends on our own effort and our own will. I must admit that, since that moment at the end of my adolescence when I discovered the overwhelming power of the Christian faith, I have always been dramatically aware of the disproportion between my being and my task. And therefore, I have always been fond of that phrase by St. Paul that expresses what the Lord revealed to him: "My grace is sufficient for you, for my power is made perfect in weakness" (2 Cor 12:9).

I had imagined that the choice of an episcopal motto would require long reflection and a deep search to find the most appropriate phrase. On the contrary, for you it was a very simple and spontaneous matter?

Yes, because I already had it in my heart, starting from my experience and also from my limitations. Besides, saying "Your grace is sufficient" was my most immediate reaction when faced with the radical life change caused by becoming a bishop.

Was this a total surprise? Did you expect this appointment to come some day?

In the preceding years, I had heard that John Paul II intended to make me a bishop, but I believed it to be pretty unlikely, given my personal history. I later learned from trustworthy people that my possible episcopal nomination had met with much resistance from the members of the Feria V of the Congregation of Bishops, the meeting where groups of three names are selected and recommended to the pope for his final choice. Thus, it was a genuine surprise to me; I didn't expect it at all. By the way, in July 1991, I was not even in Rome but studying in Fribourg when the nuncio to Italy called to tell me I had been appointed. I suddenly found myself, at 49 years of age, to be the youngest bishop in Italy. Even less did I expect to be destined to Grosseto, as I had never been there and knew nothing about it.

Your episcopal consecration, on September 21, 1991, took place in the Roman Basilica of Saint Mary Major, packed with worshippers. I remember the festive atmosphere, a little dampened by the absence of Cardinal Ratzinger, who was expected to preside over the ceremony but was impeded by an unexpected illness.

I must admit, so many years later, that it was not an easy day for me. I was certainly grateful and moved for the attending crowd, particularly for the warm and enthusiastic embrace by many CL people, and for the well over seven hundred people from Grosseto guided by Bishop Adelmo Tacconi.[2] But there were some leaders of CL who interpreted Ratzinger's absence as a way of distancing himself, to avoid an overly direct and explicit association with Communion and Liberation. This was an absurd and utterly baseless conjecture, as would be amply proven in the following years. Ratzinger had been brought to the Gemelli Hospital after suffering a mild stroke the night before my episcopal ordination. The concern for his health, and especially the pernicious interpretations of his sudden absence—speculations which upset even Fr. Giussani—made that day somewhat less joyous for me than it might have appeared from the outside. It was Ratzinger who asked Cardinal Bernardin Gantin, the prefect of the Congregation for Bishops, to preside over my ordination.[3] Thanks to this, I began a beautiful friendship with the cardinal from Benin.

You candidly confessed to your newly-met faithful of Grosseto, "My name is completely new to you, as is this city and this diocese to me." Was it a difficult start?

Being sent to Grosseto, even if it took me entirely by surprise, was a real grace. Even today, when I think back on the four years of my episcopate in Grosseto, I find myself thanking the Lord for making me live such a beautiful, intense, and valuable experience. It was an opportunity to live among common folk, immersed in the people of God, striving to build the Christian community day by day. It was a task that had kept me busy back when I led the CL university students. In Grosseto I went back to it, in an institutional role, concretely experiencing that charism and institution go together within the life of the Church, guaranteeing that pastoral action is unified and fruitful. It was an experience of grace also because of the place where I found myself working. The natural beauty of the Maremma immediately struck me: the sea, the hills, the forests, and the wonderful Uccellina Park. It is a pristine land, only marginally touched by mass tourism, and the people are very down-to-earth, practical, and hardworking, forged all through Grosseto's history by strenuous labor in the mines. A healthy people, even if largely alien to religious practice, marked by having been a borderland of the Papal States and by a strong Masonic presence; these factors later facilitated the hegemony of the Communist Party.

You were a "CL bishop" in a "red" territory of Italy.[4] The news of your appointment created some concern. Even among the clergy there were doubts about having a partisan bishop. How were you received in Grosseto? And how did you react?

I did not perceive any feelings of hostility or prejudice when I arrived. And anyway, had there ever been such sentiments, I had already decided not to pay attention to them. I threw myself headlong in every direction from the start. I met the ecclesial groups, the social movements, the civil authorities. I opened myself to all, convinced of the importance of working together. This is a method I always tried to follow, not only in Grosseto but in all of my twenty-seven years of episcopate. The record is clear: I never tried to put only people who shared my outlook in charge. I always chose people who were esteemed and regarded as authoritative in the environment where they would have responsibilities. The criterion was never closeness to me or to the movement from which I came. This is my method: synodality, a word which is often brandished in the life of the Church, but which is rarely applied to face everyday problems. It is an attitude of listening, of paying attention to needs but also to resistances being expressed, of availability to change one's mind when faced with objections or suggestions after having examined their merits. And I must say that this method works.

What does it mean to be a bishop? How did you learn to do it?

I must first say that starting out as bishop of Grosseto made my task easier. It's a small diocese, with 125,000 faithful, and therefore with the dimensions of a large parish. This allowed me to take direct, one-on-one action both with young people and adults. Anyone who wanted to come and talk had easy access, starting with the eighty or so priests of the diocese, each of whom I came to know personally. Being a bishop means showing paternity. But a true paternity can only come from being a son. It means that my complete obedience to God within the communion of the Church must shine through my episcopal function. In this, I constantly tried to refer to the teaching, repeated also by the Second Vatican Council, that identifies three characteristic tasks of the episcopal ministry—to teach, to sanctify, and to govern. In other words, announcing the Word of God, presiding over the liturgical celebration, and guiding the community. Today, there is—correctly—a great focus on the need for bishops to leave ample space for direct personal relationships, but perhaps we forget that the most effective way to speak to each one is by speaking to all.

Is not this concept of the episcopal mission a little too lofty, I daresay, aristocratic? Especially compared to Pope Francis's calls for shepherds to live among the people and have the same scent as the sheep.

Pope Francis uses very effective and suggestive images that match his sensibility, his temperament, and his Latin American formation. But it is often easy for some to turn them into slogans and use them in an ideological way. I understood this call by the pope as an invitation to practice an authentic familiarity with all, and to guide the people in an open way, getting them involved. This is something I have always tried to do. When I say—to quote a concept that the unforgettable Cardinal Giacomo Biffi once expressed—that the greatest gift a bishop can give to his Christian community is his magisterium, I certainly do not mean handing down a dogmatic treatise.[5] Rather, I refer to a capacity for judgment which penetrates reality and jolts consciences. And this happens to the extent that one lives within a people and shares their worries, struggles, and sufferings, but with a *sensus fidei* that makes it possible to see the big picture.

One of the most striking examples is John Paul II's magisterium when he first visited Poland as pope. On June 2, 1979, on the day of Pentecost, before a massive crowd gathered in Warsaw's central square, the Pope invoked the Holy Spirit and asked it to renew the face of the earth. Then he added, "of *this* earth."[6] He did not attack the Communist regime, he did not analyze the political situation, but with that invocation, which followed the words "Christ cannot be excluded from the heart of man," he triggered a dynamism of freedom and set in motion an entire people who would forever alter European history. Karol Wojtyła was as tied to Poland as he could be; his biography coincides with the enormous tragedies that his native land endured in the last century, but he did not feel the need to restate what his fellow countrymen already knew. It would have only been sterile and ineffective self-pity. Instead, by sharing the concrete situation, he subjected it to the crucial challenge of the Christian announcement. There was a true shepherd, there was manifested before the whole world the power of a magisterium that fascinated and converted.

Pope Francis's teaching also starts from his roots in the people, from the peripheries, from the poor, to reach the same goal. This is the dynamics of Jesus's preaching in the Gospel. And it is the same dynamics that every bishop should try renewing in whatever context he is called to act, aware of his own limits but also of his duties. I tried to move along this line.

Is it true that initially, people in Grosseto would call you "the German," not only for your red hair but for your fame as a bit of an abstract and difficult theologian?

Oh, but that was a refrain that always followed me wherever I went, and like all clichés, there must undoubtedly be something true about it. I will grant that because of my education and temperament, I have a tendency to speak more theoretically than figuratively. Sometimes, what I say is not immediately easy to understand, requiring a certain level of attention and availability on the part of the listener. Unfortunately, today people tend to consider easy what they already know. If you try to introduce a new perspective or a different reflection from what is out there circulating, your speech is branded as difficult and is dismissed, because no one is willing to make an effort to understand anymore. Excuse me, but if I spent ten days writing the text that I'm delivering, don't expect to understand it in the blink of an eye. Be patient enough to study it and reflect upon it.

Let's ask ourselves what it means to understand. It does not mean to grasp every sentence immediately. I always use the example of rock climbing: you have to attach yourself to the most prominent feature, pick out a foothold in order to move up. The same thing happens when you listen to a speech. If you are struck by a particular observation, attach yourself to it, treasure it. Then, calmly and patiently, you will be able to grasp the entire argument. And I believe many have understood me. Who knows, maybe I've learned to use simpler language. Anyway, in recent years the refrain about my difficult language has faded a bit.

There is a concept that often comes up in your interventions and that represents the key word of your mission at Grosseto. It's the concept of freedom, which not by chance figures in the title of your first pastoral letter to the diocese, *You will be truly free*. Wasn't this topic a bit too philosophical and theological?

Intervening at length on a theme like freedom was not an obvious choice. On the other hand, I was aware that one of the most evident reasons for the dramatic split between faith and life that had already been diagnosed by Paul VI lay in the fact that the Christian announcement no longer spoke to the freedom of the person. The letter was a sort of bet with my people—it is not possible to be truly free without Christ. Indeed Christianity, in its elementary structure, is an event that happens in an encounter and invites the subject's freedom to respond. If we forget this, the Christian fact is reduced to a doctrine and a sum of ethical behaviors which might be applicable for a while, but are ultimately neglected under the weight of other urges and necessities. Jesus is a living and personal presence who speaks to our freedom, not to human nature. He does not address humanity in the abstract, but the concrete person. He provokes him or her to a responsible adhesion, to a choice that can even result, in the end, in a rejection. For a long time, the two themes in any kind of debate, both in the Church and in society, were truth and reason. The secularization process started and then developed around these two, in a discussion on what is rational and how one can reach the truth without referring to religion.

With the fall of the walls and the end of the ideologies, the themes of truth and reason are no longer central. To be more precise, this pair, long considered decisive for Western culture and for European culture in particular, began to enter into a crisis with the events of 1968 and the rejection of the principle of authority. It marked the emergence of another thematic pair that has by now become crucial for contemporary man—happiness and freedom. The pursuit of happiness, meaning an indefinite and inexhaustible search for well-being and pleasure, in turn requires that freedom be reduced essentially to free will. The impression is that today, when we speak of freedom, we refer to an energy of the "I" that struggles to find its object.

I've often compared the freedom of today's man to the image of a high jumper, who, at the moment of clearing the bar, somehow remains magically blocked and suspended in midair. I call this a stuck freedom, an aspiration that never reaches its fulfillment. From this point of view, I find that there is a strong consonance between the Christian proposal and the more or less explicit question that emerges today from the unresolved relationship between happiness and freedom. If we read the Gospel (Luke 18:22), we find ourselves before an extraordinary fact. Jesus tells the young man who wanted to be perfect, and therefore happy, to leave everything behind and follow him. He does not add new precepts to the many that the young man already tried to follow, but instead appeals to his freedom and invites him to form a relationship with him. His "follow me" is what opens one to a freedom that brings happiness. As Balthasar wrote in a wonderful synthesis, "As opposed to those whose search for freedom urges them onwards into a barren void, the Christian stands as the messenger of freedom accomplished and a freedom attainable by all."[7] Jesus says, if you follow me, your freedom will not be stuck, because you will have a travel companion who knows the road. Therefore, I realize myself by being open to Another. The proposal of the Christian life can only become attractive on these conditions, not through the assimilation of a few formulas and norms that then need to be applied to life.

I have always bet on the freedom of the person. And I have observed that putting the theme of freedom front and center touches the hearts of all, leaves nobody indifferent. This is also the way to recover the decisive reason-truth pair.

And how was this bet received in Grosseto?

I can say with a certain satisfaction that my pastoral letter, *You will be truly free*, stirred much interest not just from the faithful, but also from nonbelievers. I remember that it was reprinted several times. It was a message that started from the experience of the encounter with Christ as recounted in the Gospels and testified to even today by those who decide to follow him. Therefore, I also spoke from my experience. I have noticed that this intrigued and evoked questions even from those who we usually judge as being furthest from the Church. I discussed my pastoral letter in rehab communities, with those stricken with AIDS (who at the time were practically under a death sentence), and with prisoners. Wherever I went, I found myself subjected to a barrage of thought-provoking questions. From these, I experienced firsthand the desire for God hidden in the heart of every man.

Another concept you often insist upon is that of education, especially the education in faith. How did you put this into practice during your years in Grosseto?

In order to educate, it is essential to hold common gestures. A particularly intense one was the pilgrimage from Roselle, the ancient Etrusco-Roman site where the first local Christian communities had been formed, to the cathedral of Grosseto. It was geared toward young people but many adults also participated. On Saturday afternoon, they walked through the city center very bravely, disregarding the jeers and insults directed at them. Such a public demonstration of faith was novel for a proudly anticlerical and red city like Grosseto. Certainly, there was and still is the ancient, traditional procession held on the vigil of the Feast of St. Lawrence on August 9, which thousands of citizens and tourists attend each year. It is a gesture that, even if its core religious meaning has not been lost, has been overwhelmed by elements of folklore, starting with the cart that carries the saint's statue pulled by the famous Maremmano oxen with their enormous horns and escorted by *butteri* on horseback.[8] Holding common gestures, with laypeople, priests, and bishop together, has an immediate educational value because it makes visible the community as a place of welcome and as a proposal for all, including young people and teenagers. With this same motivation, I proposed the Corpus Domini procession through the downtown streets.

On this topic you once cited, with some irony, Charles Peguy's judgment about "teenagers, stiffened and stunted by entire generations of catechism." You've tried new approaches, different from the traditional ones—with what results?

I did not quote only Peguy. The example I used more frequently was that recounted by Albert Camus in *The First Man*, where he remembers being sent by his grandmother to take catechism lessons when he was a boy. In the dim church, a priest spoke about the mysteries of Christianity in a way that sounded abstruse. Then he adds that the embrace of his mother when he returned home was much fuller of mystery.[9] A Christianity that does not spur affection but only boredom is an experience that has unfortunately marked entire generations.

Another text I liked to quote, talking to priests, is a story by Grosseto's most famous writer, Luciano Bianciardi.[10] In his book *La vita agra*, he describes colorfully and sarcastically Fr. Riccardo Lombardi's arrival to Grosseto. Lombardi was known as "God's microphone."[11] To bring the masses back to the Church, he would travel around Italy in a special truck that turned into an altar to celebrate Mass on the main squares. He showed great courage in publicly announcing the faith, but Bianciardi ridicules his bombastic and ultimately irritating preaching style.

I used these examples to illustrate ways of announcing Christianity that are no longer viable. I did not have God-knows-what alternative techniques in mind; I simply tried to seek direct contact with as many people as possible. I began holding informal meetings with young people, which over time became regular without losing their freshness and spontaneity. They would take the form of a conversation, with questions and answers where no topic was off limits, and they were eventually attended by more than 500 young people. The guiding thread was the desire to welcome and understand the questions people discover inside themselves, leaving out no aspect of reality. An interesting fact is that during this journey, some young people began to reflect about vocations to the consecrated life. I would tell them that if they found within their hearts the idea of dedicating themselves to God, even as a hypothesis, they had to take it into consideration because it was something that, while less apparent, was more powerful than falling in love. This is how the Verification Group began, which became a source of vocations to the priesthood, religious life, and even lay consecration. I then decided to reopen the seminary of Grosseto, which had been closed for many years. In the fall of 1995, it restarted its activity of forming future priests, after I had already been called to direct the Lateran University in Rome. My very dear vicar general, Fr. Roberto Nelli, insisted that I be the one to lead the opening ceremony of the seminary academic year, at the monastery of Vitorchiano. It was very emotional for me.

You also had the idea to open a Catholic school in a diocese that had never had one before. How was this decision received?

There were already nursery and elementary schools run by Catholics in the diocese, but there had never been a middle or high school. It became possible to create one because a group of people believed in it, quitting their jobs in the state schools to risk everything for an entirely novel experience. It began with the creation of a middle school, the only Catholic school not just in the diocese, but along the entire Tyrrhenian coast from Rome to Leghorn. I only had time to see its first steps but in subsequent years, this educational initiative grew a lot. It led to the opening of a *liceo classico*, and later of a *liceo scientifico*.

I believe that the question of freedom of education, whereby parents decide to take educational responsibility for their children by proposing a clearly Christian direction, plays a crucial role for the future of Catholicism. Once upon a time, an hour of religion a week was enough, because the social environment was still infused with Christian references. But in today's society, which totally ignores and often explicitly opposes the Christian vision of life, only a stable and structured context can guarantee an educational proposal founded on the contemporaneity of Christ with today's man. It is not a matter of creating a ghetto, but of offering everybody a clearly identifiable education, capable of attracting even those who are not Catholic. This is the challenge facing free schools—either they rise away from the logic of the protective bubble in which families hide their children to protect them from a mean and ugly world, gambling on a clear educational proposal, or they have no future, even if one day the state were to intervene, as it should, to support them.

In Grosseto, among other things, you founded a center for political culture named after Hildebrand of Sovana, the monk who went on to become Pope Gregory VII. He went down in history for his actions at Canossa. Was this meant to be a response to the crisis of the Christian Democratic party and the Tangentopoli scandal?

There was—understandably—much bewilderment among the (few, to tell the truth) faithful laypeople of my diocese who were involved in politics. They had always been in the opposition, but they were subjected to criticisms and attacks which became destructive during the era of Tangentopoli.[12] The center for political culture was established in March 1994, during the election campaign. We named it after Gregory VII because he was originally from Sovana, a town near Grosseto, and above all because he was the Church's first great reformer pope. During a lecture I was asked to give to politicians, I reminded them that a Christian engaged in public administration must bring his identity into play in a realistic manner. Quoting then-Cardinal Ratzinger, I said that "it is not refusal to compromise but compromise that in political things is the true morality."[13] In those days of inflamed debates about national politicians tainted by dishonesty and corruption, that phrase sounded decidedly provocative. I remember that when I quoted Ratzinger, in order to avoid misunderstandings, I took the liberty of slightly modifying the sentence speaking of "noble compromise."

On various occasions, I had direct public debates with local authorities—of a Marxist orientation, as is well known—who were always very respectful to me. Participating in debates was entirely natural for me. Then I noticed that the faithful were proud that their bishop was willing to dialogue with political figures and, I must confess, I even enjoyed needling them a bit, but without ever falling into squabbles or invectives. Not only in Grosseto, but everywhere I exercised my episcopal ministry, I never pulled back from public discussions. Over the years, I participated in very many debates with prominent figures and intellectuals of the secular world; just to name a few, Giuliano Ferrara, Paolo Flores d'Arcais, Ernesto Galli della Loggia, Angelo Panebianco, Gian Enrico Rusconi, Emanuele Severino, and Gustavo Zagrebelsky.[14] Sincere relationships were born from some of these encounters, with mutual esteem and frequent social interactions.

Notes to Chapter 9

1. Grosseto is the administrative capital of a large swath of Southern Tuscany, historically called Maremma. The area used to be characterized by large swamps, which were drained in the nineteenth century. It is now largely agricultural and touristic, and still relatively underpopulated.
2. Adelmo Tacconi (1915–2003) was bishop of Grosseto from 1975 to 1991.
3. Bernardin Gantin (1922–2008) was archbishop of Cotonou in Benin and a cardinal. After holding various jobs in the Roman

Curia, he was prefect of the Congregation for Bishops from 1984 to 1998.

4. In Italian political parlance, a "red" region means a region that was politically dominated by the Communist Party and by its successors. Most of Tuscany fits this definition.

5. Giacomo Biffi (1928–2015) was an archbishop and cardinal. He was an auxiliary bishop in Milan from 1975 to 1984 and the archbishop of Bologna until 2003. He wrote numerous books and was well known for his sharp wit. He is famous for having complained to another cardinal, during the conclave of 2005, that he kept getting one vote, and for promising that he would "slap that idiot" if he found out who he was. His lone voter was Cardinal Joseph Ratzinger.

6. Meaning "this land." The Italian word "terra" means both "earth" and "land."

7. Hans Urs von Balthasar, *Engagement with God: The Drama of Christian Discipleship* (San Francisco: Ignatius Press, 2008), 6.

8. A *buttero* (from the Latin, "cow-poker") is the traditional name for a mounted herder in the Tuscan Maremma.

9. Albert Camus, *The First Man* (New York: Vintage, 1996), 171.

10. Luciano Bianciardi (1922–1971), journalist, writer, and social activist.

11. Riccardo Lombardi (1908–1979) was a Jesuit priest. He became famous immediately after World War II for his open-air Masses in the squares of Italian cities and towns. He was nicknamed "God's microphone" because of his radio broadcasts.

12. Literally "Bribetown." This was the name used in the press to describe a major political scandal in 1992. A large-scale police investigation (code-named *Mani Pulite* or "Clean Hands") unearthed a vast network of corruption that involved politicians and entrepreneurs. The scandal brought down some of the major political parties that had dominated Italian politics since 1945, in particular the Christian Democrats and the Socialists. Both parties had to change name and then virtually disappeared in the subsequent 1994 national elections.

13. Joseph Ratzinger, *Church, Ecumenism and Politics: New Essays in Ecclesiology* (New York: Crossroad, 1988), 149.

14. Giuliano Ferrara (1952–) is a journalist and editorialist. He founded and edited the daily newspaper *Il Foglio.* He was also

a member of the European parliament and a minister in one of the Berlusconi governments. Paolo Flores d'Arcais (1944–) is a journalist and editor of the political journal *MicroMega*; Ernesto Galli della Loggia (1942–) is a historian and editorialist for *Corriere della Sera*; Angelo Panebianco (1948–) is a political thinker and essayist; Gian Enrico Rusconi (1939–) is a historian and political thinker; Emanuele Severino (1929–2020) was a philosopher; and Gustavo Zagrebelsky (1943–) is a jurist who served as a judge in the *Corte Costituzionale* (Supreme Court of Italy) from 1995 to 2004.

CHAPTER 10

A Community of Students and Teachers

Rector of the Pontifical Lateran University

In July of 1995, you were called back to Rome to lead the Pontifical Lateran University. How did you interpret the identity and mission of this prestigious university?

I must confess that when José Saraiva Martins,[1] then secretary of the Congregation for Catholic Education, first called me to say that the pope intended to appoint me rector of the Lateran University, I didn't feel very enthusiastic. In fact, I put up a bit of resistance. I would have preferred to continue my pastoral work in Grosseto, where I had been bishop for less than four years. It was frustrating to have to cut short a mission that I thought had only just begun. But the pope must be obeyed, always and no matter what. And then, reflecting on my new assignment, I realized that it might be an opportunity to live fully the universal dimension of the Church, not just as a figure of speech, but by the virtue of the nature of this university.

What are you referring to, exactly?

You see, the Lateran is unlike most universities, which have a campus and a set location. It's an international institution, with 45 locations spread all over the globe and organically connected to the Roman one. That means that these institutes derive their authority to grant degrees from their link with the Lateran. Some institutes are affiliated, some are aggregated, and some are even incorporated. Affiliated means they go up to a bachelor's degree, aggregated to a licenciate, and incorporated up to the highest level, that of the doctorate.

Such a structure allows the Lateran to be present at a local level in a completely original way. For example, when I visited Beirut, I discovered that the University La Sagesse, connected to us, confers degrees in canon law and also in civil law, and therefore has Islamic law as part of its curriculum. And so I, the bishop rector of the Lateran, would sign the diplomas of Muslim students! There, I discovered great opportunities to connect with the world of Islam thanks to our identity as a pontifical university. This was true for all kinds of situations. In other words, it was about valuing the local reality within a unifying, Roman Catholic vision. I gave myself the task of deepening and strengthening this type of approach.

How did you go about that?

For an organization as vast and complex as the Lateran University, the risk was that the unified cultural approach would remain a formality. It could just mean sending some visiting professors from the main campus, and supervising the committee that prepared the final examinations. Making the relationship between the many centers more substantial required above all getting the faculty involved. I tried to make this happen by incentivizing a work style based on reciprocal knowledge and cultural exchange. The most satisfying experiment took place at the John Paul II Institute for the Study of Marriage and Family, where I assumed the presidency two months after being named the director of the Lateran. In this case as well, it all started from a suggestion by John Paul II. He insisted on limiting the number of students sent to Rome from the developing nations whenever possible, to avoid the difficulties they had in adapting to an unfamiliar environment. Instead, he wanted us to create opportunities for high-quality education in their locations, so that their formation would match high standards of Catholicity and scientific rigor without having to be ripped away from the environment they were in, and where they would later be called to operate. The institute therefore assumed a unique structure among other ecclesiastical universities. It was a single institute with one dean and with several sections led by vice deans. Over the years, sections were founded in various parts of the world: in the US, Spain, Mexico, Brazil, Benin, and India, along with five associated centers in Lebanon, Columbia, Korea, the Philippines, and Australia.

It was a very demanding job. It involved training people to be competent teachers and managers so that they could go on to lead the various sections of the institute dispersed over five continents. Two people played a decisive role in this international work: Carl Anderson, the Supreme Knight of the Knights of Columbus, who founded the US section of the John Paul II Institute, and Monsignor Juan Antonio Reig Pla, who was the vice dean of the Spanish section of the Institute.[2] Each year, we met in Rome with about forty teachers for a workshop on the method and contents of instruction. Every three years, also in Rome, we held a plenary assembly of around two hundred teachers in the presence of the pope. All of this allowed the study of marriage and family to become, as people say today, "trans-disciplinary," meaning conducted with a consistent approach across various fields, striving to erase the (usually artificial) boundaries that separate them. John Paul II cared about this very much.

Let's circle back to the Lateran, the university of the pope, traditionally considered the most important center of elaboration of the so-called Roman theology. Does this expression still make sense?

The expression "the pope's university" has to be taken literally, since the teachings of the supreme pontiff are the point of reference for all ecclesiastical universities. However, the Lateran was founded in connection with the seminary of the diocese of Rome, whose bishop is the pope. This has always been a source of special pride for the teachers and even the students who come from all over the world. The expression "Roman theology," however, is more problematic and today has all but disappeared. This description was used in a mostly negative connotation, especially by some Northern European theologians who considered it to be a theology focused on commenting on the magisterium, almost second-rate, often in conflict with the European schools. This mistrust, if we are to label it such, had deep roots, but it exploded during the years of the Second Vatican Council. Think of the so-called *Nouvelle Théologie*, named by those who upheld the "old theology," namely, the neo-scholastics. Paradoxically, the Nouvelle Théologie actually included very different positions and people, and it is interesting that one of its main exponents, Henri de Lubac, always denied that he wanted to produce a Nouvelle Théologie.

When I assumed my responsibilities as the new rector of the Lateran, this opposition had eased, but the crisis in theology continued. Although the students had access to a wealth of exegetical comments as never before—translations from the Fathers, treatises on morality, on dogmatics, on systematic theology, and manuals of canon law—the fragmentation of theological knowledge had increased. There were few masters of the caliber of Daniélou,[3] de Lubac, Balthasar, Rahner, and Ratzinger, who combined a depth of analysis with an extraordinary capacity for synthesis. The most serious problem was the loss of the connection between theology and sanctity, to quote the title of Balthasar's famous essay.

In such a situation, we tried to make the university a living place, focusing heavily on daily circumstances. The excellence of a university depends upon the quality of ordinary life, comprised of research, instruction, and study. When I arrived at the Lateran, I noted that the university usually closed from one o'clock to three o'clock for lunch, then people came back for the afternoon classes. I decided to keep it open, setting up a cafeteria and new faculty offices. I upgraded the library and study spaces for students, in view of creating a community of professors, students, and staff. As Newman used to say, the university cannot be a cultural cafeteria, from which one takes what one needs, but must become a community that generates the capacity to reflect critically and organically about the faith. We tried to organize the disciplines in different ways, establishing libraries where doctoral students could work on a regular basis. We emphasized unity among the faculty and benefited from the generous availability of lay professors who also taught at state schools. People from all over the world, and not just Catholic people, were invited to hold courses and lectures. Our guest speakers included Jewish and Protestant intellectuals, along with famous politicians like the president of the Czech Republic, Vaclav Havel, who was the symbol of the Velvet Revolution against the communist regime. In order to promote the idea that all disciplines share a unifying principle, we set up a common course open to all students along the lines of Romano Guardini's course on the *Christliche Weltanschauung* (the Christian view of the world).

The years I spent leading the Lateran were an extraordinary opportunity for me to forge some very significant friendships with eminent people of culture. I will only mention Jean Guitton, to whom I was introduced by the philosopher Henri Hude.[4] My relationship with Guitton, a great French writer, intellectual, and friend of Paul VI's, grew closer and closer to the point that he dedicated *Mon testament philosophique* to me.

When you traveled across all continents, what was your experience of interreligious dialogue? This was a matter that John Paul II cared very much about.

Interreligious dialogue, along with ecumenism, is not something to be added to the act of faith, but one of its constitutive elements. For Christianity, faith cannot be cut off from its link to religiosity. The relationship with other religions is therefore an intrinsic part of its theology. Ecumenism is a necessary condition for all interreligious dialogue. If we do not strive for unity among Christians, there is no guarantee that we will be able to attempt a dialogue with other religions, independent of the results. Unfortunately, we have the tendency to reduce ecumenism and interreligious dialogue to specialized activities. We have thus created endowed chairs of ecumenism and interreligious dialogue, as if they were separate disciplines. Instead, they must be a dimension that cuts across all fields of theology.

When you find yourself in certain contexts where the Catholic Church is a numerically insignificant presence, the relationship with other religions becomes decisive. I remember one of my trips to India, in Mumbai, where I celebrated Mass with a dozen or so faithful gathered around the altar. During the celebration, I noticed that there was a large crowd of people gathered at the back of the church. I did not understand why at the time, but I later learned that they were followers of Hinduism. There were no temples in the area for them to use, so they had asked for permission to recite their prayers in a Catholic church. It was an opening that came about naturally; there was no need for sophisticated reflections on interreligious dialogue. The Second Vatican Council, with its farsighted and prophetic vision, understood that this dimension is intrinsic to the nature of

Christianity, which does not avoid relationships, but seeks them out, in order to give the reasons for our faith to far ends of the earth.

Today, there is much discussion around the challenge posed by Islam. However, you once warned us not to underestimate the cultural provocations coming from Eastern religions. What challenge do they pose to Christianity and to monotheistic religions in general?

That call did not originate with me, frankly. I heard it many years ago, at a pub in Munich, at the end of a meeting with the editors and collaborators of the journal *Communio*. De Lubac and Balthasar were also there, and they were discussing the future of religions. They both agreed that the confrontation with Islam would be very painful and difficult, but that the truly decisive challenge would come from Hinduism, Buddhism, and Confucianism. These last two, at least as they are understood in the West, are really philosophies or theosophies. For example, adhering to Buddhism does not require a conversion, in the sense of giving up one's previous religion. What Buddhism proposes is a morality founded on the idea of compassion, and it is presented as compatible with belonging to other religions. In a society that has lost its reference to Christianity as a criterion of judgment, the idea of a spiritual and bodily well-being that can be privately attained, with yoga exercises or Zen meditations, becomes an easily accessible religious experience. The same could be said about Confucianism, with its functional morality. Here, the confrontation becomes quite subtle, because it does not involve well-defined identities, but philosophies and principles of behavior that at first glance can be adopted also by a Christian.

We face the radical question of what the unity and universality of the Christian event mean in an intercultural and interreligious world. Today, we are not fully aware of it for two reasons: because we are dominated and harassed by Islamic fundamentalism and terrorism, and because the impact of Eastern religions upon Western culture is still very limited. But I fear that what de Lubac and Balthasar predicted forty years ago, when they saw Eastern religions as the gravest threat to Christianity, might come to pass. This risk, however, makes the witness of Christians in Asia even more admirable. Indeed

Catholics, with the exceptions of the Philippines and South Korea, are a very small minority in Asia. Their experiences must be carefully listened to and assimilated by the Churches of the West, where there is a harmful tendency to think that in the end, one religion is as good as another. If this relativism begins to affect the theological elaboration of interreligious dialogue, it will be a very bad sign for the Church.

Your Eminence, do you feel a bit of nostalgia for those years of cultural work and international experiences?

I really don't. First of all because those two aspects stayed with me afterwards, albeit in a different form and intensity. And also, because I have always shared Jacques Maritain's extremely important conviction that scientific knowledge is knowledge of a second degree. Original knowledge comes from *sàpere*, that is, from tasting, and is inherent to experience. There is a circularity in every kind of reflection, even theological. Reflection is useful if it starts from concrete experience and comes back to it, deepening it with rigorous and systematic questions.

Even though people have often labeled me as an intellectual, I must say that I don't consider myself to be one at all. In the common mentality, an intellectual is someone detached from everyday reality. Today, an intellectual is usually considered to be someone who, after having read hundreds of books on a given topic, writes another one. Now, obviously if you want to tackle a question, you have to do adequate research. It is a necessary but insufficient condition for cultural elaboration in the proper sense. What matters is the originality of the reflection, that thought be *sorgivo*, as I called it when I spoke of my teachers.

In this regard, I have never forgotten a remark by John Paul II. Once, when I and a small group of people were invited to lunch to discuss a text or to get some advice, the pope gave an assessment of his friend from Kraków, Stanisław Grygiel.[5] "He isn't a mere scholar, an erudite who knows many things; he is a true thinker who reflects on experience and is then able to express a profound and original point of view." From that day, I have always kept this clear distinction in mind. It has helped me, within the vortex of activities and pastoral work, to follow an idea, to reflect on a suggestion. This usually happens to me during a meeting break, during a trip or at night in bed before falling asleep. If I have written anything original in all these years of episcopate, I did not draw it primarily from reading books but from an intuition that came to me at the most unexpected moments, reflecting on something that happened to me or that I had noticed over the course of the day. Intuition is not the result of study, but instead springs from daily life, like a beautiful mushroom that one finds in the underbrush.

This is why a shared life is fundamental in a university, what was once called the *communitas docentium et studentium*. Informality creates extraordinary opportunities for intuition. And intuition is the basis of all new knowledge. To cite Maritain once again: There is no knowledge without intuition.

Notes to Chapter 10

1. José Saraiva Martins (1932–) is a Portuguese archbishop and cardinal. He was secretary of the Congregation for Catholic Education from 1988 to 1998 and the prefect of the Congregation for the Causes of Saints from 1998 to 2008.
2. Carl Anderson (1951–) is a jurist. From 2000 to early 2021, he led the Knights of Columbus, a US Catholic charitable organization with about two million members. Juan Antonio Reig Pla (1947–) is a Spanish bishop. Since 2009, he has been the bishop of Alcalá de Henares.
3. Jean Daniélou (1905–1974) was a French Jesuit, theologian, and cardinal. Like Henri de Lubac, he was an exponent of the *Nouvelle théologie* and a protagonist of the Second Vatican Council.
4. Jean Guitton (1901–1999) and Henri Hude (1954–), both French philosophers and essayists.
5. Stanisław Grygiel (1934–) is a Polish philosopher. A friend of Karol Wojtyła's, he was a professor of philosophical anthropology at the John Paul II Institute for the Study of Marriage and Family in Rome until 2019 following its refounding (see Chapter 11).

The Nuptial Mystery

President of the John Paul II Institute for Marriage and Family

As you just noted, during the same years when you led the Lateran University, you were also the dean of the Pontifical John Paul II Institute for Studies on Marriage and Family, where you had already been on the faculty. Today, this institute no longer exists. In September of 2017, Pope Francis announced that it would be substituted by an organization that, while still named after John Paul II, defines itself as the Pontifical Theological Institute for Marriage and Family Sciences.[1] How did you react to this news?

To say that it no longer exists is wrong. Rather, we can definitely say that it evolved. In order to understand the nature of this evolution, we must recall what was original about this institute, by will of its founder John Paul II himself. From the start, it chose as themes the person, marriage, and the family, meaning three topics that, by their very nature, need to be engaged by multiple disciplines. It has always been clear that the research, teaching, and study carried out by the institute involved a combination of philosophy, theology, and human sciences. I think that what Pope Francis has brought about is, in fact, an extension of a perspective that was already present, which is being strengthened chiefly in terms of a greater attention to the developments in the human sciences and to pastoral issues.

Moreover, it's undeniable that moral theology developed so much over the years that it became dominant within the institute. Msgr. Livio Melina deserves credit for creating a school of moral theology of such high caliber. But other areas of study never experienced nearly as much growth, for example, anthropology, whose chair of theology I held until 1991. Therefore, the attempt to broaden the perspective is understandable. Of course, one can raise the question of whether this goal might have been achieved with some simple changes in the statutes and regulations, without relying on the great authority of the pope and having him intervene.

But wasn't the problem that the Institute of John Paul II could no longer keep up with the times, that it was not open enough to a new vision of the family and to new pastoral practices?

This is, in fact, the most widespread interpretation in the media, but I don't believe it to be the most accurate. Of course, I'm well aware that during the two synodal assemblies on family,[2] there were heated disagreements between some faculty members from the institute and the supporters of what was considered to be a more pastoral approach to marriage and family. However, I think that the excellent work of the institute at the international level was recognized. So much so that the entire faculty, including full professors, were reappointed to their former positions.

In October of 2016, during a speech to members of the John Paul II Institute, Pope Francis said that "at times we have presented an overly abstract theological ideal of marriage, almost artificially constructed, far from the concrete situation and the possibilities of families as they are."[3] Can we read this call as an attempt to distance himself from the teachings of John Paul II?

If one examines carefully Jorge Bergoglio's intellectual biography, one understands why he wants theological knowledge to always start from the experience of Christian life—from what he calls *pueblo fiel* (faithful people)—and to be capable of directing pastoral action. Anybody who is familiar with John Paul II's magisterium on the theology of the body, and has read his writings on marriage and family from the time when he was still the archbishop of Kraków, cannot deny that this sensibility already existed in his teaching. It is an outlook that began with the Second Vatican Council and that has, in a sense, changed the language of the magisterium, necessitating a change of pace in theological work and in all aspects of the life of the

Church, starting with the pastoral aspect. Moreover, if one reads the works of de Lubac, Balthasar, and Ratzinger, he will find the same preoccupation: The theology of these great teachers steps away from the neo-scholastic framework to move as close as possible to the data of experience, trying to take up the questions and challenges that emerge from reality and relate them to the Christian event.

Of course, this also demands a systematic and critical theology which cannot but reach a dogmatic formulation. Pope Francis is telling us that this change of language is still not as developed as it needs to be. But I do not see in his words any attempt to distance himself from John Paul II's teaching method. And to support my thesis, I can cite a small personal anecdote. My first encounter with Pope Francis took place just after his election to the papacy, in the spring of 2013. He began our conversation by telling me that he had read with interest my essay *The Nuptial Mystery*, a reflection based on John Paul II's magisterium on sexuality, the body, and marriage. Then, with his typical irony, he added, "I believe I am one of the few people who actually read it all the way to the end." In short, we can say that the Holy Father knows and appreciates the profound and articulated reflection that John Paul developed on the topic of the family. This does not exclude the fact that some theologians, bishops, and even a few cardinals close to Pope Francis are convinced that the previous magisterium on the family must be rethought, as the debate over *Amoris Laetitia* has shown.[4]

The debate over the Apostolic Exhortation *Amoris Laetitia* centered on the issue of people who are divorced and remarried, and their possible access to the Eucharist. Divergent interpretations fueled polemics within the Church, which at times were sharp. Theologians, cardinals, simple laypeople, and entire episcopal conferences have taken opposing sides on the matter. You did not join either side of the argument, not taking a position. May I ask what your judgment is on this entire affair?

First of all, allow me to state a premise which is as obvious as it is important. The content of *Amoris Laetitia* is quite rich: It develops over nine very articulate and stimulating chapters. It is not fair to reduce all of it to chapter 8, and, in fact, to one paragraph. The exhortation's most decisive teaching concerns, in my opinion, the family as a direct subject of evangelization. I remember a judgment by my friend, Msgr. Corecco, that impressed me and that I quoted before: The loss of the family as a subject disincarnates Christianity. This obviously leaves ample room for secularization and dechristianization.

My judgment on chapter 8 of *Amoris Laetitia* was very clear from the start. In 2014 and 2015, in preparation for the two synods on the family, I wrote two long articles on the subject for the magazine *Il Regno*,[5] in which I clearly supported the position that the divorced and remarried cannot have access to the Eucharist. I reiterated the same theses after the publication of *Amoris Laetitia* in 2016, having requested written opinions from a dozen experts of my diocese. I also discussed this in multiple meetings of the Episcopal Council and with priests and laypeople. Lastly, I spoke about it with the Holy Father during a private audience.

That said, I want to begin from what I believe to be the heart of the matter—namely, the substantial connection between marriage and the Eucharist as the sacrament of nuptial love between Christ and the Church. The relationship between Christ and his bride, the Church, is clearly visible in matrimony. It is often held as a model for the mutual self-gift of the spouses. Instead, it is much more, the very foundation of marriage. What happens when a man and a woman go to church to say a permanent yes in front of their entire community? They would be crazy to found that "forever" on the shifting sands of their freedom. Who can guarantee to me that the "yes" of today will remain tomorrow, the day after, and for all the days of my life? A man and a woman can commit themselves to an indissoluble relationship only by virtue of the nuptial bond between Christ and the Church, whether it is explicitly recognized or not. Therefore, the reference to the Eucharist is not something extrinsic to marriage, but instead has a foundational nature.

Has this reference found room in *Amoris Laetitia*?

In *Amoris Laetitia*, as in the two synodal assemblies, the fundamental relationship between the Eucharist and marriage is not evident, and in my opinion this absence has consequences. There is a lot to get into on this point, because the exclusion of the reference to the Eucharist from the theology of marriage is not solely attributable to what happened at the synods. It comes, instead, from a canon law tradition that has legislated on marriage at various times in a scatter-shot way. In any case, this absence opened up the possibility of many reckless interpretations of *Amoris Laetitia.*

Let me explain. The nonadmissibility of the divorced and remarried to the Eucharist is not a punishment that can be removed or reduced. Rather, it is intrinsic to the very nature of Christian marriage which, as I said, lives on the foundation of the Eucharistic gift of Christ, the groom, to the Church, his bride. It follows that those who exclude themselves from the Eucharist by entering into a new union can be allowed to receive the Eucharistic sacrament only by living in perfect chastity, as affirmed by John Paul II's apostolic exhortation *Familiaris Consortio.*[6] But there is no mention of this in *Amoris Laetitia.* It neither says that the indication is no longer valid nor says that it is still valid; it simply ignores it. At the same time, it reminds us that the Eucharist, as St. Ambrose wrote, "is not a reward for the perfect, but a generous remedy and food for the weak."[7] Now it is true that the Eucharist has also a healing function, but this affirmation cannot be invoked apart from what the conciliar Constitution *Lumen Gentium* says about the ecclesial nature of the sacraments (section 11).

You speak of absence. Do you agree with the criticisms raised by many people against *Amoris Laetitia*, particularly the *Dubia* expressed in a letter to Pope Francis by four cardinals, including Carlo Caffarra, who died in 2017?[8]

Firstly, I want to say that I always had a sincere affection and a great friendship for Cardinal Caffarra, with whom I worked in complete harmony for many years at the Institute for Studies on Marriage and Family, and whose sudden death hit me painfully. I do not think anyone can call into question his theological and canonical competence, as well as his frankness and loyalty towards the pope. My criticism of *Amoris Laetitia* is, however, of another nature than that of the *Dubia,* which revealed an intellectualistic approach in which theology and morals are conceived in deductive terms. Furthermore, the *Dubia* did not, in my opinion, highlight enough the spousal nature of the

Eucharist as the foundation of marriage, which is at the origin of its ecclesial relevance.

There's a word that occurs time and time again in *Amoris Laetitia*—discernment. What is its value?

Amoris Laetitia very effectively maintains that "accompanying, discerning, and integrating weakness" is decisive. This is why when I was in Milan, I instituted the diocesan office for the welcoming of Catholics who are separated. It's a pastoral service that can, among other things, facilitate the canonical process for the dissolution of marriage or a declaration of annulment. Pope Francis, with two *motu proprios*, one for the Latin Church and the other for the Eastern Churches, codified the elimination of the second degree of trial and created the possibility of a short trial, with the bishop as judge.[9]

I must say that the office we opened in three different locations in the diocese of Milan has been received in a way that surpassed even the most optimistic expectations. In a few months, the operators have received hundreds of people, concretely helping them to verify and discern their situation. Anyone who chose to turn to the tribunal received a quick response. What must be held firm is that discernment implies a serious examination of one's situation, either in the form of a canonical trial or in the relationship with one's confessor, passing through a personal journey of conversion. There is, however, a risk of banalizing discernment to the point where it becomes an easy self-absolution.

Do you think that by now this is the most widespread attitude?

I am afraid so. I do not mean to deny the good faith of those who want to facilitate access to the Eucharist for the divorced and remarried, by invoking extenuating and subjective circumstances. But I believe that excluding perfect continence from the life of the new couple is a serious mistake. I say this based on personal observation. I know divorced and remarried people who have seriously committed themselves to living in continence. They have a new family, they have children, they live under the same roof and can therefore always fall into temptation, but they pursue the ideal of chastity and are able to receive sacramental communion. It's not a double morality—freeing oneself from sin is not something automatic. The intention to sin no more does not eliminate the awareness of our weakness. This goes for the divorcee, but also for the adulterer who goes to confession, says he repents, and then falls again.

Something John Paul II affirmed in this regard is quite illuminating. In a 1996 letter to Cardinal William Baum, then head of the Apostolic Penitentiary, he wrote: "It should also be remembered that the existence of sincere repentance is one thing, the judgment of the intellect concerning the future is another: It is indeed possible that, despite the sincere intention of sinning no more, past experience and the awareness of human weakness makes one afraid of falling again; but this does not compromise the authenticity of the intention, when that fear is joined to the will, supported by prayer, of doing what is possible to avoid sin."[10]

We see here how much the image of John Paul II as the rigid defender of abstract moral principles, oblivious to concrete situations and to the bleeding wounds in everyday life, is a caricature. John Paul II's *Familiaris Consortio* opened new perspectives for the pastoral care of the divorced and remarried, who until then had been excluded from the ecclesial communion. And again, the Apostolic Exhortation *Sacramentum Caritatis* of Benedict XVI offers nine possible ways for divorced and remarried people to participate in the ecclesial communion.[11] Unfortunately, some people's disregard for and sarcasm towards the earlier magisterium weakens the power of communion that the Church has always demonstrated in her history, even when such history was marked by tensions and disagreements.

And is this causing confusion within the Church?

What followed *Amoris Laetitia* in some ways echoes the post-council climate, when everyone felt authorized to invoke their own correct interpretation of Vatican II or, vice versa, found reasons to condemn every sentence of the Council's documents. On the *vexata quaestio* of Communion for the divorced and remarried, we are allowing praxis to decide the solution to the problem. But it is a question that we helped magnify. In truth, the divorced and remarried who question their status in order to remain faithful to the Church are a tiny minority. This is not meant to play down painful situations, even if it were only one couple. But, let us be clear: Today the majority of people who choose to live as a couple do so outside of marriage.

The statistics are staggering. According to a study by CENSIS,[12] in 1994 in Italy, there were 236,000 religious weddings; in 2004, the number had fallen to 170,000; and by 2014, the number had collapsed to 108,000. This means that the number had more than halved in only twenty years! And civil weddings are also diminishing, albeit more slowly than religious ones because the law allows divorcees to remarry. The latest CENSIS report even refers to 2031 as the year when church weddings will fall to zero.

This is the great problem we face today. Marriage has become less and less attractive, and also less convenient from an economic and social point of view. The "forever" is terrifying, the sacred nuptial bond is no longer perceived as either sacred or as a bond. And yet, having often met engaged couples both privately and during public assemblies, I can say with conviction that if we Christians propose again with courage the allure of a beautiful love, we will get a generous response from young people, whose hearts strongly desire to love and be loved forever. I will never forget the impression I felt when I heard a 16-year-old African boy in Ol Moran, Kenya— a little town without electricity where I was visiting a mission of the diocese of Venice—quote one of Shakespeare's sonnets:[13]

> Love is not love
> Which alters when it alteration finds,
> Or bends with the remover to remove.

Notes to Chapter 11

1. Francis, Motu Proprio *Summa Familiae Cura* (September 8, 2017).
2. The reference is to the Third Extraordinary General Assembly, *Pastoral Challenges of the Family in the Context of Evangelization* (October 5–19, 2014) and the Fourteenth Ordinary General Assembly, *The Vocation and Mission of The Family in The Church and The Contemporary World* (October 4–25, 2015).

3. Francis, *Address to the Academic Community of the John Paul II Pontifical Institute for Studies on Marriage and Family* (October 27, 2016), 3. Available at www.vatican.va in German, Italian, and Portuguese.

4. Francis, Apostolic Exhortation *Amoris Laetitia* (March 19, 2016).

5. Angelo Scola, "L'antropologia e l'eucaristia," *Il Regno Attualità* 16 (2014): 540–545 and "Famiglia ed evangelizzazione," *Il Regno Documenti* 16 (2015): 1–14.

6. John Paul II, Apostolic Exhortation *Familiaris Consortio* (November 22, 1981).

7. Francis, *Amoris Laetitia*, 305, n. 351.

8. The four cardinals were Raymond Burke, Carlo Caffarra, Walter Brandmüller, and Joachim Meisner. They asked Pope Francis to clarify the teachings of *Amoris Laetitia*, in particular on whether the divorced and remarried can have access to the Eucharist.

9. Francis, Motu Proprio *Mitis Iudex Dominus Iesus* for the Latin Church and Motu Proprio *Mitis et misericors Iesus* for the Eastern Churches, both August 15, 2015.

10. John Paul II, *Letter to Cardinal William W. Baum, on the Occasion of the Course on the Internal Forum Organized by the Tribunal of the Apostolic Penitentiary* (March 22, 1996), 5.

11. Benedict XVI, Apostolic Exhortation on the Eucharist *Sacramentum Caritatis* (February 22, 2007).

12. CENSIS (Centro Studi Investimenti Sociali) is a major research institute dedicated to the study on social and economic trends in Italy. It was founded in 1964. See https://www.censis.it.

13. Sonnet 116.

CHAPTER 12

The Method of Christian Life

Patriarch in Venice

Near the end of 2001, John Paul II summoned you and announced his decision to send you to Venice as Patriarch.[1] It was a gesture that showed his high esteem for you, but it was also a burdensome task, given the unique role that the Patriarch of Venice has played historically, not just in Italy but also in the universal Church. What was your first reaction to the news?

I want to tell a backstory. In the months before, as always happens for episcopal appointments, there were many rumors about me being a possible candidate for the Patriarchate of Venice. I was convinced that these speculations were absolutely unfounded. John Paul II himself had made me certain of this. In fact, when I visited him at Castel Gandolfo during the summer of 2001 for a regular scheduled meeting as rector of the Lateran, he laughingly told me, "Do you know that people here keep suggesting your name for Venice?" Then he added, "But I say that a university rector is more important than an archbishop..." So, I was very calm, having heard directly from the pope about how much he cared about the Lateran University and how happy he was with my work as rector.

However, a few days before Christmas, John Paul II suddenly invited me to dinner to tell me that the question of Venice was on the table. "It's a job that requires a person with episcopal experience, as you had the chance to have in Grosseto. However, given the particular openness to the world that the city in the lagoon always had, it also requires a bishop with international experience, like the kind you acquired during these years at the Lateran. So, I have decided to appoint you the Patriarch of Venice." A bit recklessly, but also out of a desire to return to direct pastoral work, in contact with the people, I immediately agreed. Then, feeling afraid, I asked the Holy Father,

"You know me well. What do I need to change to be as adequate as possible for what you are asking of me?" He answered me by quoting the words Cardinal Adam Sapieha had said to him when, as a young man, he decided to become a priest and enter the secret seminary of Kraków: "Don't change anything: be yourself." [2] I must add that once again, just as when he had appointed me to Grosseto, the pope encountered much resistance. But the pope's determination gave me strength and serenity in facing a task that was by no means easy.

Is it true that when the pope appointed you, he made a special recommendation: "Always remember that Venice must be Rome's wingman."[3] What did he mean?

Yes, it's true. I believe he was referring to the cultural (not just spiritual) contribution that Venice has always made to the Universal Church, demonstrating in an extraordinary way faith's capacity to generate art and beauty. Venice is a patrimony shared by the East and West, a bridge between worlds, open to everybody. Every day it is visited by enormous crowds from every corner of the planet. Saying that Venice is the city of humanity is not a rhetorical statement. By the power of its past and present, Venice speaks naturally and constantly to the entire world. On the other hand, we should not ignore the local dimension, with its tangle of well-known problems—environmental, logistical, and social.

What were your first impressions?

I immediately realized that the Patriarchate of Venice is rather complex, being an agglomerate of various, very different entities. There is Venice in the lagoon, and there is the mainland of Mestre and Marghera that represent an entirely new reality relative to historical Venice. Marghera was designed to be a model city where sea trade, industry, and nature could coexist, although things did not turn out as planned. Then there is the Riviera del Brenta, characterized by small, family-owned businesses. Lastly, there is the Adriatic Riviera, now a popular tourist destination. These are four different realities that are not easily brought together, and this also creates problems from the standpoint of governing the diocese.

To give one small example: I noticed that the clergy born in the lagoon tended to look down condescendingly upon the priests from the mainland (who were called "those from the countryside"). Hence, it was always a big struggle for me to move a priest born in the lagoon to the mainland and vice versa. Otherwise, during my ministry in Venice, I found the clergy well-prepared, with some extraordinary priests. There were men of great faith and exceptional culture such as Fr. Antonio Niero and Fr. Bruno Bertoli. Another example was Fr. Germano Pattaro, who passed away in 1986 before my arrival.[4] He was a self-taught theologian, whose cultural and spiritual legacy I appreciated, thanks to the cultural center named after him and through his stimulating and often original writings on the Church's journey in the world.

The archdiocese was undeniably marked by the experience of the worker-priests. They had produced, in Marghera, one of the most radical expressions of the experiment that had begun in France. However, their experience produced a division within the clergy. It was only thanks to the patient mediation of my predecessor in Venice, Cardinal Marco Cé, that it had been possible to heal this painful fracture. I arrived later and benefited from the fruits of his intelligent and generous labor.

And yet, when he handed the reins to you, the relationship between you and Cardinal Cé was rather cold and distant.[5]

We did not know each other personally beforehand. Perhaps the memories of past clashes between CL and the Catholic Action (of which Msgr. Cé had been assistant general) still created a barrier. But once in Venice, I appreciated his personality right away, along with the work he had done as patriarch. We developed a rapport based on mutual esteem, which became a sincere and intense friendship, visiting one another regularly to discuss the problems at hand and the decisions to be made. He was deeply immersed in the Sacred Scriptures, which he particularly loved and knew deeply. This faithful attachment to the Word of God marked his pastoral style. He founded a diocesan center where, still today, more than a thousand laypeople (at different times) attend a special type of retreat. He also gave special attention to "listening groups." These were meetings among families, often in people's homes, where they would read the Sacred Scriptures and reflect upon them. It was an effective approach that spread rapidly and is now present in many Italian parishes.

In Venice, you organized a great pastoral visit around the entire diocese which began in 2005 and ended six years later in the presence of Benedict XVI. When you announced it to the faithful you said, and I quote: "I would hope that those among the baptized who are a bit forgetful may suddenly feel, moved by the arrival of the patriarch, the attitude (which was more than mere curiosity) of the Unnamed before the arrival of Cardinal Federigo Borromeo."[6] You were referring to a famous episode in Manzoni's *The Betrothed*. That's no small presumption. Was not this comparison a bit too bold?

Perhaps I should have added the ancient Latin maxim, *"si parva licet componere magnis"* (If it permissible to compare something small to something great).[7] I certainly did not mean to place myself on the same level as that of Cardinal Federigo. The reference was not to my person but to my task, to the mission I was about to undertake. My wish was that the arrival of the patriarch not be perceived by the people as an administrative act, as just one of the functions the bishop somehow has to perform. Such a perception nips in the bud the Christian proposal, which springs from an event and can only be communicated through an event. Witnessing the multitude of people who are running to see and listen to Cardinal Federigo, the Unnamed is curious to learn "what it could be that communicates the same impulse to so many different people." This is the dynamic I wanted to evoke by citing Manzoni's passage. But to set something like this in motion, each individual must participate as both a personal and communal subject, without identifying themselves with any sort of role.

This was, in a way, the thread running through the pastoral visit. It was long and structured, prepared by two ecclesial assemblies and carried out in every single parish of the diocese from Friday afternoon to Sunday. Basically, for six years I spent all of my weekends going around the cities and towns of the diocese, except for summers and major liturgical periods. I wanted to meet not just church groups but also civil realities, ranging from institutions to corporations (like the oil refinery and the port) and from unions to schools. And then I wanted to meet associations of every kind, from the gondoliers to cultural and senior centers. In short, I tried to leave nothing and no one out. And I must say, I myself learned a lot from this pastoral visit.

What lesson did you take away from it?

I wouldn't speak of lessons as much as stimuli, or, even better, intuitions. The first was the intuition of pastoral community. It came to me while visiting a small coastal town where the pastor introduced me to some nuns and two families who lived with him in an expanded rectory. It was a life together that involved every state of life: priest, consecrated people, families. This experience, as I was later able to observe, had a very positive impact on people, facilitating the involvement of laypeople in the parish. I understood from this that it is much easier to talk about the communal dimension, a topic the Church keeps stressing, if you make it immediately visible and concretely accessible to the faithful.

Traditionally, the Christian people view the priest as a single man. A man of God, of course, but single, while life in a community is typically considered to be monastic, something entirely different than the parish. Yet this gives the faithful an idea of communion as something abstract. At best, communion is the result of an individual effort, instead of being the way God cares for us by placing us beside men and women with whom we can face daily life. I then had the opportunity to see just how feasible this is in Mestre, in the Sacred Heart parish run by the Minor Friars. In addition, knowing that Cardinal Dionigi Tettamanzi was doing something similar in Milan, I called his vicar general, Monsignor Carlo Redaelli,[8] later the archbishop of Gorizia, to explain the proposal to the priests of my diocese. The term "pastoral community" originates from the fact that the model of the "expanded rectory" is easier to implement on the level of not just one, but multiple parishes where there are more opportunities to find people willing to live together. In Venice, I made various attempts in this regard. The most successful was the experiment in the Lido, where a stable pastoral community was born.

Another intuition born from my pastoral visit was the School of the Method of Christian Life, which lasted from 2005 to 2011. It addressed three hundred leaders of parishes, movements, and associations of the archdiocese. The theme of the first lecture cycle was "How the Christian community is born and lives." This was later turned into a booklet which spread beyond the borders of the diocese. The theme of the second cycle was "The circular relationship between faith and culture." The choice of the word "school" was deliberate. The point was to reflect upon the implications of the mysteries of the Christian faith in daily life.

This is a concept you often talk about, a sort of *leit-motiv* of your reflections and of your preaching. If I may, isn't this a bit of a fancy way to describe what we usually call the consequences of faith in practical life?

The word "implication" is not the same as the word "consequence." An implication is an aspect which is contained—indeed, implied— in a reality that precedes it, whereas a consequence is something extrinsic that one can draw or not draw, depending on convenience and on circumstances. The idea that the Christian mysteries have implications originates from Henri de Lubac's famous work *Catholicisme,* which bore the subtitle "the social aspects of dogma."[9] The implications demonstrate that when the Christian revelation meets human experience, it makes it more true. In this regard, I often speak of anthropological, social, and cosmological implications. When we live the Christian mysteries, we discover that it is possible to face questions about how to conceive ourselves as humans, how to tackle social problems, and how to think about our relationship with creation. Because of these implications, faith and culture act back and forth on each other (they have a "circular relationship"). On the one side, as Cardinal Ratzinger once said, "Insofar as faith tells man who he is and how he should begin being human, faith creates culture; faith is itself culture."[10] On the other side, faith is in turn interpreted by the various cultures that act in history.

So, for example, you find anthropological and social implications even in a mystery of faith like the Trinity, which seems very distant and entirely inaccessible?

This idea was already supported by Romano Guardini, one of the greatest Christian thinkers of the last century. For example, he considered the dogma of the Trinity as the "Magna Carta of the duty and dignity of every human community" and he wrote unforgettable pages showing "how alive the relationship is between the most unapproachable of all mysteries and our daily life."[11] Here we see firsthand the power of the social implications of the mystery of the Trinity, which provide the correct perspective in a confused world.

The anthropological implications seem even more decisive. There is an analogy between God's existence in the relations of the Trinity and the existence of humankind in the form of the dual unity of man and woman. A world that cannot conceive the Trinity has a harder time understanding sexual difference. The debate over this topic that marks our age is undermined from the start by the current confusion about the terms "diversity" and "difference," which are now taken to be synonyms. In this way, people delude themselves into believing that they can overcome the insuperability of sexual difference by making it similar to other kinds of diversity—ethnic, national, or religious. By way of contrast, the notion of diversity involves multiplicity and is entirely unrelated to the relationship of identity-difference. Already these examples show us that reflecting on the Christian mysteries and all their implications is not a way to step out of the world but rather a clear witness to how fruitful our faith can be when it becomes culture.

In this aspect, the Orthodox Church is way ahead of us. I always remember the speech by the Ecumenical Patriarch Bartholomew I when he came to Venice.[12] His visit marked the conclusion of his journey across the Mediterranean, which was part of a brilliant initiative in which he ran conferences on the environment by traveling around one sea each year on a ship. The patriarch impressed me with how he framed his talk on that occasion, which took place at the Hall of the Council of Ten during an event that John Paul II also joined via live video.[13] He began by speaking about the relationship between the Trinity and creation, moving next to the topic of the redemption of the world carried out by Christ, and then tackling the question of protecting the environment as an implication of the mysteries of faith. His speech was far removed from the typical dualism of us Westerners, for whom the invocation of religion is at most a way of introducing a topic, in this case ecology, which is then developed within an exclusively scientific and environmentalist logic. The words of the patriarch of Constantinople revealed an effective and courageous way that Christians can work together on concrete questions in a truly ecumenical spirit.

Earlier you mentioned that Venice is the city of all humanity. Can we also say that it is the city of ecumenism?

I'll go further: Venice is the city of religions. And not just because all monotheistic confessions are represented in it. In Venice, the relatively small size of the congregations can make the dialogue between people of different faiths easier. Venice is, together with Paris, one of the two European sees of the orthodox Ecumenical Patriarchate. The relationships with its permanent representative, Metropolitan Gennadios, have always been very cordial and fraternal. The same holds true with the patriarchate of Moscow. The then head of the foreign department, Kirill, who became patriarch of all Russia in 2009, visited Venice twice during my tenure.[14] Once troubles ended in post-Communist Russia, there was an exponential increase in the number of Orthodox pilgrims, to the point that the church in San Niccolò al Lido cannot now contain all the faithful. There is also the community of Catholic Armenians on San Lazzaro island, where the documents that attest to the birth of the world's first Christian nation—which is precisely Armenia—are preserved.

Furthermore, Venice belongs to the history of religions. I have always admired the Jewish community, which is small but vivacious, both on the cultural and religious levels. There are five synagogues, which are among the most beautiful in Europe, along with the library and the museum in the Ghetto quarter. I visited all these institutions by official invitation of Rabbi Elia Richetti.[15] We also maintained an intense dialogue with the local Islamic communities, proving that Christians, Jews, and Muslims can not only live in peace but are also capable of being a public presence which strengthens the democratic life of a city and a nation.

Notes to Chapter 12

1. In the Latin Church, the title of patriarch is traditionally conferred to two archbishops: that of Venice and that of Lisbon. The Patriarchate of Venice was instituted in 1451.

2. Adam Sapieha (1867–1951) was a cardinal. He was archbishop of Kraków from 1911 to 1951.

3. Andrea Tornielli, *Il futuro e la speranza: vita e magistero del cardinale Angelo Scola* (Milano: Piemme, 2011), 105.

4. Antonio Niegro (1924–2010) was a priest. He was a historian of the Venetian Church and a professor at the Patriarchal Seminary of Venice. Bruno Bertoli (1928–2011) was also a priest. He founded the Biblical School of the Archdiocese of Venice. Germano Pattaro (1925–1986) was a priest; from 1957 to 1986, he taught fundamental theology, patristics, and ecumenism at the Patriarchal Seminary of Venice.

5. Marco Cé (1925–2014) was a cardinal. He was patriarch of Venice from 1978 to 2002 and was succeeded by Scola. From 1976 to 1979, he was the ecclesiastic assistant of the Catholic Action.

6. The quote is from *Oggi devo fermarmi a casa tua. Prima visita pastorale del Patriarca di Venezia cardinale Angelo Scola*, Venice, April 2005, p. 9. The "Unnamed" is a character from the novel *The Betrothed* by Alessandro Manzoni (1785–1873), a classic of Italian literature. An evil man, he marvels at the crowds who are going to meet Cardinal Federigo Borromeo of Milan on a pastoral visit. He himself goes to meet the cardinal and converts.

7. "If I may compare small thing to big ones" from Virgil's *Georgica*, IV, 176.

8. Dionigi Tettamanzi (1934–2017) was an archbishop and cardinal. He was CEI general secretary from 1991 to 1995, then archbishop of Genoa from 1995 to 2002, and finally archbishop of Milan from 2002 to 2011. Carlo Maria Redaelli (1956–) is a bishop. From 2004 to 2012, he was auxiliary bishop in Milan. Since 2012, he is the bishop of Gorizia, near the Slovenian border.

9. Henri de Lubac, *Catholicism* (San Francisco: Ignatius Press, 1998).

10. Joseph Ratzinger, *Christ, Faith and the Challenge of Culture: Address to the Doctrinal Commissions in Asia* (Hong Kong: March 3, 1993).

11. Translated from the Italian in Romano Guardini, *Scritti politici,* *Opera Omnia* VI (Brescia: Morcelliana, 2005), 97–98.

12. Bartholomew I (1937–), is an Orthodox archbishop. Since 1991, he has been ecumenical patriarch of Constantinople.

13. The Sala del Consiglio dei Dieci is in the Doge's Palace in Venice. The Council of Ten was the highest government body of the Venetian Republic (1310–1797).

14. Gennadios Zervos (1937–) is the metropolitan archbishop of the Greek Orthodox Church in Italy; Kirill I (1946–) is a Russian Orthodox archbishop. He is the former president of the Department for External Relations of the Patriarchate of Moscow. Since 2009, he has been patriarch of Moscow and all Russia.

15. Elia Enrico Richetti (1950–) was the chief rabbi of Venice from 2001 to 2010. He is currently a member of the Rabbinical Tribunal for central and northern Italy.

CHAPTER 13

A New Educational Subject

The Marcianum Foundation

In Venice, you also had many contacts with the political world. What were the results?

These contacts were an important element of my pastoral action. They were fruitful relationships which I maintained with all the institutional authorities. On a personal level, they were characterized by an esteem which I believe was mutual, in a context of great fairness. There was a constant dialogue about the needs of the city, so structurally fragile because of the inherent problems of tidal flooding and the mass invasion of tourists, who treat the city as if it were disposable. The days of Thomas Mann's long vacations at the Lido of Venice are long gone. By now, visitors only stop for a day and want to see everything, as if dashing to the supermarket. In a city perennially on display, every problem becomes a wound, a *vulnus* that affects every single inhabitant and the entire community.

During one pastoral visit, I was struck by a young woman's comment in a parochial assembly. She said that there was a risk, especially for residents of the lagoon, of losing the "zest for life." A paradox, in a city that for the whole world is synonymous with astonishing beauty. I always tried to stress the value of dialogue and involvement among all parties. I bet on civic friendship as the key factor in bringing back the zest for life and halting the exodus from the lagoon. Obviously, it's not the patriarch's job to come up with political and technical solutions. Nevertheless, to help look for them, I once initiated a gathering of the highest authorities from several areas, about thirty people, for an absolutely informal and completely free exchange of opinions, without the presence of the press and with a strict commitment that no one would make any public declarations at the end of the daylong meeting. It was a very interesting experience, attended by everyone invited, that overcame the typical rigidity and role-based schemes that inevitably play a part in political debate. Sincere and constructive dialogue is fundamental for civic life. This by itself seemed a satisfactory result to me.

You remained on good terms with Mayor Cacciari even after you left the Patriarchate of Venice.[1]

My friendship and collaboration with Massimo Cacciari grew over time. Not only was he a good mayor, he is also a prominent intellectual. An acute and passionate philosopher, he has studied the Sacred Scriptures in depth, has read Balthasar, and has always had an intense dialogue with important Church figures like Cardinal Martini.[2] Christianity is something Cacciari confronts every day, as he himself has admitted. He defines himself as a nonbeliever, but his research borders on faith. I daresay he is a man who has his own sort of faith. At the risk of being indiscreet, I'll reveal that he once told me he considers himself a Christian up to Good Friday, but that for him the resurrection is an insurmountable obstacle.

Cacciari once described you as "a manager bishop." Do you recognize yourself in this definition?

If he meant to say that I'm a gifted organizer, I am not going to deny it. Jokes aside, I will admit that I'm inclined to create projects and to weave networks to make them happen. Had I not become a priest, I would have probably been a politician in the sense that I have always wanted to build something connected with life in community. My father had this civic passion in his DNA; he also passed it down to my brother. Certainly, however, the most exciting undertaking is to contribute to the construction of the Christian community. The truth is, whenever a priest or a bishop has a nonclerical vision of reality and shows a capacity for social analysis, he is immediately labeled a manager, or even a politician, in the negative connotation that has become so common. In short, if you give a judgment or launch a project, there will be people who think you are doing it not out of the desire to incarnate the faith in real life but for your own personal advantage. Unfortunately, this attitude of suspicion is very widespread in the Church.

One large project you started in Venice, beginning in 2004, was the Marcianum. It was an educational and academic institution, an integrated system from preschool to the university. What motivated you to start such a massive and complex enterprise?

I did not found the Studium Generale Marcianum just to have a school of theology or canon law that did not previously exist or to combine and reorganize a number of already existing schools. The true motive behind Marcianum was different—the unity of the human subject.

Let us start from an undeniable fact. We face a serious fragmentation, which today affects the investigation, dissemination, and study of the various fields of knowledge. It's something very different from the necessary demarcation of fields Karl Popper talked about. By now the various disciplines, including theology, have become so specialized we no longer see their connections. This results in the weakening of the organic and vital bond between the object of knowledge and the subject of knowing. In other words, the extreme fragmentation of the object has provoked the fragmentation of the subject who teaches it or learns it. The Marcianum was an attempt to overcome this situation by implementing a new, unified subject—spanning primary and secondary schooling, university education, and research. It thus reclaimed the original intuition from which university scholarship was born. Starting from a well-defined, dynamic identity—that of Christianity—with a rigorous respect for the rules and methods of the sciences, we offered an independent public proposal for education and learning that was open to everybody, believers and nonbelievers, Christians or followers of other religions.

We began by strengthening what already existed: the preschools and elementary schools run by nuns, which had fallen into hard times. Then we revived the middle schools and the high school, which had all recently closed. And then we added a university level with the establishment of the Saint Pius X School of Canon Law and the Higher Institute for Religious Sciences, which worked in connection with the Theological School of Triveneto.[3] Lastly, we created centers of excellence, along with postgraduate initiatives such as the Man-Polis-Economy Project, the Master in Ethics and Business Management, and ASSET.[4] Many books have been published as a result of the Marcianum's research activities, testifying to their quality. The university, high school, and seminary were located in a large complex next door to the Basilica of Santa Maria della Salute. This iconic Venetian site designed by Longhena on the Punta della Dogana, flourished once again after a long period of abandonment, with a daily flow of 600 students, teachers, and researchers. The Marcianum has become a concrete example of how to halt the decline of the historic downtown area, something many considered inevitable. It was an undertaking that helped reawaken some of the city's hidden energies, and it was generally looked upon with great interest and sympathy by the Venetians, in particular by the Ca' Foscari University and the Venice University Institute of Architecture.

For this reason as well, I consider the foundation a positive experience, in which all participants were actively involved. Much credit goes to the theology professors from the patriarchal seminary as well as to various professors from the Venetian universities. This joint project, in some ways unprecedented in the Italian academic panorama, also gained international recognition as the years went by. The small Marcianum had faculty from twenty-four different countries, including many teachers from abroad, such as Ignacio Arrieta and Brian Ferme, who became the deans of the School of Canon Law.[5] It was easy to convince famous professors to participate in a conference or a lecture series in a city like Venice!

You used to push the students to "dare more" and to throw themselves into the study of theology even if they wanted to become doctors or economists. Why did you do that?

We created two university curricula within the Higher Institute of Religious Sciences, one traditionally designed for seminarians, and another, more innovative one where the theological aspect was combined with the study of topics that involved the faith, such as bioethics. If someone wants to be a Christian and chooses to become a doctor, where will they find an answer to the many crucial questions they will face? The same thing applies to other professions—the engineer who cannot ignore environmental issues, for instance, or the business manager and the economist who wish to take the social teachings of the Church into account.

Cardinal Newman once said, "I want a laity, not arrogant, not rash in speech, not disputatious, but men who know their religion, who enter into it, who know just where they stand, who know what they hold and what they do not, who know their creed so well, that they can give an account of it."[6] Though written in 1851, Newman's sentence is still very relevant. If we consider the changes that are taking place in this digital era, what is happening in the health field, the upheaval in the world of business and economics, or even the central place of the so-called "new rights" in the legal professions, it seems evident that there is much work to be done on the educational level so that Christians may enter the fray of civil society as expert, mature subjects. Hence the idea of transdisciplinarity, which recognizes the contribution of theology. We implemented transdisciplinarity at the Marcianum by creating two new degree programs in Religious Sciences: Biothethics and Cultural Heritage.

To keep the Marcianum running, you asked for help and financial support from public institutions. You also involved politicians and entrepreneurs who led the MOSE project,[7] for which they were later investigated. Do you regret this choice?

I wanted to involve civil society directly into the management of the Marcianum Foundation, by asking for the support of the public and private institutions that joined the board of directors. We offered two ways to participate: They could choose to be founding institutions that committed to a contribution of 300,000 euros a year, or they could be supporting institutions which gave 50,000 euros a year. Among the founding institutions, the patriarchy had two of the six shares, maintaining its right to nominate the president and to set the cultural direction. To me, this provided an adequate guarantee against the risk that anyone might try to alter the Marcianum's educational proposal. I do not regret that decision, and I defend it still today because it showed that we fully accepted the principle of secularity and were not afraid to enter into civil society as an institution in our own right. In any case, the Patriarchate of Venice is small and limited, even from a financial point of view, and could not have sustained something like the Marcianum all on its own. I consider it a success that both public and private institutions were willing to make a significant financial commitment. It enabled us to pay for the restoration and to recover the artistic and architectural heritage of the great complex by Longhena—which housed the seminary and the Studium Marcianum—and of the Basilica della Salute. Everyone acknowledged this.

The legal brouhaha that involved the Consorzio Venezia Nuova, as the main actor in the MOSE scandal, exploded in 2014, when I was long gone from Venice. The consortium was accused of illegal contributions and kickbacks to parties and politicians. But the financial contributions our Foundation received from Consorzio Venezia Nuova, like the contributions from our other donors, were always acquired, accounted for, and spent in a transparent and correct way in accordance with the statutes. The insinuations made by journalists trying to drag the Marcianum into the MOSE scandal hurt me because they were false and utterly unfounded.

In any case, the Marcianum was effectively shut down by your successor in Venice, Msgr. Francesco Moraglia.[8] Do you agree with his decision?

Patriarch Moraglia believed that the costs of running the foundation were too high, without a stable endowment to guarantee its maintenance over time. The fact of the matter is that I always tried to position the Marcianum as an institution that operated by secular market rules in the sense that our projects relied on constant fundraising and sponsorships. Msgr. Moraglia told me that the sponsors were disappearing partly because of the aftershocks from the scandals in Venice. I responded that, in any case, there was a path that had to be followed and that if anyone pulled out, new sponsors would have to be found. Apparently, he did not feel he could take on that task. It was his choice, and it was entirely legitimate. All that is now left of the Marcianum is a center that deals with the culture of work. However, it is important that the Saint Pius X School of Canon Law continues its work. It is the only one in Northern Italy, and it functions very well.

Tell me, in all sincerity, do you really regret nothing about this affair?

Are you asking whether I made any mistakes regarding the Marcianum? Other than, perhaps, my, let us say, megalomania [*laughs*], yes, I have to admit that I did make a very serious mistake. I was not able to find someone rooted in Venice who had the competence and the authority to lead the foundation after I stopped being patriarch. In short, I needed a person, ideally a priest, who would have been able to take responsibility for the whole Marcianum so that the burden of managing it did not fall directly upon the shoulders of the patriarch. To tell the truth, I had selected my general vicar, Auxiliary Bishop Beniamino Pizziol,⁹ as the man for the job. He was appointed as the bishop of Vicenza only a few months before I was transferred to Milan, however. I learned about it from the nuncio in Italy after the decision had already been made. I was very disappointed to see the project end the way it did, but I believe that the Marcianum has still been a very positive experience for Venice and for the Church.

Notes to Chapter 13

1. Massimo Cacciari (1944–) is a philosopher and politician. He was mayor of Venice twice, from 1993 to 2000 and then again from 2005 to 2010.
2. Carlo Maria Martini (1927–2012) was a Jesuit, Bible scholar, theologian, and cardinal. He was archbishop of Milan from 1980 to 2002. One of his initiatives was the *Cattedra dei non credenti* (presentations for unbelievers), a series of events addressed to all men of good will, even if not Christian.
3. The word *Triveneto* indicates the three North Eastern Italian regions: Veneto, Trentino-Alto Adige, and Friuli-Venezia Giulia.
4. Man-Polis-Economy was a three-year training and research program on anthropological questions in today's culture. ASSET stands for "Advanced Studies in Society, Economy and Theology."
5. Ignacio Arrieta (1951–) is a Spanish bishop and canonist. A member of Opus Dei, he was dean of the Saint Pius X School of Canon Law in Venice from 2003 to 2008. Brian Ferme (1950–) is a British priest and canonist. From 2008 to 2014, he was

rector of the Marcianum and Dean of the Saint Pius X School of Canon Law. In 2014, Pope Francis appointed him Secretary of the Vatican Council for the Economy.

6. John Henry Newman, "Lecture 9. Duties of Catholics Towards the Protestant View," in *Lectures on the Present Position of Catholics in England*, 363–403 (London: Longmans, Green and Co., 1908), 390.

7. The MOSE (*Modulo Sperimentale Elettromeccanico*, Experimental Electromechanical Module) is a project designed to protect Venice from tidal flooding. It is managed by a government agency called *Consorzio Venezia Nuova* (Consortium for a New Venice), which has been investigated for corruption.

8. Francesco Moraglia (1953–) is a bishop and theologian. In 2012, he succeeded Angelo Scola as patriarch of Venice.

9. Beniamino Pizziol (1947–) was auxiliary bishop of Venice from 2008 to 2011, when he was appointed bishop of Vicenza.

CHAPTER 14

A Different Approach to Islam

The Oasis International Center

Eminence, in 2004 you took the initiative to start the Oasis Foundation, together with an international journal which is an important point of reference for dialogue with the world of Islam.[1] When did you begin to think about this? Was it after the tragedy of 9/11?

The first idea dates back to over a year before 9/11. The occasion was a meeting in Damascus, in May 2000, when I was still the rector of the Lateran. The encounter was informal, organized by the Vatican nuncio in Syria with seven representatives of the different Middle Eastern Catholic rites. During lunch, there was a very fiery discussion on Western Christians, and I found myself the target of some very harsh criticisms. "You do little or nothing to help us live here in the East," they told me. "You do not know our churches and are even more ignorant about Islam. You ignore us. We do not even have access to the fundamental documents, the encyclicals, or the catechesis of the pope." I objected. "But how? You know English, all the texts of the Vatican are immediately translated." At that point, their criticism became an open accusation of my ignorance of their world and of their struggles to communicate without using the local languages, not only with the people but with the intellectuals, because it was so hard to overcome the cultural and political invasion by the West. I was left shaken. I met those brethren again several times in my visits to the Middle East, but could do nothing more.

When I was appointed patriarch of Venice, I thought of creating an instrument to bring about closer ties between the Christians of East and West because of the role that the city has historically played as the gate to the Levant. That is how the *Oasis* journal was born, to foster understanding and dialogue with the Islamic world and to support the Christian minorities in the Middle East. It's not an instrument for interreligious dialogue, which would require a high level of specialized competence, nor is it an instrument for intellectuals. The journal is simply an attempt to get to know each other better because the mutual ignorance still existing between us is huge. *Oasis* would have never been born without that provocation from my brethren in Damascus. Their criticisms became the criteria for our work. Contrary to the usual way of facing the tumultuous situation of the East from our Western perspective, as a debate about Islam among Europeans, we decided to constantly compare our judgments with those of our Eastern Christian brothers. This is why *Oasis* is published not only in Italian, English, and French, but also in Arabic, and up until recently in Urdu, the language of Pakistan. This is intended precisely to involve the Christian minorities in the dialogue with Islam.

You launched the notion of a "*métissage* of civilizations," a neologism that initially received various criticisms, but later became a common expression in the debate over migrations. Where did this definition come from?

From experience, because ideas are always born by going along with reality. I became aware of the issue in three stages. The first happened long ago, in 1966, when I traveled to Brazil. I spent an entire afternoon waiting for some friends in a large square in the center of São Paulo, curiously observing people's faces. Their features revealed a German ancestry, but the skin tones were dark. They were mixed race, with light colored eyes. Then, some years later, I had the opportunity to travel to Mexico to the shrine of Our Lady of Guadalupe, and I saw the faces of the crowd of pilgrims reflected in the face of the Virgin, "*La Morenita*," in a mix of cultures and ethnicities. Finally, in Venice, during a pastoral visit, I had a conversation with a black teenager who spoke in Venetian dialect with a perfect accent. It was then that I realized that the process of mixing of peoples and cultures had by then become an immediately observable fact, even in Italy.

When I started talking about these things and using the word "métissage," I met fierce resistance. People interpreted my arguments as an invitation to syncretism and multiculturalism. Even some of my collaborators thought that the term was ambiguous and, moreover, difficult to translate into English. But I have always used "métissage" to describe an actual *process*, not to theorize a *project*. Processes happen without asking for anybody's permission. They must be accepted, studied, and, to the extent possible, guided with creative and constructive patience.

Today, what you call "métissage" is happening, but in a tumultuous and chaotic way, as mass immigration which is putting Europe to the test. How can we direct, how can we govern this process?

Like all processes, we cannot know a priori how they will develop. However, we do have standards and values that originate from the great European tradition. Even if today they are in a crisis, they must be rediscovered and reformulated. First of all, we need a much clearer and more explicit awareness of the three subjects that have to face this phenomenon. The first are the charities, meaning all the various voluntary organizations, ranging from NGOs to churches, which carry out their sacrosanct work of welcoming and rescuing. Every attempt on their part to go beyond this level, however, risks generating confusion and complicating problems rather than solving them. That is the task of the second subject. Political institutions must guide and govern the mass immigration that has grown to a global scale. At the end of 2017, the UN reported that 258 million people have left their countries of origin, about 50 percent more than in the year 2000. It is clear that such a massive phenomenon must be monitored and governed on several levels—locally, nationally, on the European level, and globally. We must go beyond short-term politics and the lack of vision that have until now characterized various interventions.

Here, we can see a great naiveté among us Westerners. I said this already in 2001,[2] before the tidal wave of immigration from Africa and the East, reflecting on the arrival of tens of thousands of Albanians on the Italian coasts in the nineties, after the fall of Communism. Our TV channels broadcast images of our well-being and way of life around the globe, and we presume that those poor people will stay put and admire us, without moving. It is obvious that they will start moving, doing everything possible to come to us, at any cost, because they have discovered that the world is full of places where life is better. By now this is simply a fact, which has revealed the hollowness of the "one day at a time" political approach. We have been blind and deaf for many years. For example, I remember how in the seventies small cultural centers were born in Southern Italy, in which people spoke about how necessary it was for Italy, within Europe, to take a leadership role in the Mediterranean, promoting friendly politics and economic policies to help North Africa. But those calls remained unheard.

I am not saying that our governments have remained passive in the face of mass immigration. I am saying that for a long time they have been reacting without any global vision or ideal motivation and that they have only recently noticed the serious limitations of their actions aimed purely at containing the phenomenon. Think, for example, of the much-proclaimed distinction between refugees and economic immigrants. How can we realistically think of welcoming only the first group and turning away the second? It's like one of those movies set in medieval times in which a castle is being besieged. Initially, the people inside believe themselves invulnerable. Protected by thick walls, they defend themselves by throwing down pitch from the battlements. But the crowd attacking from outside is so immense that they find a breach; a flood of people rushes in. The European Union is now trying to develop a plan, but its member countries are disoriented and divided. Some even consider using force and building walls to try to keep the phenomenon at bay. Lastly, there is the third subject, after charities and institutions, which, perhaps, works the best. It is civil society, where—albeit slowly and painfully—integration is taking place in schools, neighborhoods, and ecclesial communities.

The truth is that mass immigration, most noticeably in Europe, causes fear and closed-mindedness in large sections of the population. How do you assess this reaction?

It is nothing to be surprised about. These feelings of fear and closed-mindedness are not new. Northern Italians already experienced them in the fifties when people immigrated from the south. I remember how the adults would talk about it when I was a boy: Sure, they might even be good people, but they are different, they will always be *terroni*.[3] And, of course, if someone living in tough circumstances is suddenly surrounded by ten-person families packed into small apartments, by veiled women, or by foreign languages, habits, and music, it would be unrealistic to expect any reaction but indifference and closed-mindedness. Not to mention the fear of terrorism. These feelings are understandable, but that is precisely why a patient work of education is necessary in order to rediscover what I like to call "civic friendship." It consists not only in a welcoming attitude but in an openness to the other as a benefit to me and a resource for all. What must be condemned is the political exploitation of these fears. I consider such manipulation gravely wrong, because it appeals to people's most despicable sentiments and cuts off at the root any possibility of living together, that is, the *civitas* where the new arrivals must find their place, too. From this perspective the question of citizenship is extremely important. A state cannot treat children born and raised within its borders like aliens until they reach eighteen years of age.

Even within the Church, there are those who stress the duty of hospitality and those who deny it, emphasizing the need to defend Europe's Christian identity. Is this a normal debate, or is it a scandalous rift?

There is nothing wrong with recalling the value of history and tradition, but the crucial question is about the future. This means that we must realistically recognize changes as they happen and be able to concretely show that Christianity, precisely because of its great past, is capable of accompanying the process of métissage and of giving Europe new life. The defense of Christian identity risks becoming an abstract defense of a value if we do not conceive identity in a dynamic, intelligent, and welcoming way. On the other hand, those who believe that the Church's only task is to be indiscriminately welcoming reduce Christianity to a generic spirit of compassion. Believers will have a role to play in a new Europe only if they start again from the mysteries of faith, with their cultural and social implications. The new Europe will inevitably be racially mixed, but this will not take away its identity. Christians cannot help but see a providential provocation in all of this.

Regarding the controversial topic of dialogue with Islam, you once said that we should not so much talk "about Muslims" but rather "with Muslims." With which Muslims?

In order to talk with them, we must first learn again how to talk in a different way among ourselves. I mean that we must learn to question each other about the most adequate meaning for life, based on what we Europeans believe. If we rediscover this renewed capacity for dialogue among ourselves, we will find that, actually, there is no sharp division between us and them. Europe and Islam have been in relationship for a very long time. Of course, this relationship has often been conflictual, but real nevertheless. History is there to show it. There are entire parts of Europe—ideas, architecture, and institutions—that have been transplanted in the Middle East and vice versa. Usually, people think of the mosques of Toledo, or the Islamic invasion of medieval Spain, but we must not forget the strong influence that European states have had upon Muslim-majority countries.

This is where we hit a sore spot, which is rarely spoken about. I'm referring to the question of postcolonialism. The manner in which Europe stepped away from colonialism ought to be investigated in greater depth. It was right and sacrosanct to recognize the colonized nations' legitimate aspirations for independence. But the interplay of spheres of influence which had the effect of drawing the new countries' boundaries with a yardstick, the support for authoritarian regimes that at a certain point mutated into the presumption of exporting our forms of democracy, the dominance of market logic combined with ignorance and even contempt for the customs and traditions of others—all of this has undermined the possibility for dialogue and collaboration, which were replaced by mistrust and hostility. This topic is often discussed in small circles of experts and scholars, but is completely ignored in the great debate over Islam within our societies. Now, when we talk about dialogue with Islam, we must not forge a path *ex novo*, but instead resume a cultural exchange that has been interrupted by both sides. From this point of view, the EU would do very well to promote chairs of European studies, Euro-Islamic relations, or, dare I say it, Christianity in the most important universities of the Arab world.

You still have not answered my question: With whom should we talk? Moderate Muslims?

I think that "moderate Muslims" is an inadequate category. In general, when people speak of moderate Muslims, they are referring to isolated individuals, often Westernized intellectuals. I prefer to speak about an Islam of the people, or, even better, of peoples. At Oasis Center, having worked for so many years in various situations, we have realized that there are great differences within the Muslim world. This is why we introduced the idea of using the word "Islam" in the plural. There is a line of separation between Sunnis and Shiites, but there are also ethnic and historical differences. The Islam in its birthplace, Arabia, is not the same thing as the Islam we find in the Balkan countries or around Indonesia, even though the main difficulty specifically concerns the question of doctrine.

Are you referring to the interpretation of the Quran?

There are two main reasons for this difficulty. Islam considers itself the fulfillment of Revelation, the completion of Judaism and Christianity, which represent previous stages on the timeline. In short, they think of themselves as the only true monotheistic religion. The second reason resides in the fact that according to Islam, the Quran was handed down directly from heaven. It therefore becomes very difficult to investigate by historical-critical methods a document whose author, according to the Muslims, is God himself, without human mediations.

Personally, I tried to push the dialogue to the doctrinal level in an international symposium among Christians, Jews, and Muslims. I organized it in the Holy Land when I was rector of the Lateran, with the title "Thinking about God in Jerusalem."[4] On that occasion, however, we made no progress with the Muslims on doctrine. I learned then that it may be better to deal with some issues that can help prepare the ground. For example, in a meeting of the Oasis scientific committee in Amman, we brought up the topic of freedom of conversion.[5] The main counterpart was the Islamic foundation directed by the cousin of King Abdallah II of Jordan, Prince Ghazi bin Muhammad bin Talal.[6] So, it was a prestigious institution, respected for its openness to dialogue. Still, even though they favored freedom of conscience in principle, our interlocutors in Amman could not get themselves to clearly acknowledge the freedom to convert. However, in recent years, the approach of having doctrinal discussions has perhaps become a bit more viable.

Many in the West demand that Islam reform itself, accepting the modern principle of the secularity of the State. Do you agree?

In principle, it is right to stress the distinction between the civil and the religious spheres, but in practice, it risks being an abstract argument that fails to take into account how Islam was born and developed. Think of Atatürk's forced secularization, and how it produced the opposite outcome in Erdogan's Turkey. But consider also France, the land of *laicité*, where still today an extreme secularism dominates. All religious symbols, be they a statue of the Virgin or a cross on the gate of a cemetery, are viewed as an offense against civil society. French President Emmanuel Macron's speech at the Collège des Bernardins showed promise for a different attitude.[7] We shall see. We Europeans are the first to fall into contradiction when it comes to the concept of secularity. To hope that Muslims will take a purifying cleanse in secularism—just as we are starting to complain about its effects on the life of Christian communities and on society in general—would be naive and wrong.

I must admit that I initially found the position of those who proclaim the need for so-called European Islam both abstract and artificial. But I had to change my mind when one day, we invited the leader of the Islamic communities in France to a meeting of the scientific committee of *Oasis*.[8] He did not talk about European Islam, but instead outlined what he considered to be the fundamental criteria for being a good Muslim in Europe. The first was absolute autonomy from the great Sunni powers—the Emirates, Saudi Arabia, and Qatar—and from the Shiite power of Iran. These countries fund the construction of mosques and control religious teaching. According to him, the economic independence of European Muslims could be ensured—besides the traditional form of almsgiving, *the zakat*—by the organization of travel to Mecca and by the transportation of the dead to be buried in their homelands. This autonomy, the Imam of

France concluded, would be decisive in order to support the credibility and dignity of the Islamic religion in the eyes of non-Muslims. It seemed a very interesting perspective to me, although I imagine that it will be quite difficult to break that umbilical cord with the financing countries.

Is there not also a need for reciprocity regarding the freedom of Christians in Muslim-majority countries?

Yes, certainly. We need to ask those countries to do everything in their power to make sure that the freedom of every believer who lives and works in their territory is respected. But the just request for reciprocity must not become, in my opinion, any sort of ultimatum. In the Christian faith, the aspect of gratuitousness, which may touch the heart of another, is very important. When the Catholic Church made new gestures of forgiveness and openness to other religious communities, it did not ask for anything in exchange.

Is Jihadist fundamentalism a political ideology that abuses religion, or is there something unresolved in Islam's relationship to violence?

The idea that religions always bring peace while the holders of political and economic power are responsible for war and terrorism contains an element of the truth, but does not explain everything. The relationship between Islam and violence is a complex question, which must be faced first of all from a historical point of view. It is undeniable that the expansion of Islam by Mohammed took place by force. On the other hand, anyone reading the Old Testament will be shocked by the amount of violence committed in the name of Yahweh. Even Christianity, which spread under a hailstorm of persecution and martyrdom, has known periods of violence, such as the wars of religion. It is an age that we have definitively left behind us, but it did terrible damage to the European consciousness, in which the prevailing idea is that peace can only be guaranteed by weakening the religion dimension.

The idea that monotheistic religions are violent by nature has been revived by the Egyptologist Jan Assmann.[9] He traces the origin of conflicts back to the commandment, "You shall have no other gods before me," whereas allegedly only polytheism can guarantee freedom for all. But this negates the very essence of religion, which aims to be an access to the truth. Religious freedom cannot be confused with indifferentism or relativism. On the contrary, freedom of conscience always implies the duty to welcome the truth. It's what we find expressed in the constitution *Nostra Aetate* of the Second Vatican Council, in which the Church solemnly affirms the principle of religious freedom as the point of arrival of a long and tormented journey. Islam has yet to do that. God only knows how and when it will. It remains true that the Muslim world is being called to think about the question of freedom in a new way.

The question of freedom forced its way into the spotlight with the Arab Spring of 2011, a brief interlude which has by now been filed away and even discredited. Do you think this question might actually become relevant again in the Muslim world?

I'm convinced that this will be the real question of the future, even more so than terrorism. The lack of freedom is the great, unresolved knot, the source of so many tensions among Muslims, including precisely the tragedy of Jihadism. If Islam fails to face this crucial question, it will continue to bounce back and forth between authoritarian governments and religious dictatorships. This wretched choice blocks the development of those peoples and suffocates the Eastern Christian Churches.

The Arab Spring was a cry for freedom, but it lost its way in the convulsive and dramatic stages that followed the initial enthusiasm. The Islamist parties came to power, only to be crushed by the iron fist of the military, as happened in Egypt, while in other countries the result was civil war. Apart from the political outcomes, I believe that the fragility of the Arab Springs lay in their pursuit of a Western model of freedom, which showed all its limitations. I remember what Cardinal André Vingt-Trois, then archbishop of Paris, said after the terrorist attack on Bataclan,[10] commenting on the slogan "We will not change our way of life," which was used as a provocation against the terrorists. He said, "Is this how we are going to resist? By doing things as we did them before? Shouldn't we instead be asking ourselves about what we live for, about what we rely on to remain free people, about what we believe in?"[11] This is the challenge that we find ourselves facing today.

How can we overcome this challenge?

By practicing love for every person while respecting diversity, but above all, by giving concrete and visible testimony to the truth in which we believe. For a Christian, this means to embrace the logic of martyrdom, a reality that we thought no longer belonged in our experience as men of the third millennium, which on the contrary has become dramatically relevant again.

As Pope Francis often points out, there are more martyrs today than there were in the Church of the first centuries. I had the opportunity to visit some Iraqi Christians who had fled from Mosul and the Nineveh plain.[12] They had survived the massacres, rapes, and kidnappings carried out by Daesh, the black army of the Caliphate. It is hard for us Europeans to imagine such a thing—professionals, teachers, entrepreneurs, and people of every social class who lost their lives or were forced to flee their own homes overnight to end up in a container at a refugee camp in Erbil, in 120-degree weather with no running water. I saw in them a dignity, a pride, and a rootedness in the faith that moved me. Now, they are finally beginning to return to their homelands after the defeat of Daesh, but everything must be rebuilt, beginning with trust in the future, which is always very uncertain in a country that lives according to sectarian logic. Helping them means helping ourselves to rediscover our reasons for living, and to remember, as Balthasar said, that "persecution constitutes the normal condition of the Church in her relation to the world. . . . This does not mean that the Church will be necessarily persecuted at all times and in all places, but if it does happen at certain times and in certain places, then it should be remembered that this is a sign of that special grace promised to her."[13]

And perhaps we should stop using the expression "Christian minorities"—a penalizing definition that they reject. "We must claim our place as full and rightful citizens of our country," I was told unanimously by the faculty of the Saint Joseph University in Beirut during a meeting I had with them.[14] Visiting the Shrine of Harissa was an experience that went beyond my expectations. This is the place where the Holy Virgin, proclaimed the Queen of Lebanon, is venerated not only by Christians but also by Muslims.[15] It is significant that in the country of the cedars, March 25, the feast of the Annunciation, is considered a national holiday. I remember arriving at Harissa by car with the Maronite Patriarch Boutros Raï.[16] It was already late at night, but we were not able to reach the parking lot, so great was the crowd of pilgrims.

From our brothers in the Middle East, I learned Christian realism. It is not resignation. It creates a hierarchy of goals to pursue, taking into account one's limitations and weaknesses. Msgr. Jean-Clément Jeanbart,[17] the Greek-Catholic archbishop of battered Aleppo, told me: "You Westerners fail to understand that if we want to survive, we will have to bite the bullet and accept certain facts." He was referring to Syria's despotic and authoritarian system. This painful realism highlights how abstractly we often judge the tragedy which has befallen that people.

Will Christians and Muslims someday get to the point of embracing and accepting each other, without exception, as brothers?

We know that God has a plan for history and that this plan is good. Of course, both the freedom of God and the freedom of man enter into play here, as well as (let us not forget) the work of the devil. In my work with *Oasis*, I have often asked myself by what mysterious plan of God over a billion men and women are faithful to Islam. It is the question I found in the spiritual will of Fr. Christian de Chergé, one of the monks of Tibhirine, in Algeria, who were killed in 1996 and for whom Pope Francis has begun the beatification process.[18] "If it should happen one day—and it could be today—that I become a victim of the terrorism which now seems ready to encompass all the foreigners living in Algeria, I would like my community, my Church, my family, to remember that my life was given to God and to this country," he wrote with shockingly prophetic words. And he continued, "My death, clearly, will appear to justify those who hastily judged me naive or idealistic: 'Let him tell us now what he thinks of it!' But these people must realize that my most avid curiosity will then be satisfied. This is what I shall be able to do, if God wills—immerse my gaze in that of the Father, to contemplate with him his children of Islam just as he sees them, all shining with the glory of Christ, the fruit of his Passion, filled with the Gift of the Spirit, whose secret joy will always be to establish communion and to refashion the likeness, delighting in the differences."[19] I first read Fr. Christian's testament in 1997, a few months after his martyrdom. Since then, his curiosity has stayed with me and has pushed me to be interested in this reality that affects and overshadows more and more our way of living and thinking.

Notes to Chapter 14

1. The journal is also called *Oasis*. The name was inspired by John Paul II's *Address to Meeting with the Muslim Leaders—Omayyad Great Mosque, Damascus* (May 6, 2001), 3: "Both Muslims and Christians prize their places of prayer, as oases where they meet the All Merciful God."
2. In a conference to the Banca Popolare di Sondrio on January 19, 2001.
3. Derogative term used in Northern Italy to denote people from the south. *Terrone* derives from *terra* (land) and suggests that people who work the land are somehow inferior.
4. The conference took place in Jerusalem at Easter time in 1998.
5. This happened in the context of a conference on "Religious Freedom: A Good for Every Society," organized by *Oasis* in Amman in June 2008.
6. Abdallah II (1962–), king of Jordan since 1999, is a supporter of interreligious dialogue between Christians and Muslims. Prince Ghazi bin Muhammad (1966–) is a first cousin of the king and a professor of philosophy. He is also known for his initiatives in favor of interreligious dialogue.
7. French President Emmanuel Macron was invited by the French Conference of Bishops to give a talk in Paris on April 9, 2008. Addressing French Catholics, he said, "Your faith is something politics needs." This was widely interpreted as a rejection of the most rigid interpretations of the French principle of *laïcité* (secularism).
8. Dalil Boubakeur (1940–) is the rector of the Great Mosque of Paris. He was president of the French Council of the Muslim Faith from 2003 to 2008.

9. Jan Assmann (1938–) is a German Egyptologist who has written extensively on monotheistic religions. See, for example. *The Price of Monotheism* (Stanford: Stanford University Press, 2010).

10. On November 13, 2015, members of the Islamic State terrorist organization attacked the Bataclan Theater in Paris, killing ninety people. It was the largest massacre in France since World War II.

11. André Vingt-Trois (1942–) is a French archbishop and cardinal. From 2005 to 2017, he was archbishop of Paris and primate of France.

12. In 2015, Cardinal Scola visited Erbil, the capital of Iraqi Kurdistan, where on June 19, he met a group of Christian refugees from Mosul and the Nineveh plain.

13. Hans Urs von Balthasar, *The Moment of Christian Witness* (San Francisco: Ignatius Press, 1994).

14. The University of Saint Joseph in Beirut was founded by the Jesuits in 1875.

15. The Shrine of Harissa was built at the beginning of the twentieth century near Jounieh, twenty kilometers from Beirut.

16. Béchara Boutros Raï (1940–) is a bishop and cardinal. Since 2011, he has been the Maronite patriarch of Antioch, leading one of the most important Eastern Catholic churches.

17. Jean-Clément Jeanbart (1943–) is a bishop of the Melkite Greek Catholic Church. Since 1995, he has been the Melkite archbishop of Aleppo in Syria.

18. The seven Trappist monks of Tibhirine have been proclaimed blessed by Pope Francis. Their beatification, together with that of twelve other Algerian martyrs, was celebrated in Oran on December 8, 2018.

19. Christian de Chergé, "Last Testament," *First Things* (August 1996).

CHAPTER 15

A "Humble Servant in the Vineyard"

The Relationship with Pope Benedict XVI

In April 2005, after one of the shortest conclaves in history, Cardinal Joseph Ratzinger was elected pope with the name of Benedict XVI. Could it be said that, and forgive my expression, you were one of his "Great Electors"?

I know I will disappoint your curiosity, but conclaves cannot be discussed. There is a clear rule that binds the participants to secrecy. It is a law that in my opinion still has its own profound reason to exist, as a supreme guarantee of freedom. For this reason as well, I do not see why we should violate it. In any case, the term "Great Elector" seems inappropriate. We are allowed to exchange opinions during a conclave, without giving in to any dubious motives, like trying and using our votes to influence the behavior of a future pope.

But there have been many stories about different parties, dramatic turns, even the number of votes of various front-runners.

Stories, exactly. Stories and suppositions that often did not correspond to the facts and that were intended to depict power struggles that have nothing to do with the good of the Church. What I can say is that Ratzinger easily collected the majority necessary for his election, a fact easily deduced from the brevity of the conclave. His homily during the Mass *Pro eligendo Romano Pontefice*, with that reference to the winds of doctrine and the currents of thought that have rocked the small boat of the Church, left a great impression on the cardinals called to choose John Paul II's successor. This explains why so many people supported Ratzinger.

Weren't there other valid candidates at the time?

If we let the imagination run free, I, for example, thought that the archbishop of Paris, Cardinal Jean-Marie Lustiger, would have been a great pope, if only he had been a little younger and not already very ill. I knew him back when he was a simple pastor. Later, when he was appointed the bishop of Orléans, I had several chances to visit him and to befriend his three closest lay collaborators—Jean-Luc Marion, Rémi Brague, and Jean Duchesne. As I have already mentioned, they had taken part in the project of the international journal *Communio* back in 1973.

Lustiger was a truly extraordinary figure. I was fascinated by his sense of the Christian people, his intelligence, his cultural and theological background, his open-mindedness, and his genius for launching new initiatives. But the thing that impressed me most was the way he converted to Christianity from Judaism. He had a fruitful bond with his origins, causing him many problems even inside the Church, because he publicly affirmed that he had never turned his back on Judaism and had embraced faith in Christ as its continuation. His adolescence was tragic. His mother and sister were deported and killed in Auschwitz. At fourteen years of age, he converted to Christianity and had himself baptized. As de Lubac pointed out to me when I interviewed him, it is absolutely extraordinary that someone manages to encounter Christ just by reading and learning Sacred Scripture. That's exactly what the very young Lustiger did. I believe that only a person who combines brilliant intelligence with a passionate search for life's meaning can follow such a route.

Our friendship became closer towards the end of the nineties, when I was the rector of the Lateran University. At that time, Cardinal Lustiger wanted to create a school of theology in the École Cathedrale educational complex that he had founded in Paris. It was not an easy task, especially since a school of theology already existed at the Institut Catholique, besides the Centre Sèvres of the Jesuits. However, he cared very much about the formation of seminarians and deemed it absolutely necessary that there be a different style and emphasis in theological studies for future priests. He asked me to give him a hand, and I helped him obtain authorization from the Holy See. He made a habit of refuting commonplaces, like the belief that there has been a progressive de-Christianization of France.

The last time I saw Lustiger was shortly after the conclave of 2005. I went to Paris with some younger Venetian priests to introduce them to the city's ecclesial community, and he, already very weakened by sickness, wanted to spend time with us anyway. By then, speaking was a struggle for him, but his judgment was as lucid and lively as ever. He loved to repeat that "nothing is impossible with God."

Let's circle back to Pope Benedict XVI. You had met the future Benedict XVI when he was a professor at Regensburg. Then you had the opportunity to spend time with him when he was appointed the prefect of the Congregation for the Doctrine of the Faith, for which your Eminence was a consultant. Could you tell me a little about your personal relationship with Joseph Ratzinger?

There was a rapport that has continued to grow since our first meeting, almost fifty years ago, when we immediately felt an affinity of judgment, which then became a personal closeness that has proven decisive for me. An atmosphere of confidence and friendship marks our relationship, although for me it is accompanied by what I would call a sense of awe toward him. Probably because Ratzinger has a timid and reserved personality, his cordiality is sincere but sober, and his judgments can be sharp, and at times even cutting. I remember having a private meeting with him in the eighties, during which I spontaneously gave him a suggestion. He did not react at the moment, but at the end of the conversation, before taking his leave, he told me in a tone both good-natured and stern: "My dear Fr. Angelo, remember that there is nothing worse than giving advice to those who do not ask for it."

Working with him as a consultant of the Congregation allowed me to observe up close his very special relationship with John Paul II. It was not just that of a cardinal and a pope. Ratzinger did not regard the pope only with loyalty, esteem, and respect, but also with an unconditional admiration because he recognized in him the power of sanctity. For his part, John Paul II would often admit, even publicly, that Cardinal Ratzinger was his greatest theological asset, of whom he could not do without. So much so that he never let him go away. When, upon reaching seventy-five years of age, Ratzinger expressed his firm intention to retire from his position as the prefect of the Congregation,

John Paul II was so upset that he turned to Cardinal Joachim Meisner of Colonia,[1] a very close friend of Ratzinger, begging him to convince Ratzinger to stay. He said that "without him, I cannot continue being the pope." And so, he stayed, out of pure obedience. The most on-the-nose, realistic, and profound way to define Ratzinger is how he presented himself to the world just after his election to the papacy, "a humble servant in the vineyard of the Lord."

What struck you the most about Ratzinger's personality?

In all my encounters with him, both public and private, on the most solemn occasions and in the dozens and dozens of work meetings at the Congregation, I always learned something. I used to visit him regularly when he was a cardinal. I met him often during his pontificate and, even after his retirement, I go to see him whenever I am in Rome. And no encounter I ever had with him has been routine. Ratzinger's interventions have always been characterized by great strength and originality; they are never banal. I believe that this is due to his deep immanence in the mystery of Christ. His pontificate made this evident to everyone.

The image many people have of the pontificate of Benedict XVI is that of a doctrinaire papacy.

Anybody who reads one of Ratzinger's texts will find a style and an argumentative method that are anything but doctrinaire, if by doctrinaire we mean the type of theology that dominated up until the seventies. Ratzinger would never have anything to do with that. In fact, he criticized it as "purely systematic thought, which only allows for the present juridical form of the Church."[2] From his very first writings, he joined the theological trend characterized by two fundamental elements: a research closely connected with the Bible—no longer used as a mere starting point but deepened as the true source of reflection—and an acute sense of the history into which the Christian message is inserted. From this point of view, Ratzinger has been a very innovative theologian. This is evident from the way that he chose to organize his most famous work, *Introduction to Christianity*.[3]

A rootedness in Scripture and sensitivity to current problems also characterize the three volumes on Jesus of Nazareth written during his papacy.

More generally, it can be said that the entire teaching of Benedict XVI rests on these two pillars. Hence his ability to get to the heart of the Christian announcement and to repropose it to our contemporaries, beginning from the unanswered questions and the contradictions of today's society. The way in which he faced the crucial relation between faith and reason, his awareness of the variety of cultures, his invitation to stop identifying the Church's message with its reception in the West—all this shows us very clearly how far Benedict XVI has been from that doctrinaire mindset concerned only with organizing the discourse of faith into neat geometrical shapes. On the contrary, he has been very attentive to the cultural and social implications of Christianity.

At times, however, this attention to current questions has caused Benedict XVI some trouble. I'm thinking of the famous speech in Regensburg,[4] where he quoted a very harsh judgment on Islam which prompted angry reactions from the entire Muslim world. What is your opinion of that episode?

On that occasion, Benedict XVI was addressing the faculty and students of the University of Regensburg, where he had taught. In his *lectio*, one can detect the typical professorial taste for refined quotations, precisely like that of the erudite Byzantine emperor Manuel Paleologus, who until then was almost unknown. He accused Mohammad of having brought "only bad and inhuman things." Perhaps the quote was not essential to the purpose of the talk, which would have worked well in its logical development even without it. If today we go and read it in the *Acta Apostolicae Sedis*, we find that the emperor's attitude is judged to be "blunt to the point of being unacceptable to us." So, it would have been better not to quote him, also because the ensuing polemics obfuscated the authentic meaning of that papal lesson, which described in a powerful and original way the unbreakable link between truth and freedom. However, I must say that, apart from the Regensburg speech, the magisterium of Benedict XVI has not always been understood.

Do you mean that it did not get the attention it deserved?

I have the impression that it was set aside a bit too quickly. But I believe that very soon, we will find ourselves coming back to the contents of Benedict XVI's teaching, particularly to his invitation to respect the breadth of reason that does not exclude faith. I mean that we believers must recover the historical intelligence of Christian thought, to which Benedict XVI called us back. It is an approach that certainly does not replace, but integrates, the one promoted by Pope Francis on the necessity of a new ecclesial subject. The former cannot exist without the latter, of this I am firmly convinced. Otherwise, we fall back in the simplistic opposition that reduces Benedict XVI to a somewhat abstract German thinker and Francis to a Latin-American populist. These caricatures fail to do justice to either of them, and, more importantly, harm the Church.

The weak side of Ratzinger's papacy was curial governance. There was a lack of resolve in making decisions, which he himself admitted in his *Last Testament* with Peter Seewald.[5] How much damage did this weakness do to Benedict's pontificate?

That Benedict XVI was not very interested in governing, and was not very adept at managing practical problems, is certainly not news. In the book you cited, *Last Testament*, there is a statement which goes a long way to explain his pontificate. "What matters is preserving the faith today, I consider it the crucial task," Ratzinger said. "All the rest are administrative issues."[6] I saw this personally when I worked with him at the Congregation. He was focused on the contents of the faith, to preserve it in the noble sense of the word. To preserve, one must anticipate changes, safeguarding the flow of tradition, which Ratzinger always understood in the manner of philosopher Maurice Blondel as a fact of experience.[7] Let us not forget that when John Paul II called him to Rome from Munich, overcoming his strong resistance, Ratzinger agreed on the condition that he be allowed to continue studying and writing books, despite the burden of his job as prefect for the Congregation for the Doctrine of the Faith. And he continued to do so even as pope, with a clear distinction between personal reflections and pontifical magisterium.

Benedict XVI never had other interests, other concerns than this: to preserve the faith. It is what makes him a truly free man, one who has nothing of his own to defend, thus allowing other people to do what they think best when the supreme value, the message of the Gospel, is not at stake. He was an extraordinarily humble pope, a pope who had little inclination not only to authoritarianism, but even to impose his will, which would have been more than legitimate as far as Church governance is concerned. For that, he always delegated to people who fit two criteria: management ability and personal trustworthiness—in short, people who could govern the bureaucratic machine but who were also friends he could trust completely. This is why, when he was prefect, he chose then Msgr. Tarcisio Bertone as secretary of the Congregation for the Doctrine of the Faith.[7] Later, when he became pope, he wanted Bertone to remain at his side and appointed him secretary of state. After choosing the person he considered most suitable, Ratzinger trusted him totally, with great loyalty, even to the point of inverting the famous maxim of Cardinal Giovanni Benelli,[8] "Whatever happens in the Vatican, the pope is not responsible and the secretary of state must take the blame." The opposite happened with Benedict XVI. He always intervened to save his closest collaborators even when they had obviously made mistakes.

Is it true that you, your Eminence, and some other cardinals tried to have Benedict XVI change this approach, suggesting that he send away Cardinal Bertone?

No, that is absolutely false. What most newspapers reported about the meeting held at Castel Gandolfo in 2009 between the pope and four cardinals (Camillo Ruini, Angelo Bagnasco, Christoph Schönborn, and myself)—namely, that we asked Benedict XVI to change the secretary of state—does not correspond to the truth.[9] It was an entirely informal meeting, like those we used to have when Ratzinger was still prefect. At that time, we would meet with him every four months at Cardinal Ruini's house, along with Cardinal Schönborn of Vienna when he was in Rome, and myself, then the rector of the Lateran. After his election to the papacy, we asked him to continue that tradition, less frequently, of course. After 2007, the new president of the CEI, Cardinal Bagnasco, was also invited. The meeting at Castel Gandolfo in the spring of 2009 took place in this context.

Perhaps it is worth recalling that that meeting happened after the Williamson case.[10] Pope Benedict revoked that Lefebvrite bishop's excommunication, ignoring his anti-Semitic statements. These caused protests from the Jewish world and eventually forced the pope to cancel the revocation. The polemics that followed focused on the errors made by the Curia and the responsibilities of the secretary of state, and there were rumors of his possible dismissal. This is why your meeting at Castel Gandolfo was interpreted as an attempt to pressure Benedict XVI in that sense.

Let me say that we were dealing with a very deep and unjust prejudice. I do not think any of us wanted to pressure him. In any case, at that meeting we discussed many things but not Cardinal Bertone, never mind his possible dismissal. Benedict XVI was clear about this from the start. Even before sitting down he told us, "We are not talking about the secretary of state." And so, we did not, obviously. All the recreations of that conversation that appeared in the newspapers were completely fictional, with no basis in reality.

Besides the Williamson case, the eight years of Benedict XVI's papacy saw the exposure of what, as a cardinal, he had called "the filth in the Church." Sexual and financial scandals, plots, "crows," leaks, later called "VatiLeaks."[11] There was a widespread impression that the pope was being held hostage by a Vatican bureaucracy in shambles. What is your assessment?

To begin, I would not use the word "hostage," because it implies passivity, and to some extent even connivance. Benedict XVI fought very hard against the filth within the Church. He took measures and tried to change things. I am thinking of the decisions he put into practice regarding priests accused of pedophilia and of the way he powerfully and explicitly admitted the Church's fault on multiple occasions, for example in the letter he wrote to the bishops of Ireland.

Regarding intrigues and financial scandals within the Roman Curia (the so-called VatiLeaks), he started an investigation entrusted to three wise men, Cardinals Julián Herranz, Jozef Tomko, and Salvatore De Giorgi.[12] Their report was submitted to Benedict XVI in the last days of his pontificate, but its contents were never made public. In the general preparatory congregations of the last conclave, in March 2013, some people asked about it. The response was that the report (which was otherwise kept secret) raised no suspicions and had no negative information about any members of the College of Cardinals. This response clarified, without a shadow of a doubt, that no cardinal was unworthy of being elected the next pope. After this, nothing else was revealed about the report which I now imagine is in Pope Francis's hands.

My impression—definitely blurred and perceived from afar, since I do not know the details of these events—is that the problems Benedict XVI faced in the Curia are still essentially the same ones Francis is dealing with. I think that the Church has a long way to go yet in regards to financial management and the IOR,[13] which is for all purposes a small bank. As far as I have been able to see—first in Rome, then Grosseto, Venice, and finally Milan—from the standpoint of financial management, the Church is still a sort of large parish where people lend their help, often freely, but there are not enough competent people. Moreover, the larger the parish, the more self-proclaimed experts and adventurers sneak in, taking advantage of our naivete.

Otherwise, power cliques and intrigue are unfortunately a constant element of any center of power, including ecclesiastical power. But in the Vatican, there are very many people who work with honesty and dedication. When I was a consultant of the Congregation for the Doctrine of the Faith, I admired people like Fr. Benoît Duroux, Fr. Karl Josef Becker, Fr. Umberto Betti,[14] and many others who, even though they were first-rate theologians, sacrificed recognition to serve anonymously, writing texts and correcting mountains of official documents. It was clear that they were putting all their energies at the service of the Church in a selfless way. Unfortunately, as the saying goes, one falling tree makes more noise than a thousand growing ones.

Beyond the financial scandals, however, there is something much more serious happening in the Church. I'm referring to the scandal of pedophilia. How does the Church face it? How can the Church overcome it?

We must honestly admit that there was too much delay in recognizing the enormous gravity of this type of behavior. This underestimation occurred not only in the Church but in society and culture at large. Even the tragedy of one case of pedophilia is one too many. Let us say that this phenomenon, which is an odious crime that marks its victims for the rest of their lives, was tacitly tolerated. It is a very grave sin that betrays the bond of trust that is intrinsic to an educational relationship, especially when it is committed by a person consecrated to God. It is a scandal that causes dismay and remorse and that touches the entire Church, which is called to profound penitence and radical change. Pope Francis, taking up Pope Benedict XVI's resolute initiative, is carrying out this reform with great rigor and determination.

From outside, people often do not appreciate the full scale of the Church's commitment to help victims and to identify and bring to justice those who bear responsibility for the crime of pedophilia, directly or indirectly. Zero tolerance is a drastic but just provision. As soon as there is a justified suspicion, a bishop is obligated to start an investigation. When it comes to the sexual abuse of minors, even negligence by the ecclesial authorities is no longer tolerated, not only cover-ups and complicity, as Pope Francis mandated with his June 2016 motu proprio, *As a Loving Mother*. Condemnation, justice in sincere cooperation with civil authorities, and expiation are the key words that make it possible to deal with every single case. The prominence given to these revelations by the media is entirely understandable. What is less understandable is the strategy of discrediting the entire clergy, which obscures the shining commitment of countless worthy priests in the field of education. The true task we are facing is prevention, and therefore education. To this end we must have the courage to tackle with careful consideration the way in which we priests live the sexual dimension, witnessing the beauty of virginity and celibacy.

Among the many events that occurred during the papacy of Benedict XVI, there is one which, unlike those we have recalled so far, was not widely reported but did leave its mark on the life of the Church. I'm referring to the Synod of Bishops on the Eucharist held in October 2005. You, Eminence, were the general rapporteur. That was not a coincidence, since you have reflected and published much on the Eucharistic mystery. What is the origin of your interest in a topic which is usually considered very obscure and difficult?

The origin is a very simple and evident fact, that I can only be saved by someone standing before me who is my contemporary. As Kierkegaard once said, "The only ethical relationship one can have with Christ is contemporaneity. Relating to a dead man is an esthetic relationship: his life has lost its sting, it does not judge my life, it allows me to admire him and lets me also live in entirely different categories. It does not force me to judge in a definitive way."[15] The issue of Christ's contemporaneity is decisive for the question of salvation. Indeed, the greatest problems for the European churches began between the end of the eighteenth century and the beginning of the twentieth, when the process of secularization affected theological reflection itself. It allowed Jesus Christ to be reduced to a myth, something that served for many centuries as a crutch for the moral conscience of humanity, which today can allegedly walk on its own. Then Christ becomes an idea of mine, or in the best-case scenario, a memory of what happened in the past. But woe if we reduce "memory" to a mental or emotional recollection. That is a very serious mistake. The Eucharist reproposes the perennially present reality of the single and unrepeatable event of the passion, death, and resurrection of Christ. It thus grants to the freedom of every man in every age and in every place the possibility to anchor itself to this salvific event.

Let us ask ourselves what the genesis is of the mysterious structure of the Eucharist. Rereading the Gospel account of the Last Supper, I make sense of it as follows: Jesus knows that the hour has arrived, and lets it be known with various quotations from Scripture. With the loving gaze that always characterized him, he thinks of what will happen to his disciples, of the confusion and discouragement that they will experience before the tragedy of the Cross. And it is at this point that the institution of the Eucharist takes place, an event that expresses the genius of Catholicism. We can say that, in a sense, Jesus lets his disciples benefit in advance from the saving power of his death and resurrection, in order to sustain them during the trial to come. But if he was able to do that in advance, this means that he can also do it afterwards. Therefore we, too, can benefit from it today two thousand years later. The truth of the original event, the death and resurrection of Christ, is known through another event: the Eucharist. It has the nature of a mediation, but still maintains the objective character of the original event. It is not an automatic mechanism that applies to the present something that happened many years ago; it is not a sort of magic that brings back someone from the past. In fact, it touches the essence of my freedom.

How does the Eucharist concretely touch the freedom of every man?

In the Eucharist, the infinite freedom of God leans down to touch the finite freedom of man, like a mother over her child. This is how man's freedom can be fulfilled. In the Eucharist, where the event of Christian Revelation concentrates, we are given the possibility to recognize and truly actualize our condition as free men, adhering all the way to the saving design of God. Here we see that Christianity is not an ethical imperative but a process of making oneself one with another. St. Augustine would tell his flock, "You must not become Christians, you must become Christ."[16] We could say that in the Eucharist, God takes a step towards me, allowing me to participate in the freedom of the dead and risen Christ.

You do admit that this is quite difficult to understand, is it not?

As a dear friend of mine who is also a great thinker, philosopher Jean-Luc Marion, wrote, there is nothing to "understand" in the Eucharist—also because wishing to capture the mystery of God present in the Sacred Host would be a gnostic presumption. What we need is to allow ourselves to be in constant awe of the Eucharist. From this point of view, I believe that one way to educate ourselves to this dimension is through the experience of Eucharistic adoration. Unfortunately, for a long time, adoration has been regarded as a mere devotion.

I discovered what it means to be in adoration of the Blessed Sacrament when I was a student in Fribourg, in Switzerland, at the end of sixties. In the *basse ville*, the lower part of the city, there were tenements of foreign workers, nearly all construction workers. One of those buildings housed the MOPP (Saint Peter and Paul Laborer's Mission), the movement founded by a Dominican priest named Jacques Loew, who had worked as a dock worker in Marseille.[17] In Fribourg, there were about twenty worker priests. Every Thursday night, they would hold a Eucharistic adoration, and we students would also join in. The priests sat on pillows and most would end up fast asleep by the end, exhausted by a hard day of work. Many of those priests had become construction workers. Once, while I was chatting with Fr. Loew, I asked him why they did not do the adoration on Sundays, so that they would not end up asleep before the Blessed Sacrament. His response was blunt and I have never forgotten it. "You do not understand anything. Adoration is just staying with Jesus, spending time with Him." From that day, I began to reflect on the beauty of such a simple gesture. In particular, I learned to value perpetual adoration.

I remember how the Synod of 2005 was deeply impressed by the testimony of the bishop of León, Mexico. He related the moving experience of five million of his countrymen who since 1967 have taken turns practicing perpetual adoration day and night in the sanctuary of Christ the King (which is located over 2,000 meters above sea level). This is a custom I also found in the United States, even in Washington where, on more than one occasion, I went with Msgr. Lorenzo Albacete—a brilliant American theologian and friend of Karol Wojtyła—to one of the local churches for Eucharistic adoration after dinner.[18] This tradition used to be very widespread also here in Italy, and now is flourishing again after it almost disappeared following the Council. I saw this in Venice, and even more so over the last few years in Milan. It is interesting to note that adoration is practiced predominantly by young people. The impulse came from Benedict XVI during the World Youth Day 2005 in Cologne, when he decided to change the traditional vigil of song and prayer into a whole night of Eucharistic adoration. The tradition has continued ever since. I remember what Pope Francis said to the young people gathered in Kraków in 2016. "Before Jesus present in the Sacred

Host you must not worry about looking, but rather let yourselves be looked at by him."

The Eucharist is fundamental for the life of a Christian. Let us imagine for just a moment what our churches would be without Sunday Masses, the gesture that still today keeps the Christian community together. Unfortunately, a factor that has contributed to emptying the Eucharist of its meaning has been an excess of Biblicism—namely, the attitude that says, "Let's give more space to reading Scripture than to the Mass." It misinterprets Vatican II, which affirmed that Word and Sacrifice must be bound together in the liturgical celebration. Without the Eucharist, without the contemporaneity of Christ, the event of Salvation becomes a pretext, a suggestion for our dreams and plans, which ultimately renders the very existence of the Church useless and superfluous.

Notes to Chapter 15

1. Joachim Meisner (1933–2017) was a German archbishop and cardinal. From 1980 to 1988, he was bishop of Berlin. In 1988, John Paul II appointed him archbishop of Cologne, against significant opposition from the progressive wing of German Catholicism, which is quite strong in the Rhine region. Meisner retired from the post in 2014.

2. Joseph Ratzinger, *Opera Omnia*, vol. 7, tome 1 (Rome: Vatican Publishing House, 2017). The work has not been translated into English.

3. Joseph Ratzinger, *Introduction to Christianity,* 2nd ed. (San Francisco: Ignatius Press, 2004).

4. "Faith, reason and the university" originally a lecture by Benedict XVI to the students and faculty of the University of Regensburg in Bavaria. It is available in the *Acta Apostolicae Sedis* (the official compilation of papal texts by the Vatican) and also in the volume *A Reason Open to God* (Washington, D.C.: The Catholic University of America Press, 2013), 7–19.

5. Benedict XVI, *Last Testament,* ed. Peter Seewald (New York: Bloomsbury, 2017).

6. Benedict XVI, *Last Testament,* 221.

7. Maurice Blondel (1861–1949) was a French Catholic philosopher who influential on Catholic theology.

8.   Tarcisio Bertone (1934–) is a Salesian priest, archbishop, and cardinal. He was secretary of the Congregation for the Doctrine of the Faith from 1995 to 2002. He became archbishop of Genoa until 2006, when Benedict XVI appointed him secretary of state, a position he held until 2013.

9.   Giovanni Benelli (1921–1982) was an archbishop and cardinal. He was the substitute of the Secretariat of State under Paul VI from 1967 to 1977, and then archbishop of Florence from 1977 to 1982.

10.   Camillo Ruini (1931–) is an archbishop and cardinal. From 1991 to 2008, he was the pope's vicar for the Archdiocese of Rome. In 1991, Pope John Paul II appointed him the president of CEI, and he was subsequently confirmed in that position until 2007. Angelo Bagnasco (1943–) is an archbishop and cardinal. From 2003 to 2006, he was the military ordinary for Italy and then archbishop of Genoa from 2006 to 2020. In 2007, he succeeded Cardinal Ruini as president of CEI, and held that position until 2020.

11.   Richard Williamson (1940 –) is an English traditionalist bishop. He was originally excommunicated in 1988 after being ordained without papal permission by Archbishop Marcel Lefebvre. Benedict XVI lifted the excommunication in 2009 without knowing that Williamson had made Holocaust-denying statements. The excommunication was reimposed in 2015 after he illicitly ordained another bishop.

12.   The expression "VatiLeaks" is meant to echo "WikiLeaks" and refers to the unauthorized release in the public domain of a trove of Vatican confidential documents in early 2012. An internal investigation led to the arrest of Paolo Gabriele, the pope's personal butler. He was tried and convicted for aggravated theft, and he spent two months in prison before Benedict XVI pardoned him in December 2012.

13.   Julián Herranz (1930–) is a Spanish archbishop and cardinal. A member of Opus Dei, he was president of the Pontifical Council for Legislative Texts from 1994 to 2007. Jozef Tomko (1924–) is a Slovak archbishop and cardinal. He was prefect of the Congregation for the Evangelization of Peoples from 1985 to 2001. Salvatore De Giorgi (1930–) was archbishop of Palermo, in Sicily, from 1996 to 2006.

14. Istituto per le Opere di Religione (Institute for Religious Works) is a Vatican financial institution.

15. Benoit Duroux was a Swiss Dominican and one of the theologians who assisted Pope Paul VI in writing *Humanae Vitae*. Karl Josef Becker was a German Jesuit and cardinal who taught at the Gregorian University. Umberto Betti was an Italian Franciscan and cardinal who served as an expert at Vatican II and then as president of the Lateran University from 1991 to 1995.

16. Søren Kierkegaard, *Journals and Papers*, Vol. 3 (Bloomington, Ind.: Indiana University Press, 1967), 419.

17. "Therefore let us rejoice and give thanks, not only that we have been made Christians, but that we have been made Christ." Augustine, *Tractates on the Gospel According to Saint John, 11 –27*, translated by John W. Rettig (Washington, D.C.: The Catholic University of America Press, 1988), tractate 21, par. 8, pg. 186.

18. Jacques Loew (1908–1999) was a Dominican and the first French worker-priest.

19. Lorenzo Albacete (1941–2014) was an American priest, theologian, and author. He taught at the John Paul II Institute in Washington, D.C., and was one of the more visible figures of Communion and Liberation in the United States.

CHAPTER 16

The Church and Public Life

The Ruini Era

Benedict XVI will go down in history as the pope of "nonnegotiable principles"[1] regarding the defense and promotion of life. Today, this expression has fallen out of use and is a target of criticism, even inside the Church. Is this formula outdated?

As Benedict XVI himself explained, these principles are inherent to human nature, and therefore the action of the Church in their defense does not have a confessional character, but addresses all citizens, regardless of their religion and beliefs. According to Ratzinger, the moral contents at stake here concern the dignity of the person as such, and therefore cannot be diminished or erased.

I completely agree with this correct and sacrosanct affirmation, even though I prefer to speak of "unrenounceable" principles. "Nonnegotiable" may give the impression that the Church is closed off to discussion. Personally, over the years I have reached a more nuanced conception of how the Church should intervene in a pluralistic society. I think that it is currently very difficult to prove the benefit of the Christian position unless it is backed up by the power of witness—with a caveat. The witness I refer to is not something individualistic and interior, as those who place it in opposition to presence and action seem to think. I mean witness as a fundamental attitude of the believer who knows how to communicate the reasons for his faith in the public sphere, telling his life story and letting his life story be told by others.

For example, it is by witnessing the beauty of family life and the fullness of the nuptial mystery that Catholics show that they have something decisive to say about civil unions and so-called homosexual marriage. This is not a road to disengagement, quite the opposite. The confrontation may even become severe, especially when the debate becomes political and concerns legislative intervention. In any case, the manner and instruments of these debates, which the Church cannot walk away from, must be decided each and every time in a realistic way.

The manner and instruments used to defend the nonnegotiable principles theorized by Benedict XVI were those deployed by then-president of CEI, Cardinal Camillo Ruini. Under his guidance, the Italian Church once again became a protagonist in public life. In 2005, it called for abstention in the referendum on assisted fertility and in 2007, for mass street protests against DICO (the law on civil unions drafted by the Prodi administration). This strategy succeeded. The referendum did not pass and the DICO bill was withdrawn. You, your Eminence, agreed with Ruini's approach, openly supporting it. Do you still believe it was the right approach?

Cardinal Ruini's interventions in the public square had their premise in the change of course at the ecclesial congress in Loreto. As I have already said, such change was authoritatively and effectively proposed by John Paul II, to whom the necessary (also public) role of faith for the good of all society mattered very much. With the end of the Catholic party and the loss of the political mediation that had existed until then, the president of CEI was forced to take up the task—which was certainly heavy, and in many ways unpopular—of directly and publicly representing the concerns of believers, defending the fundamental values of the person, life, and the family in the civil domain. Cardinal Ruini did it intelligently and realistically, positioning himself as a voice for fundamental anthropological issues to politicians and to the government. He did it not to obtain favors or privileges for the Church, but to safeguard the health of society from a dangerous drift towards nihilism. His aim was to defend not the particular interest of his own side, but the general interest of all society. As Benedict XVI said in an address to members of the European People's Party in March 2006, "When Churches or ecclesial communities intervene in public debate, expressing reservations or recalling various principles, this does not constitute a form of intolerance or an interference, since such interventions are aimed solely at enlightening consciences . . . even when this should conflict with situations of power." It was within this context that Cardinal Ruini, as then-president of CEI, made his choice, and it was absolutely understandable.

In order to affirm that certain values are indispensable at a general level, Ruini leveraged various forces in civil society, such as the Movement for Life and the Forum of Families.[2] He also suggested entirely legitimate actions, such as abstention in the referendum on artificial fertilization. Those who accused him of intolerable meddling and political horse trading understood nothing. He was not pursuing a *do ut des*; he did not barter the Catholic vote, for example, in exchange for more money for private schools. Contrary to what his critics assert, Ruini acted not to impose the supremacy of the Church upon society, but following a logic of service and witness. I cannot deny that certain people entertained hegemonic ambitions at the time, but Cardinal Ruini was certainly not one of them. He was aware that the manner in which the Church could intervene in public life heavily depended on the historical situation, which in Italy was rapidly deteriorating. He knew how to assess the situation and was successful in making the public and courageous testimonies of millions of Catholics, together with many nonbelievers, both decisive and effective. It is unfair and anti-historical to judge Ruini's presidency as a step backwards to a hegemonic mindset, thus setting up Pope Francis's magisterium against it as a return to the authenticity of the Gospel.

In summary, what is your assessment on the long ecclesial era of "Ruinism"?

Cardinal Ruini's leadership was authoritative. He sometimes expressed his protagonism in imperfect ways, as when he responded to criticisms against Catholics with the famous line, "Better controversial than irrelevant." Some people found it a bit too arrogant. But the action of the Italian Church under his guidance, in close unity with John Paul II, turned out to be eminently suited to and effective in that particular historical period. The net result was more than positive, not only in terms of political action.

Ruini transformed the CEI, turning it into a full-fledged episcopal conference, both in terms of content and organization. Furthermore, with a brilliant initiative like the Cultural Project—which unfortunately has been underrated by part of the Catholic world—he was able to reassert the centrality of the anthropological question, by gathering together intellectuals of all backgrounds to freely and openly debate this crucial topic.[3] In this regard, the international conferences "God Today: With or Without Him Changes Everything" in 2009 and "Jesus, Our Contemporary" in 2012 are still memorable. Over two thousand people participated in them.

You, Eminence, were considered the natural successor of Cardinal Ruini as leader of the CEI. Your name was on the top of the list of candidates but then, in March of 2007, then Monsignor Angelo Bagnasco, the archbishop of Genoa, was appointed president of the Italian Bishops' Conference. How come?

At the beginning of 2007, there was the widespread opinion that both Benedict XVI and Cardinal Ruini were favorably disposed to my appointment as the next president of the CEI. Then, supposedly, there were some difficulties because Cardinal Bertone was sharply opposed. The fact is that Monsignor Bagnasco was appointed leader of the CEI, and I must acknowledge that it turned out to be the right choice—dare I say even a providential one—because his personality was certainly more suitable than mine for a role that requires such a great and patient capacity for mediation, and that must rely on the largest possible consensus within the Italian episcopate.

The end of the Ruini era saw a change of strategy for the Italian Church. How do you explain it, and above all what is your assessment of it?

The change of strategy, to use your expression, did not depend on Cardinal Ruini's retirement, since his style and approach were kept essentially the same by Cardinal Bagnasco. If there is a clearly visible discontinuity between the Ruini era and the current phase of the Italian Church, it is due, in my opinion, to two fundamental factors. The first is that the instruments chosen by the Church to intervene in public life in order to safeguard the unrenounceable values of the person cannot be used in the same way anymore. What was very effective fifteen or even ten years ago risks becoming a blunt tool today. The process of secularization has rolled heedlessly onward and the ability of believers to bear witness to the social value of faith has unfortunately weakened. This is why we need to be very careful in choosing our moves. Some choices may turn out to be counterproductive in the end, while it is advisable at times to reach a compromise and cut our losses. For example, in a pluralistic society, the principle that marriage is an indissoluble union between a man and a woman, and is open to life, can be safeguarded even as the State recognizes other kinds of unions in some form as long as they are in no way equated to marriage. And if dialogue is fruitless and the law undermines the unrenounceable principles— as happened with the law on living wills approved by the Italian parliament in 2017— then we have the duty to fight for the recognition of conscientious objection (as was granted for abortion).[4] On this point I believe it important to highlight the social dimension of conscientious objection. I have in mind the movie *Hacksaw Ridge*, which tells the story of the first conscientious objector in the United States Army, Desmond Doss, who managed to save dozens of his comrades from the Japanese attacks at Okinawa during the Second World War without using any weapons. I mean to say that the individual's right to invoke freedom of conscience must be embedded into the life of a people or a group of people. Besides this sociological and cultural factor, there is another decisive factor of discontinuity in the Church's actions, namely the papacy of Francis.

Does Pope Francis mark a sharp break with the past?

The introduction of elements of discontinuity is vital for the Church. It has always been so in history and especially today. This does not contradict the essential element of continuity, which for a believer is called Tradition. In this sense, the Church's discontinuity must never become a complete break with the past but must instead be a shot of strength and vitality. When Pope Francis says he does not like the expression "nonnegotiable values" and refrains from starting great battles for the defense of life or the family, it does not mean that he does not care about them, he is just showing that he has a different set of priorities.[5] It is enough to go and see all the positions he has staked, even quite recently, against abortion, or his declarations about gender theory's "ideological colonization," or his resolute and moving intervention in the case of little Alfie,[6] to easily recognize that there is absolute continuity between his preaching and the traditional teachings of the Church. The fact that he does not repeat them every day does not mean that the doctrine has changed!

But Francis strongly highlights other issues as well—social justice, preference for the poor and those viewed as "throwaways," welcoming immigrants, care for the environment. This does not mean that the pope considers abortion a lesser evil. Rather, I think he is convinced that in our current ultra-secularized societies, it is good to repropose the entire range of unrenounceable principles, giving more space to the topics that people are more sensitive and aware of, with the goal of provoking a change of heart that will make it possible to promote them all. It seems to me that Pope Francis, compared to his predecessors, has chosen a path that is not different on the level of substance, but on the level of how to propose it. We shall see whether he will be more successful!

Therefore, in this new era, does it no longer makes sense for Catholics to take to the streets and protest against laws or state interventions considered gravely harmful to the values of life and family?

I am not opposed a priori to Catholics getting out in the streets and protesting. I say this knowing well that there is a dominant idea in our society that a believer has the right to hold his own convictions and act accordingly, but must not express them publicly lest he hinder other people's freedom. It is a rule that has triumphed in Italy since the time of the referendum on divorce. But this is not how a pluralistic society should work. Everyone needs to tell his life story and allow his life story to be told by others, striving as much as possible for a mutual recognition, as philosopher Paul Ricoeur once said.[7] For example, if I am convinced that a certain concept of family is beneficial for the entire society but I fail to share that publicly, I am taking something away from the debate and making it poorer and narrower.

Therefore, we must reiterate that it is completely legitimate to take public stances, especially when it comes to unrenounceable principles, as long as a few conditions are respected. The first is that the logic of witness must be clearly visible, that we don't just wave flags and shout slogans. Secondly, we must judge wisely whether the moment is opportune and the chosen method is effective. This is a historical assessment that cannot be decided once and for all. In a pluralistic society, especially one as fragmented as ours, jumping headlong into a "battle for values," regardless of what outcomes one can reasonably expect, perhaps doesn't make much sense. If we choose the wrong method to present our ideas, there is a risk that it will produce an effect opposite to the one we desire. It matters whether an initiative comes from above, from the ecclesial hierarchy, or from the leadership of an association, or if instead, it comes from below and progressively spreads, involving groups, movements, and social aggregations—as happened in France in 2012 with *Manif pour tous*, which had (dare I say it) an insurgent type of origin, and which seriously embarrassed the powers that be.[8]

It is a fact that in a pluralistic society different views of the world meet, debate, and even clash. Believers must not be afraid to publicly offer their contribution to build a good life for everyone, in ways that must be evaluated on a case-by-case basis.

We have discussed the CEI's interventions in public life. You, however, have paid much attention to politics in the strict sense of the word. In the spring of 2009, at Riva del Garda, you gave a lecture and participated in a national meeting of *Rete Italia*, a group that brought together center-right politicians close to the president of the Lombardy region, Roberto Formigoni.[9] Once you also said that you were always fascinated by politics. Where does this interest come from?

First, let me clarify that I appeared not only at the meeting of Formigoni's group that you mentioned. I also attended conferences promoted by various political entities, from the UDC to the ACLI and the MCL.[10] The most interesting initiative I participated in was the one organized by the so-called *Intergruppo parlamentare per la Sussidiarietà*, which gathered around fifty politicians from the right and left, from Quagliariello to Enrico Letta, from Lupi to Bersani.[11]

To get to your question: Yes, it is true, I have always been interested in politics. When I said that I was fascinated, I was referring to the way politics was lived by my father, a Socialist, and above all, by my brother, a Christian Democrat. My brother was involved in Lecco's political scene for over twenty years, ten of those as mayor of the town of Malgrate where we were born. They worked for free, a characteristic shared by many activists and local administrators I knew when I was young. In my opinion the crisis of political Catholicism began back in the seventies, precisely when people abandoned the principle of engaging in politics without payment. Something similar also happened in the labor movement. At that time, I started traveling around Italy, and every time I met a politician, I was struck by how much money seemed to be available to their staffers. And it was a short step from being compensated for political work to engaging in politics purely for the money.

The second factor in the crisis of the Christian Democratic Party was the abandonment of culture. Augusto Del Noce, one of the most lucid as well as one of the most unheeded minds of the Catholic world,[12] remarked with some irony that the party began to crumble when it stopped holding its conferences in San Pellegrino—meaning, when it began to regard cultural reflection as a waste of time. Not that there was a great depth of ideals before. However, there was the European ideal, which somehow managed to provide ever greater goals with the prospect of unification. In the last few years, even this ideal seems to have faded away—the introduction of the single currency and then the global financial crisis have shifted the focus from the ends to the means, leaving us in the hands of a political class that has lost its way in the labyrinths of technocracy.

As a matter of fact, today people no longer believe that politics has anything to do with ideals. And we must admit that the Church has limited herself to merely condemning political ills—the cancer of corruption, the growing injustices, and so on—without being able to create the necessary conditions for a renewed involvement of Catholics in public life.

Is this the reason you recently invited the Catholics of your diocese of Milan "to overcome the fear that for too long has caused the topic of politics to be censored in the Christian community"?[13]

At the root of this fear there is a lack of organic reflection on what the Christian proposal can mean in a pluralistic society. It is a lack that affects every level of ecclesial life, from the missionary announcement to the building of social works and initiatives to political action in a proper sense. If we are incapable of realizing what I have called "civic friendship," that is to say a sincere openness to others based on the constitutive factors of our faith experience, then sparking a genuine interest in political work will obviously not be possible.

I am aware that there are many entirely understandable reasons why this topic has been off limits in our communities. However, after we leave behind the negative effects of corruption cases, and our embarrassment over political practices in the recent past that had little or nothing Christian about them, either we find the courage to offer our contribution of a good life to all of society and in all contexts, or else the organization of our existence will be determined more and more by those who hold financial and economic power—because while politics emptied of ideals turns into cynicism and oppression, an ideal that does not become a project will prove vacuous. The classic example is that of Europe's founding fathers, who belonged to Catholic parties. After the war, they began the unification process by facing very concrete issues together, such as the production of coal and steel, which until then had been a source of constant conflict between France and Germany.

The Italian elections in March 2018 marked the disappearance of the last, residual political forces subscribing to the values and symbols of the Catholic political tradition. Was it the end of a history and the beginning of an era characterized by the total irrelevance of believers in the public sphere?

It does seem that we have gone back to year zero. It is a crisis that affects not only political Catholicism but all the parties connected in some way to the history of the labor movement as well. It is the umpteenth symptom of a change of era that requires a new conception of politics. Political action has become so warped that it has lost its fundamental meaning.

For a believer, it is entirely evident by now that the way forward cannot be the creation of a new Catholic party. The future belongs to pluralistic forms and assemblages that are internally capable of freely welcoming people. We need forces with dynamic identities, aimed at realizing a common vision. It is very important to forcefully restate that politics cannot exist without ideals. If there are no ideals, politics becomes subordinate to processes that it has a hard time understanding, and it struggles even more to govern.

I am thinking of the big questions raised by genetic engineering and neuroscience, of the problems associated with the digital revolution and the new media, of the climate crisis, of the disconnect in the economy between production and finance, of the phenomenon of mass immigration, and more radically, of the injustice in the distribution of resources, which is forcing a large part of the global population into poverty and even starvation. On every single one of these issues, politics is oscillating dangerously between simplistic recipes and a powerlessness that hides behind empty promises and vague plans.

I was deeply struck when, in a recent symposium among experts, the need arose to discuss *ex novo* the theme of the "political" in its full sense, referring to the great texts of Aristotle and Plato as examples. Such a research work would be very important today, even if in a totally mutated scenario. If we accept the fact that in history, processes assert themselves and do not ask for our permission to happen, I believe that even in the current context, we can look towards the future with hope. In particular, I think that there are many in politics who still intend to remain attached to the Christian vision, thank God.

Does this judgment also apply to your friends, with whom you shared the experience of Communion and Liberation since youth, who engaged in politics with various ups and downs (even legal ones)?

When, in the midseventies, some of my CL friends decided to run for office within the Christian Democrat party (though with very different styles and goals from those of the declining Christian Democrats), they had the complete support of the leaders of the movement, and thus also mine. When I became a bishop, I decided to publicly and clearly distance myself from them. This was not just for the very obvious reason that all political commitments are primarily the personal responsibility of those involved, but also to safeguard my pastoral mission from the prejudice that I was still associated with my friends who had gone on to have political careers. I reaffirmed this distance when Roberto Formigoni, the ex-president of the region of Lombardy, was the object of accusations, which I hope will be quickly clarified by the judiciary. This does not mean rejecting our common history, or breaking a friendship which endures in the deepest sense of the term, as affection and prayer.

Notes to Chapter 16

1. The expression "nonnegotiable principles" appeared for the first time in Catholic magisterium in the *Doctrinal Note on Some Questions regarding the Participation of Catholics in Political Life* published on November 24, 2002 by the Congregation for the Doctrine of the Faith, presided over by Cardinal Ratzinger. After Ratzinger became Pope Benedict XVI, he used the expression again several times, in particular in his address of March 30, 2006 to representatives of the European People's Party (which gathers together various parties with a Christian inspiration in the European Parliament). On that occasion he listed the following as nonnegotiable principles: "protection of life in all its stages, from the first moment of conception until natural death; recognition and promotion of the natural structure of the family as a union between a man and a woman based on marriage … ; the protection of the right of parents to educate their children."

2. The Movement for Life is the largest Italian pro-life organization. The Forum for Families was born in 1992 with the goal of focusing the cultural and political debate in Italy on the family and its needs.

3. In 1997, Cardinal Ruini started the Cultural Project of the Italian Catholic Church with the purpose of presenting a Christian worldview in dialogue with contemporary culture.

4. See note 12 to chapter 7.

5. In an interview with *Corriere della Sera* on March 5, 2014, Pope Francis stated: "I never understood the expression 'nonnegotiable values.' Values are values, period. I cannot say that among the fingers in my hand one is less useful than another. Thus I do not understand in what sense some values could be negotiable."

6.   Alfie Evans was an English child who suffered from a degenera-
     tive neurological disease. His doctors decided to take him off life
     support against the will of his parents. After a protracted legal
     battle, the British judiciary ruled against the Evans family and
     Alfie died on April 28, 2018. A few days earlier, Pope Francis
     received Alfie's father at the Vatican and supported him publicly,
     stating that it is "our duty to do everything we can to protect
     life." See Steven Ertelt, "Pope Francis Speaks Out for Alfie Evans
     After Meeting His Father: 'It's Our Duty to Do Everything to
     Care for Life,'" LifeNews.com (April 18, 2018).

7.   See Paul Ricoeur, *The Course of Recognition* (Cambridge, Mass.:
     Harvard University Press, 2007).

8.   *Manif pour tous* is a French organization born in 2012 with the
     goal of "defending marriage and the procreation of children
     based on human sexual reality, which is threatened by politi-
     cal reforms inspired by gender ideology." It brings together over
     thirty associations, mostly of a Christian inspiration. In early
     2013, it organized protests in Paris, which were joined by hun-
     dreds of thousands of people, to protest the law on "same-sex
     marriage" introduced by then President Hollande.

9.   Roberto Formigoni (1947–) is a former politician. A mem-
     ber of Communion and Liberation, he was a founder and
     first president of Movimento Popolare in 1975 (see note 18 to
     chapter 3). He has been a member of the European Parliament
     and a senator in Italy. From 1995 to 2013, he was president of
     the Lombardy region.

10. The UDC (*Unione Democratici Christiani*) is a small centrist
     party. The MCL (*Movimento Cristiano Lavoratori*) is an associ-
     ation of Christian workers which was born in 1970 when mem-
     bers of ACLI left the organization because they disagreed with
     its embrace of Socialism (see note 17 to chapter 3).

11. Italian politicians belonging to, respectively, Berlusconi's *Forza
     Italia* party, the Democratic Party (center left), *Noi con l'Italia-
     UDC* (center right), and the Democratic Party.

12. Augusto Del Noce (1910–1989) was a philosopher and political
     theorist. One of the most prominent Italian Catholic thinkers in
     the second half of the twentieth century, he predicted the collapse
     of Communism and the advent of a new type of post-Marxist

capitalistic society as the end result of the western process of secularization. See *The Crisis of Modernity* (Montreal: MQUP, 2015) and *The Age of Secularization* (Montreal: MQUP, 2017).

13. In the document *Per la città* addressed to the Ambrosian Church on January 14, 2016.

CHAPTER 17

A Church of the People

Archbishop of Milan

Eminence, in 2011 you became the archbishop of Milan. What events led to such a prestigious appointment?

My appointment was very normal, in the sense that it came through the ordinary procedure. There was an inquiry conducted by the nuncio to Italy, who proposed a list of candidates to the Congregation for Bishops, whose plenary chose my name by a wide majority. Based on this vote, which is not binding anyway because the pope can always change the decision, Benedict XVI went ahead with the appointment. He insisted on a very scrupulous investigation to make sure that the appointment had broad support. In exact adherence to all the proper procedures, I myself received the news from the nuncio, not from the pope, with whom I discussed the appointment to Milan only at the end of the process.

Did Benedict XVI intend to signal a break with the past, by appointing you archbishop of Milan?

The word "break" implies something traumatic, and I do not think that was the case. Like I already said about Pope Francis, also in this case, I prefer to speak of a discontinuity. This is a very important issue which is worth tackling head-on without beating around the bush. Appointing a new bishop to guide a diocese is not a routine action that recurs periodically and never changes anything. This is why in the end it is the pope who makes the decision with unchallengeable authority. Well, I believe that one of the strong points of the ecclesial institution is precisely the coexistence of the elements of continuity and discontinuity. In the transition associated with a succession—not only in the case of an episcopal seat, but also of the throne of Peter—these two elements are intertwined. There has to be continuity in regard to the Tradition of the Church. But, regarding pastoral guidance, change is often necessary, and it is one of the ways in which the life of the ecclesial community is continually regenerated. Now, it is clear that with my appointment as archbishop of Milan, Benedict XVI intended it to be a signal of discontinuity.

Are you talking about your predecessors, in particular Cardinal Martini, who governed the Archdiocese of Milan for over twenty years and left a deep mark both inside and outside the Ambrosian Church?

I have always been on good terms with both Cardinal Tettamanzi and Cardinal Martini. Tettamanzi and I had a very close relationship which began in the eighties, when we worked together at the Congregation for the Doctrine of the Faith alongside John Paul II. It continued at the CEI and endured through the last years of his life with a sense of affection and gratitude. I also won't forget that when I arrived in Milan, Cardinal Martini welcomed me with great openness, giving me advice that turned out to be very valuable and offering suggestions—at my request—about the first important appointments that I had to make.

Everybody knows that Cardinal Martini possessed a big personality. He had a powerful influence, not only on the Milanese Church, but on the universal Church. I think that his most important contribution was to communicate to priests and laypeople his authentic passion for the Word of God. He creatively reformulated the *lectio biblica* and contributed to notably improve the quality of the homilies we hear in the churches of our diocese. Cardinal Martini and I never hid our disagreements from one another, but that did not diminish our mutual respect. I met him for the last time ten days before he died. He struggled to speak, but found the strength to tell me that I was wrong to think that the Church had no power over the sacraments. I imagine he was mostly referring to the ordination of women. But such a position, in my opinion, is not compatible with the awareness, which the Church has always maintained and even formally taught, that we have received the sacraments in their most essential elements from the Lord.

With due distinctions, I must say that I feel my intellectual temperament is similar to his. Faced with the most burning anthropological and social problems, both of us always delved into them to their extreme conclusions. Martini, dissecting doubts with great subtlety, just gave glimpses of solutions, which practically always were interpreted in "progressive" terms. This approach made him an icon of a prophetic, modern Church in the eyes of the media. I, on the other hand, even though I try to address every doubt with realism, am convinced that I must always point to the certainties that the Church has reached, even if they may evolve in the future. Without certainties men cannot move.

Eminence, how did you react when you were appointed to Milan?

I had "mixed feelings" as the British say, a tangle of contradictory emotions. On the one hand, I did not want to leave Venice, where I'd thought that I would be able to conclude the work begun more than nine years before, remaining until the canonical retirement age. On the other hand, I was happy to come back home, because Milan is the mother Church where I was born and raised in life and faith. At the same time, I was well aware that the pope was entrusting me with a difficult task. In the beginning, I had to face some understandable uneasiness among a majority of people, along with a negative bias among a minority.

Was this due to your dramatic departure from the diocese of Milan, which you had to leave in order to become a priest, and which now saw you coming back to the highest position of authority?

No, my departure from the Venegono seminary played absolutely no part in this. That was a forty-year-old story, water under the bridge. In fact, every time I met my former classmates from the seminary, both in personal encounters and for annual class reunions, I had very beautiful and moving experiences. No, what caused unease and raised old prejudices was an incident that came out of the blue and, I must admit, deeply disturbed me.

Are you referring to the letter written by Fr. Julián Carrón,[1] Fr. Luigi Giussani's successor as the leader of CL, which, besides supporting your appointment as the next archbishop of Milan, contained some very critical judgments about Cardinals Martini and Tettamanzi?

I am referring, to be more precise, to the publication of that letter. Signed by Fr. Julián Carrón and addressed to the pope, it was a sensitive document which was supposed to remain secret. Instead, it was made public in 2012, among the first of the Vatileaks documents. I knew absolutely nothing of this letter. I was surprised, and so I sent Msgr. Mario Delpini, my vicar general at the time, to meet with Fr. Carrón and clarify the situation and then report it to the episcopal council. I have the impression that Fr. Carrón, as part of the consultations conducted by the nuncio, had meant to express legitimate concerns regarding the dwindling strength and power of the Christian witness in our times, but his phrasing was imprecise and somewhat clumsy. This is something he himself acknowledged.[2]

I must say, however, that the hailstorm of polemics that followed, which hurt me a lot, was not shared by the clergy except to a minimal extent, contrary to newspaper reports. Questions about Carrón's letter and my relations with CL were only ever brought up twice in the assemblies I held with priests of the diocese during that time. It is possible that some tried to use it against me, but in general saw the greatness of the Ambrosian clergy in their spontaneous attitude of respect and admiration towards their archbishop in filial obedience. In any case, I did not pull back, and it was actually in one of these assemblies with the priests that I said, "It is rare for someone to be burdened by two original sins as happened to me," speaking of my belonging to Communion and Liberation. On that same occasion, I explained that "my ecclesial sensibilities certainly bear the mark of the charism of Fr. Giussani, as well as of people like Wojtyła, Balthasar, and Ratzinger, but my only concern is that the Ambrosian Church grow in faith and charity on a common journey."

The most convincing answer to those who worried that I would act as a "CL bishop" came from the facts. In all my six years in Milan, as in my previous assignments, no one had cause to raise such an objection or managed to stir public dissent against my person. One of the things that pleased me most was something Pope Francis told me during the last meeting I had with him before I left my position in Milan: "I was deeply impressed by the fact that everybody recognized that, in all your years of episcopacy, you never played favorites with CL."

How did you mark the beginning of your mission in Milan?

Right after my Mass of installation and my meeting with the priests of the diocese, I set out to listen to the living reality of Milan. I did so with four gestures which I think expressed my desire to dialogue with everyone. I had meetings with people involved in politics, culture, the economy, and charitable works.

You were the archbishop of Milan for six years. What imprint did you want to give to your pastoral ministry in one of the largest dioceses in the world?

We are talking about the Church of St. Ambrose and St. Charles Borromeo, rich with history and educational, charitable, and cultural works. It is a complex and articulate reality, with over a thousand parishes and five million baptized and thus, one of the largest dioceses in the world by number of faithful (more than all the Catholics in countries like the Netherlands or Croatia). So, in front of all of this, my first reaction was that there was no new imprint to leave, only the attempt to deepen more and more the knowledge and love of Christ, trying to show how it impacts ordinary life.

I put great emphasis on the need for a renewed conversion of our Church in the fundamentals of the Christian life, reproposing the method described in the second chapter of the Acts of the Apostles (Acts 2:42–47). This is where we are given the four fundamental pillars to build the ecclesial community: the Eucharistic memory of Jesus, striving to share our own life with all our brothers, assimilating Christ's thought, and missionary action. In all my years of episcopate, not only in Milan, I have realized that in Europe, the idea of method is muddled for the most part. Method gets confused with a set of techniques—even very sophisticated techniques from the psychological and sociological standpoint—designed to adapt the Christian proposal to so-called modernity. Hence the frantic search for new languages and approaches, which has generated an overabundance of artificial and largely useless talk, contributing, in my view, to the worrisome decline of the European churches. By way of contrast, I have always been convinced that the question is much simpler. We must go back to the elementary Christian fact, identifying ourselves with the person and the history of Jesus and witnessing that Christianity is the most fascinating way to live one's own humanity. Do not get me wrong, it's obvious that the form and the language must constantly adapt. No one, for example, would dream of talking to today's youth about sexuality in the same way as when I was a teenager. But these are indeed techniques, which must not be mixed up with the method of Christian life, and cannot replace the witness of the encounter with Christ, which I experienced, and which as a consequence I want to propose to others.

What did your insistence on the fundamentals mean, concretely, for the life of the ecclesial community? Do you think your message got through?

I tried to communicate this message through my preaching, and above all through gestures, in both my personal and public encounters. From this point of view, the strongest and in some ways most surprising experience was undoubtedly the pastoral visit that involved all of the deaneries of the diocese over the two-year period from 2015 to 2017. I was struck by the quantity and quality of the participants. In all the assemblies I presided over, held at the end of the visits to the various districts, there were always hundreds of people, sometimes over a thousand, including people who did not regularly attend Church. They were well-prepared assemblies, first at the parochial level and then at the deanery level, to which people brought witnesses, questions, and proposals. I tried to answer them by entering into a dialogue in which I strove to bring out as much as possible the method of Christian life which I have just described. I particularly insisted on the importance of having the same mentality and sentiments as Jesus. And I was positively surprised by how a spontaneous sense of faith had endured among the people at these events. Many of them later thanked me, pointing out how novel the assemblies were. However, this doesn't mean my message was understood in its entirety. Let us say that I sowed the seeds and perhaps the fruits will come sometime later. Only a minority embraced my proposal for the method of Christian life. Many others, although they were not opposed to it, remained in the same position they were used to.

If I had to make a quick overall assessment, I would say that some of my suggestions were well received—for example, the importance of having a personal and communal subject who must give a public witness, the proposal of an educational community, the overcoming of the opposition between traditional associations and new movements, and the value of a constant dialogue with all the groups present in a pluralistic society, striving for civic friendship. But I must honestly recognize that the discussion of these fundamentals did not penetrate in depth.

Do you have an explanation for that?

First, we have to recognize that many believers lack the awareness of being a personal and communal subject. This is probably the main reason why it is difficult to repropose gestures that make the Christian announcement in a simple and decisive way. Let's be honest—even today, the parish remains the inevitable starting point. However, beyond providing the sacramental life, parishes are at risk of being boiled down to a network of initiatives and services. A French author published a book titled *The Pastor has Gone Insane*,[3] in which he recounts in a tongue-in-cheek way, the often-absurd conflicts between different parish groups—which may well offer wonderful services, but do so in complete isolation from each other. Then communion becomes, in the best-case scenario, a habit of being kind and polite, a form of religious and political correctness that depends on our initiative, rather than on a gift that comes to us from above and changes our lives.

When I speak of the fundamentals, I'm not referring to abstract concepts, but to the essential kernel of the life of a Christian community. For example, I have strongly emphasized the education to gratuitousness, but I have noticed a radical misunderstanding, whereby gratuitousness is confused with service or with charitable work:

"There are needy people and I make myself available to help them." That is sacrosanct. But education to gratuitousness means to learn to love the other and to give part of myself, so that the other may become a part of my life in the communion generated by Him who holds us together, by Christ. Just like the method is destroyed by confusing it with technique, so gratuitousness is emptied out when it is reduced to mere service. In the Italian Church, and in the Diocese of Milan in particular, *Caritas* and other charitable organizations have become very important. This is undoubtedly a positive fact, tied to the admirable generosity of thousands of volunteers. I was able to observe that many priests have found a convincing reason for their ministry by investing their energies in charitable works. But there is a risk of partiality. This is why, as archbishop of Milan, I constantly pointed out the unbreakable connection between charity and culture, in the sense that the preferential option for the poor lies within the overall proposal of the fundamentals of Christian life. It cannot be reduced to providing services.

I could go on and on with examples, but I will stop here. I also have to add that the invitation to go back to the fundamentals of Christian life echoes Fr. Giussani's proposal. In a way, this connection is inevitable, given my formation. To be blunt, the accusations of being a "CL bishop" are gone, but there is still diffidence about my history in Communion and Liberation. Even though CL is no longer subject to hostility the way it was forty years ago, and many of its adherents actively participate in parish life and collaborate with other ecclesial groups, some people still feel they must distance themselves from its method of educating one to the Christian life.

You have also affirmed, though, that the Ambrosian Church is still a Church of the people.[4] Doesn't that contradict what you just said?

Not at all. What we have discussed up to now concerns a laborious process of growth, and an image of Christian maturity that we must strive for. But this does not mean that we live in a desert. A strong religious sense imbued with Catholicism still endures in the Ambrosian people, regardless of statistics. Just think of the over one million people who go to Mass every Sunday, or of the vitality of our oratories, attended by thousands of young people. These are macroscopic facts that cannot be ignored, but there are also the smaller, every-day realities of which the archbishop of Milan is a privileged witness every time he is approached after a celebration or assembly by people who confide in him their sorrows and ask for a prayer. Certainly, once people walk out of the church, their criteria for judgment and their behavioral models have little to do with the Christian vision. But the growing chasm between faith and life signal precisely a dichotomy which does not erase the tension between belief and action.

This is why, in my farewell homily, I said that the Ambrosian Church is still, at its roots, a church of the people. This fact has two important consequences. As long as the roots are healthy, the tree can grow and flourish again, even if we cannot know how and when in advance. Also, a church with popular roots can truly be a church for everybody, because every man and every woman by encountering it can always find the life perspective that will lead them to happiness. We need to get rid of the depressing mystique about "people far from the Church" and the nebulous strategies to bring them closer. No one is far from the human experience of affection, work, and rest. The more believers are able to live these three aspects conforming to Christ, the more they immediately find themselves close to everybody. In other words, the fact that the Ambrosian Church remains a church of the people contradicts the idea that Catholicism is on retreat and faith is on the road to extinction.

Based on this perspective, we decided to compare our efforts with the attempts at church reform in a few great cities of the world. Thus, I invited four authoritative ecclesial personalities from four different continents to speak in the Duomo—Cardinal Schönborn of Vienna, Cardinal Luis Antonio Tagle of Manila, Cardinal John Onaiyekan of Abuja in Nigeria, and Cardinal Seán Patrick O'Malley of Boston.[5] Each spoke at two separate events—one for priests and another for laypeople. And in a certain sense, Pope Francis's visit to Milan gave us an indirect look at the Church in Latin America.

Notes to Chapter 17

1. Julián Carrón (1950–) is a priest, biblical scholar, and author. Since 2005, he has been the president of the Fraternity of Communion and Liberation, as recommended by the late founder Fr.

Luigi Giussani. His letter to Benedict XVI in March 2011 was addressed to the apostolic nuncio to Italy, Msgr. Giuseppe Bertello. Together with other Vatileaks documents, it was published by Gianluigi Nuzzi in *Sua Santità—Dalla scrivania del Papa le prove degli scandali del Vaticano* (Milano: Chiarelettere, 2012).

2. Julián Carrón, *Dov'è Dio?* (Milano: Piemme, 2017), 175–76.

3. Jean Mercier, *Monsieur le curé fait sa crise* (Paris: Ed. de l'Emmanuel, 2016).

4. In his farewell homily in the Duomo, on September 8, 2017.

5. Luis Antonio Tagle (1957–) is a Filipino archbishop and cardinal. From 2011 to 2019, he was archbishop of Manila. Since 2019, he has been the prefect of the Congregation for the Evangelization of Peoples. John Onaiyekan (1944–) is a Nigerian archbishop and cardinal. From 1994 to 2019, he was archbishop of Abuja. Seán Patrick O'Malley (1944–) is an American archbishop and cardinal. Since 2003, he has been the archbishop of Boston.

CHAPTER 18

A Metropolis in Search of its Soul

The Church and the City

Being a Catholic in Milan means being a part of the Ambrosian Church. Does the adjective only refer to a past history, or does it denote a distinctive character even today?

The first thing I want to emphasize is that an Ambrosian rite actually exists. This is the main reason why the Archdiocese of Milan—unlike other very large dioceses such as Mexico City or Madrid—maintained its original unity without losing parts of its territory. As we know, the Ambrosian character originates from the figure of St. Ambrose, a Roman prefect. He was a government official who suddenly found himself in a new role as a religious authority, without quite knowing what this new responsibility even meant, so much so that he asked for the assistance of old Simplicianus, who would go on to be—if only briefly—his successor. Ambrose was well aware of the distinction between the ecclesial and the civil spheres, but he also knew that in real life they intersect. Here lies, in my opinion, the root of the Ambrosian character, which would be further deepened by the magisterium of St. Charles Borromeo. His great work of Church reform concerned the priests and their formation (the seminary), the organization of parishes, the introduction of pastoral visits, and the importance of Christian doctrine and of the sacraments for the daily life of the people of God. And all this was accompanied by a preaching on the virtues that radically impacted civil society as well.

The "Speech to the City" that the archbishop of Milan gives every year on the feast of St. Ambrose, which is both a civil and a religious holiday, is part of this tradition. I tried my best to make my speeches relevant to the current "change of epoch," risking some judgments about our society and offering to all the proposal of the Christian life, with a desire to contribute to the common good. But if there is a project that, in my view, can be considered a beautiful fruit of the Ambrosian spirit, it is definitely the initiative of the Dialogues on the Good Life, which was born over a breakfast with Professor Cacciari. In these events, we invited people engaged with various aspects of the city's social life to discuss the great issues of our time—from migrations to the new forms of poverty, from the economy to the overbearing power of technology—trying to come to a shared judgment. I think I can say that with these Dialogues on the Good Life, we created a virtuous circle between a Church attentive to what moves in civil society and a civil society attentive to the proposal of the Church.

You have lived through and responded to the major events and the profound transformations that the city of Milan has experienced over last few years. What struck you the most about this change?

When I was a young university student in the sixties, I would often walk across the Piazza del Duomo and be intrigued by the little knots of people chatting and arguing among themselves, at times even vociferously, about Milan's and Italy's problems. Then came the Years of Lead,[1] of terrorism, which threw our country into fear and agony, and swept away that kind of social interaction, so that it has now been forgotten. Well, if there is something positive that I observed in major events like the 2015 Expo and other initiatives such *Tempo di Libri*, the Milano Music Week, or the *Salone del Mobile*, just to give some examples, it is that they helped bring many citizens together again out in the open.[2] I'm not talking about going for a walk or window shopping, but about occasions for social interaction.

As I have often stressed, man is a person-in-relation and he cannot renounce coexistence, that is, sharing the adventure of existence with other people. It seems to me that the taste for being together has returned, and this facilitates the spontaneity and informal creativity that are so decisive for the life of the person and the community. It is one of the signs—in my opinion, actually the most significant sign—of Milan being reborn, even though we must not forget the old and new problems that await solutions.

In this regard, you said that Milan is searching for a new soul.[3] That statement met with much controversy. Wasn't your judgment a bit too harsh?

That was the reproach I got. But I didn't intend to deny the passion and energy of a city that is flourishing again. I wanted to stress the need for Milan to communicate what the criterion is that can give guidance and unity to all these changes. The word "soul" precisely means the principle that gives life and makes it grow. We could also use the word *senso*, understood as the meaning of life but also as the direction to take. We cannot content ourselves with finding it only in economic growth, also because there remain places of great poverty, both in the city and in the suburbs. Some peripheral areas bore the weight of the first wave of immigration from Southern Italy, and today, they are in the midst of a second migratory wave from the Southern Mediterranean and from Europe's poorest countries. There is a tradition of generosity and dedication in Milan that has prevailed to help these newcomers. Just think of how associations, parishes, and civil institutions and organizations have welcomed them. The phrase *Milan col coeur in man* still applies.[4] But generosity is not enough; a vision is needed.

Etymologically, Milan means "middle town." It has a central role that goes beyond the borders of Italy; it is a laboratory of the future of Europe, and more so than the other capitals can be, because its cosmopolitanism is open and evolving, without the ideological incrustations of London or Paris, whose models of integration have so visibly failed. This central role of Milan and its region also holds in relation to European Catholicism, and for the challenges that the Church faces in the Old World. Benedict XVI reminded us of this when he received the Lombard bishops for the *ad limina* visit in February of 2013, the last audience before he resigned. "Lombardy must be the believing and beating heart of Europe," he told us.

Because of immigration, Milan—and, more generally, the entire diocese—has seen a rapid growth in the presence of various religious faiths, particularly Islam. What has that meant for the Ambrosian Church?

It has meant that interreligious dialogue, whose importance has grown in a way that ten years ago was unimaginable, has matured. First of all, the ecumenical dialogue with our Christian brothers. I was able to participate in strong gestures of unity with the Orthodox world, welcoming the patriarch of Constantinople, Bartholomew, to Milan on the occasion of the Constantinian Year in 2013. We also commemorated the fifth centenary of Luther's Reform with the Protestants. The pope of the Orthodox Coptic Christians, Tawadros II, visited Milan several times.[5] We have a long-standing tradition of friendship with the Jews, which was greatly and enthusiastically promoted by Cardinal Martini and Rabbi Laras (who recently passed away).[6] This tradition still continues.

In regards to the world of Islam, there is something interesting that I want to emphasize: Not only has the Church maintained open the dialogue with Muslims, but it has also facilitated the encounter between different Islamic groups that tend to either ignore each other or to have conflictual relationships due to their nationalities or religious traditions. In order to meet and talk to each other, the Milanese Islamic communities often go through the Catholics. The Ambrosian Church has taken on an increasingly important role in this regard.

Msgr. Delpini, my successor, decided to hold a minor synod called "Church of the Peoples" to discuss how the Milanese Church needs to change in front of the arrival into our land of believers from many ethnic backgrounds. It is a farsighted decision. It's no longer enough to talk about multiethnic challenges or about integration without thinking about the ways in which who we are and how we live will have to change. A new configuration of the Milanese Church is on the horizon, determined also by the presence of these new brothers. The future of our communities will depend to a large extent on this next step.

There is always the question of building one or more mosques in Milan.

Yes, this is still a problem, and quite frankly I don't understand it. I have always said, since I was in Venice, that we cannot continue to pay lip service to beautiful ideas like religious freedom without giving people the chance to worship in accordance with their beliefs.

Obviously, in the case of a mosque, it will be necessary to verify who is behind the request, to see whether it is a local community or a foreign power, just as it is right to demand that all preaching be delivered by a well-prepared, qualified imam and be given in Italian, with the exception of prayer in the strict sense. Our tradition must also be respected, but I do hope that no one plans to build a mosque near Piazza del Duomo. Among other things, it is important to assess whether it would be preferable to build multiple places of worship suitable to the different Islamic communities in our territory, rather than one big mosque for the entire Milan area. I have to say that I have not encountered pertinent objections to these observations of mine but then when we tried to implement these principles, we ran into trouble also because the bureaucratic process to carry out this new initiative is unfortunately very long and complicated. Anyone not on board with the proposal was able to use that as an excuse.

"Being the archbishop of Milan is a terrible job," Cardinal Schuster used to say back in the fifties.[7] What was the greatest difficulty you met doing this "terrible job"?

I think it is the lack of face-to-face interaction, which at times became painful. It is difficult to personally encounter the faithful and especially priests. In a diocese like Milan, which has five million baptized Catholics, you don't have the opportunity to go beyond a quick greeting and a handshake most of the time. Every year, I would meet with all the priests—nearly two thousand of them—in liturgical or formational assemblies, plus several hundred private audiences. In any case, the numbers are so vast that they require a synodal form of government. This is a necessity even more than a choice. In fact, the episcopal vicars of each region are the ones who "bishop" the territory. Only a few of the vicars are actually auxiliary bishops, but in my opinion they should all be.

And what was the biggest satisfaction?

There were many things that gave me satisfaction. Perhaps it was because of my advanced age, but the numerous opportunities I had to meet young people were a source of great and deep consolation to me. They filled the Duomo several times a year, responding to my invitation. And they invited me to schools and universities, and even to the great hall of Malpensa. One particular source of joy was the relationship with the seminarians of Venegono. An ongoing conversation developed with them, as we reflected together on the beauty of the priestly vocation. I was positively surprised by the welcome I received from the secular world and civil institutions, right up to the last, unexpected recognition of the *Grande Medaglia d'Oro* unanimously awarded to me by the City of Milan.[8] And I was moved by many gestures, first of all by the opening of the Holy Door of the Duomo that marked the beginning of the Jubilee Year of Mercy.[9]

I remember above all the joy and the emotion I shared with tens of thousands of people during two events on Piazza Duomo. The first, called "Come See this Spectacle" (referring to the Cross), was held in 2014, with the exposition of the Holy Nail. The second, called "You are All Invited," in the context of the 2015 World's Fair, centered on Jesus, the food of man, that is, the Eucharist. These were events that united art and faith under the banner of beauty, with music, songs, prayers, and witnesses, which could be described as a sort of sacred representations for our time. Even some famous personalities participated for free. Some people discounted these events as ephemeral and faddish emotional experiences. I am convinced, on the contrary, that the Christian experience also gives value to these aspects of our communal life.

Your ministry in Milan began and ended with papal visits, by Benedict XVI in 2012 and by Francis in 2017. Was this only a coincidence, or did it mean something more profound?

I would remind you that I had already welcomed Benedict XVI in Venice in May 2011. I believe that very few of my brother bishops had three papal visits over the course of their episcopate, and I regard this as a privilege of grace and a priceless gift. I think that certain events do not repeat just by chance, but instead reveal the thread of a providential design. And this is the case of the papal visits to Milan.

Benedict XVI came at the beginning of June in 2012, a few months after my arrival in the Ambrosian diocese. It was a visit that had been planned for a long time on the occasion of the 7th World Encounter of Families. He spent an entire weekend in Milan. One of the most beautiful moments, which remains fixed in my memory, was Pope Benedict XVI's dialogue with the families at the Bresso airport. I was particularly struck by his wonderful unscripted answer to a question about divorced and remarried couples. He said that it is not enough for the Church to intend to love these people, but that "they must be able to see and feel this love." And he added that "their suffering, if truly and internally accepted, is a gift to the Church." These moving words displayed an attention and sensitivity to this problem that did not suddenly pop up with *Amoris Laetitia,* as a crude and superficial narrative has suggested.

If I remember correctly, Benedict XVI's visit to Milan took place during a particularly difficult and painful moment.

It's true. Only a few days before, the pontiff's butler, Paolo Gabriele, had been arrested. He was accused of stealing and releasing Benedict XVI's private documents, the so-called Vatileaks scandal. Then, exactly on the vigil of his visit to Milan, there was the earthquake in Emilia.[10] On the night of June 1, a concert had been planned to honor the pope at the Teatro alla Scala, with Beethoven's Ninth Symphony directed by maestro Daniel Barenboim. Immediately, some people questioned whether it would be appropriate for the Holy Father to participate in a celebration just as Italy mourned the earthquake victims. In the afternoon, the Secretariat of State suggested to Benedict XVI not to go to the Scala to avoid controversy. I told him that it would be a big mistake, that Milan would not understand his absence. At the moment he did not answer, and he retired to his room. When he came out, he told me, "I have slightly modified the speech I had prepared for la Scala. Yes, I will go." It was a short but absolutely extraordinary speech. Benedict XVI commented on the *Hymn to Joy* in the context of the pain and suffering of that day, which revealed that "we are not in need of an unreal discourse by a distant God," such as could be found precisely in Schiller's *Hymn*, but rather, "we seek a God who is close."[11]

To me, it was the latest of many demonstrations of Pope Benedict XVI's genius and his striking ability to subvert the usual way of looking at things. And, I'd like to add, it was also a demonstration of his freedom to make a different choice than what his entourage suggested. At the end of the visit, I told him, "I imagine that Your Holiness must be very tired after these busy days." He responded, "Yes, I am very tired. But I also feel quite consoled," pointing to the crowd that flanked his popemobile on the road to Linate airport. And indeed, the participation of the people was truly remarkable. It was exactly the same on the occasion of Pope Francis's visit.

In this case, the preliminaries were a bit complicated. After a first announcement, the trip was postponed, but then Francesco's visit to Milan succeeded beyond the most optimistic expectations. Could it be said that after a suspenseful start there was a happy ending?

It was clear from the beginning that Pope Francis wished to make a pastoral visit to Milan. He told me so in one of my first private audiences with him. "One cannot not go to Milan," he said. The year 2015 was mentioned as a possible date, but the pope was not thrilled with the idea of having his visit coincide with the World's Fair. He limited himself to sending a video message on the occasion of its opening. The visit was set for May 2016, but it was postponed because he had too many back-to-back commitments in the year of the Jubilee of Mercy.

In any case, his visit, which lasted little more than 10 hours, turned out to be a formidable event.[12] And it is not true that the pope changed the program we proposed to him. His visit to the Case Bianche neighborhood,[13] to show his closeness to those left behind, was proposed by us, not imposed by him, as some foolishly insinuated. The most emotional moment was undoubtedly the pope's encounter with the prisoners at the San Vittore prison,[14] whom he insisted on greeting one by one. Personally, I was struck by his direct way of introducing himself: "I am here because every one of you right now is Jesus for me." In all of his encounters, he was able to cut right to people's hearts, inviting them to overcome the resignation that renders us unable to share in Christian joy. The Milanese immediately took to him, coming to greet him along the roads and participating in large numbers in the celebrations.

The large crowd was not a surprise to me, since I know how well-loved Francesco is. The crowd at Mass in the Parco di Monza was estimated at a million people.[15] It was moving to see them smiling, in spite of the strain of having had to walk several miles. The true surprise, also for the pope, was the reception he got from the crown of around 80,000 candidates for Confirmation gathered in the San Siro stadium. It was the final moment of a grueling visit, and Pope Francis was visibly exhausted. "I am afraid I may not be able to make it," he confided to me on the way to San Siro. Then, before the incredible spectacle of so many spontaneously happy and joyful teenagers, I saw the weariness disappear from his face. The Holy Father was regenerated, so to speak, allowing him to address the youth in an effective and convincing way, like a grandfather to his grandchildren.

Milan was fascinated by Francis, but Francis was also very struck by Milan. I remember how, as we drove in the popemobile through the crowd at the Parco di Monza, he kept asking, "But how many are they, how many?" Then, privately, he told me that he had only seen such popular mobilization in Latin America and that he would have never expected it in Milan.

You once said that being the archbishop of Milan helped you know yourself better. Can I ask what you discovered?

Milan resized me, in the sense that it brought me back to my correct and better size. Being the archbishop of Milan involves a frantic agenda that brought to light, besides my ability, all my personal limitations as well. In my encounters with simple people, in my visits to places marked by suffering and marginalization, but also in my relationships with the cultural and civil institutions of such a big and complex place like the Ambrosian diocese, I was able to measure the distance between the enormous task I was called to and the little I was actually able to do. I believe that this experience is typical of all archbishops of Milan: The more you adhere to reality, the more you realize the true "size" of your own personality. You cannot fly away; you have to stay there with your feet on the ground. It is what all of my predecessors must have lived through, and it is written in the coat of arms of St. Charles: *humilitas*, (humility). I, too, was able to learn this humility a little, day by day, feeling the burden but also the wonder of living the grace I had been given of guiding the Ambrosian Church for six years.

Notes to Chapter 18

1. The expression *Anni di piombo* is used to describe the period from the late sixties to the early eighties, which was marked by street violence involving both left-wing and right-wing political extremists, political assassinations, bombings, and other forms of terrorism.

2. The 2015 World's Fair, which took place in Milan from May 1 to October 31, 2015 on the theme "Feeding the Planet, Energy for Life." *Tempo di Libri* is a book fair; Milano Music Week is a live music festival taking place in many different venues around the city; and *Salone del Mobile* is one of the largest furniture trade fairs in the world.

3. In the address to the city on December 7, 2014, *Un nuovo umanesimo per Milano e le terre ambrosiane* [A new humanism for Milan and the Ambrosian lands]. See Angelo Scola, *Percorsi di vita buona. I discorsi di Sant'Ambrogio* (Milano: Centro Ambrosiano, 2017), 72.

4. Milanese dialect for "Milan presenting its heart in its hand," referring to the city's traditional spirit of generosity and openness to strangers.

5. Tawadros II (1952–) is an Egyptian Orthodox bishop. Since 2012, he has been the pope of the Coptic Orthodox Church and patriarch of Alexandria.

6. Giuseppe Laras (1935–2017) was a rabbi and academic. From 1980 to 2005, he was chief rabbi of the Jewish community of Milan.

7. Alfredo Ildefonso Schuster (1880–1954) was a Benedictine monk, archbishop, and cardinal. He was archbishop of Milan from 1929 to 1954. In 1996, he was beatified by John Paul II.

8. The Great Gold Medal is the highest honor bestowed by the city of Milan. It is best known as the *Ambrogino d'Oro* (Little Golden Ambrose) because it bears an image of St. Ambrose, the patron saint of Milan, and is awarded on his feast day, December 7. Cardinal Scola received it on December 7, 2017, at the end of his

active episcopal ministry, "for his contribution to build a stronger and more integrated city."

9. The Extraordinary Jubilee of Mercy was proclaimed by Pope Francis on March 13, 2015, on the fiftieth anniversary of the end of the Second Vatican Council. The jubilee began on December 8, 2015 and ended on November 20, 2016.

10. Emilia is a region south of Milan, across the Po River. The 2012 earthquake consisted of several tremors (up to magnitude 6 on the Richter scale) between May 20 and May 31. About thirty people died and thousands lost their homes.

11. Pope Benedict XVI, *Address at the La Scala Theater in Milan* (June 1, 2012).

12. In the end, Pope Francis's pastoral visit to Milan took place on March 25, 2017.

13. The Case Bianche is a residential project on the southeastern outskirts of Milan, mostly inhabited by impoverished people and recent immigrants.

14. San Vittore is the best-known prison in the Milan area. It is also the most centrally located and overcrowded.

15. A large historic park north of the city. It includes a former royal palace and an autodrome, which hosts every year a Formula One Grand Prix.

CHAPTER 19

A New Kind of Papacy

The Conclave of 2013 and the Relationship with Pope Francis

Your Eminence, how did you experience Pope Benedict XVI's resignation from the papal ministry, which he announced on February 11, 2013? Had you received any indication that Pope Benedict XI was about to make such a shocking decision?

For me, as for everyone, it was an absolute surprise. When I received the news, I was bewildered. Then, upon reflection, a few things came back to mind. I remember that, already before reaching the canonical age of seventy-five, Ratzinger as a cardinal had repeatedly asked John Paul II to allow him to leave his position as prefect of the Congregation for the Doctrine of the Faith. In vain, because as I described, the constant reply by the Holy Father was, "You will stay here as long as I am here. I cannot be the pope without you next to me." If he already felt under strain when he was a prefect, I can imagine the deep, not only physical, fatigue that must have built up in Ratzinger during his almost eight years of pontificate, and now at an old age. Then I thought how increasingly difficult long-distance air travel had become for him, due to the small strokes he had suffered, the first taking place in 1991 precisely on the day that I was scheduled to be consecrated bishop at his hands. In 2012, his secretary, Fr. Georg, confided to me that after his trip to Mexico and Cuba, Benedict XVI had suffered some health complications and the doctors could not find the right therapy. Therefore, they had advised him against future intercontinental travels. Finally, what happened with Vatileaks, with the problems involving the Vatican bureaucracy, definitely did not help him. I believe that all these objective factors together made him feel the disproportion between the huge weight of the responsibility that he had obediently accepted when he became pope and his strength, which he felt was dwindling. I already said that Benedict XVI was one of the humblest popes in history. Well, in my opinion, his resignation can only be understood from the perspective of a humble acceptance of reality. His was a gesture of obedience to an objective situation.

Some people have objected to the fact that he is being called "pope emeritus." Is that an appropriate title, in your opinion?

If a serious and rigorous personality like Ratzinger approved this title, it means that he thoroughly examined it, and it was not improvised. To tell the truth, during the congregations immediately before the conclave, a few cardinals stressed the need for new canonical norms to define better the issues involved in the resignation of a pontiff. Instinctively, I am against the mania of legislating everything, even though a collegially developed approach might be of some use in the future. In the present, it seems to me that Ratzinger's behavior is very transparent and exemplary. He chose to retreat to a monastery, specifically to the *Mater Ecclesiae* that John Paul II opened inside the Vatican, to be a contemplative and prayerful presence that accompanies the pontifical ministry of Francis. And this is what the pope emeritus is doing, without lending himself to be used in any way, while maintaining a cordial relationship with Pope Francis, who professes himself grateful for his prayers and advice.

You entered the conclave of 2013 as pope and left it as a cardinal. This is, at least, the interpretation by the mass media. Tell me honestly, did you suffer because of this image as the defeated candidate?

Let me clarify. This interpretation came only from the media. The reality was always very different. There was no objective reason for that statement. Today, we might say that it was a piece of "fake news," designed to sound plausible. As Cardinal Walter Kasper said once,[1] the conclave of 2013 started without an obvious candidate, unlike the conclave of 2005 in which one name came immediately to the fore—namely Ratzinger's, who would go on to be elected. This is the pure and simple truth.

A person I trust told me a story. At the moment of saying goodbye to your collaborators before leaving for Rome to participate in the conclave, you said: "The resignation of Benedict XVI is an unprecedented fact in the history of the Church of the last few centuries, and it preannounces a new pope who will be just as unprecedented." You started off, but then turned around and added, "And you can be at peace that it will not be me." Is that true?

Yes, that is what I said and what I always thought. I said it also during those days talking to the journalists who asked me for predictions—probably the next pope would not be European, much less Italian. This because Benedict XVI's totally unexpected step was not just about the past, but contained an indication for the future, namely, that in that moment, the Church needed something outside the conventional wisdom. But journalists did not give up on their conventional wisdom, quite the contrary.

However, you still did not answer my question. Did you suffer for being depicted as the loser?

The answer is implicit in what I just said. I never believed in the possibility of becoming pope. And thus, I did not suffer for that reason. I must admit, though, that because of what the newspapers wrote, I suffered a degree of marginalization. After the conclave, I was considered the adversary who lost the race with Bergoglio, the cardinal who was nostalgic for the previous popes, the man of the past. Obviously, I was not happy about that.

I imagine you were also not happy about the CEI press release immediately after the election of Pope Francis, wishing well to "Cardinal Angelo Scola, elected to be the successor of Peter." How do you explain this blunder? And how did you react?

I have been told that somebody in a hurry clicked on the wrong press release, among those that had been prepared beforehand with the names and bios of about ten candidates. Staffers at the CEI Press Office apparently had taken seriously what the newspapers were writing, so I was one of the *papabili*. Many people called me to say it was a scandal and that I should intervene and ask for the resignation of whoever was responsible. Perhaps, contrary to appearances, I am a bit naïve, but I did not take the incident too seriously. Given that the story was refuted by the facts, it seemed useless to complain about a blunder by a press person. It would only have the effect of going from the ridiculous to the pathetic.

Do you think that mass media have an outsize influence on what goes on in the Church?

You see, in Church history it happened more than once that the powers-that-be interfered in the conclave. At the beginning of last century, and thus not too long ago, Emperor Franz Joseph of Austria vetoed the election of the secretary of state at that time, Cardinal Mariano Rampolla, to the papacy. But then the Holy Spirit knows how to write straight with men's crooked lines, and that conclave elected Cardinal Giuseppe Sarto, who took the name Pius X, a holy pope.[2]

My impression is that today the mass media end up—in a very analogical sense, for sure—playing the role of a modern emperor, or even think that such role belongs to them. Sadly, all of us carry some prejudices with us, but those who have an ethically sensitive job such as a journalist should, at least, not let prejudice fossilize into ideology and fantasies replace reality. I myself have been burned by this, as I already said in reference to my belonging to CL. However, I must say that I always had a good relationship with many journalists, including those of a secular orientation, and that I have felt comfortable talking to them directly and personally, something I have never tried to avoid. Once, in New York, I was invited by the editor of the *Wall Street Journal* to a meeting with the editorial board of that prestigious newspaper.[3] It was not an interview, but an informal conversation in the editorial office because, as the editor explained to me, for those who work in the news, face-to-face dialogue is fundamentally important, despite all the new media. I thought it was a very poignant remark. Moreover, as we well know, for a journalist the temptation of a scoop is harder to beat than the sexual temptation.

Once you said that we must "learn" every pope, trying to understand his logic, his style and his message. What has your personal learning about Pope Francis been like?

When we say that the election of the pope is assisted by the Holy Spirit, who ensures the essential infallibility of the Church, it is not just a way of speaking. The various interventions that succeed or fail, the great deeds or many weaknesses of the men of the Church, all the vicissitudes that seem to push in one direction or another, they are all means the Holy Spirit uses to steer the boat of Peter. Therefore, I believe that it is absolutely necessary to unite ourselves with the figure of the pope, with a feeling of deep and sincere empathy. This learning process is even more necessary for a pontiff who is not European but Latin American, with a mentality and an approach that for us is unusual. On the other hand, I would like to recall that something similar already happened when Pope John Paul II was elected. He presented himself immediately as a very different personality compared to previous popes, even though his philosophical and theological elaboration was still rooted in a robust European cultural tradition. Even more so, the appearance of Francis as pope has been a healthy punch in the stomach that the Holy Spirit has used to wake us up.

Personally, when I went through the learning process I was talking about, I identified a number of elements that characterize the action and the thought of Pope Francis, precisely in that order because he starts from doing and then arrives at saying, he begins with gestures and then gets to teachings. The first element is his extraordinary ability to give signs of closeness and affection to everybody, in particular to those who are marginalized and left out, against what he calls "throw-away culture." Secondly, he relies on a very Christocentric style of preaching, which emerges clearly in all his speeches, but especially in the homilies at Santa Marta and the Wednesday catecheses. Pope Francis tackles all questions in genuinely evangelical terms, and does it with a communicative power that relies on examples, and with a temperament that is not afraid of making judgments. He says what he thinks and he strikes people precisely because he puts himself at stake and lets himself be called into question by the Gospel he announces, and this is very convincing. The third element is a culture of the common people, from which we Europeans have a lot to learn. Let us not forget that Bergoglio was one of the promoters of the transformation of liberation theology. He made it evolve towards a theology of the people, without the Marxist ideological superstructure that two documents of the Congregation for the Doctrine of the Faith had warned against in the eighties.[4] His way of thinking is typical of a form of popular Catholicism that had to face enormous social and environmental problems.

Finally, there is his magisterium, which is not in the least naïve from the standpoint of thought. Even though he never was an academic in a strict sense, Bergoglio has a solid intellectual formation which is founded not only on having assimilated the message of St. Ignatius within the Society of Jesus, but has been nourished by the texts of great theologians and philosophers, like Möhler, Przywara, and Guardini; French Jesuits like de Lubac and Fessard; and Balthasar.[5] He also took advantage of the studies of important Latin American thinkers like Miguel Ángel Fiorito, Amelia Podetti, Lucio Gera, Alberto Methol Ferré, and Juan Carlos Scannone.[6] He thus arrived at formulating a "polyhedric" thought marked by an overall harmony which preserves the specificity of each part.[7] This has been highlighted well by Massimo Borghesi's recent book on the intellectual biography of Jorge Mario Bergoglio.[8] We need to keep into account all the factors I listed if we want to truly understand the features that Francis is giving his pontificate.

Did you know Bergoglio before he became pope?

When I was rector of the Lateran University, I went several times to Buenos Aires, because of the very close relationships I kept with UCA, the Pontifical Catholic University of Argentina. I had an occasion to go and meet Bergoglio as a visit of courtesy. I can say that I started to know him better, however, only in subsequent years, working with him in the congregations of the Holy See and of the General Secretariat of the Synod of Bishops, of which we were both members. I remember the subtleness of his contributions and his serious and courteous manners. During meeting recesses, he almost always remained seated at his place, quiet and focused on his notes, which suggested a very reserved personality. Or at least that was my impression. For this reason also, I was struck by the open, jovial, and ironic temper that he has displayed since he became pope. I see in this a confirmation of the special "grace of state" imparted to those who are elected to the throne of Peter. As Balthasar used to say, it is the mission that dictates the form of vocation and molds the personality. In the case of Pope Francis, this phenomenon has been so evident that it cannot but fill us with awe.

The impression is that your personal relationship with Francis went from awkwardness mixed with coldness—evidenced by him missing meetings, or canceling them at the last minute—to great reciprocal esteem, until the moving embrace before the crowd in Milan. Is that so?

If I remember correctly, there were two canceled meetings, and in both cases, they were public—one at Policlinico Gemelli for the anniversary of the foundation, and the other with the representatives of the World's Fair from Milan. The pope did not show up because he was slightly indisposed, but some people chose to speculate, insinuating that he did not want to meet me. If that were true, he would have refused to meet me also privately, whereas precisely in those two periods I had several personal meetings with Pope Francis. I must say that every time I asked him for an audience, he received me promptly, giving me all the time needed and entertaining me with great familiarity. Furthermore, he did ask me for some advice, for example during the breaks at the two synodal assemblies on the family, and a few times even by phone. His cordial availability was for me an intimate consolation, when I was facing the gossip I just mentioned. It took the pope's visit to Milan to put an end to all those baseless insinuations.

Everybody remembers Cardinal Scola's voice cracked with emotion and teary eyes while he thanked the pope after the celebration at the Parco di Monza.

Oh, no, I just suddenly lost my voice . . . I am joking, obviously. Indeed, it was a truly emotional moment. I was looking at the pope and starting to see signs of exhaustion due to a grueling visit, in which he had not held back anything, and this moved me once again to recognize the great strength of faith of this man, who has already accepted to pay the price of a total gift of himself. At the same time, I had in front of me the spectacle of an incredible crowd who cheered him and showed him its affection. The combination of these elements produced in me a storm of emotions, certainly facilitated also by my not-so-young age.

You spoke earlier of a learning process about Pope Francis. Has this meant also a change in your way of being a bishop, and a transformation of your pastoral style?

I am not one of those who changed their pectoral cross, replacing it with one made of tin, in order to imitate the pope. I kept the one I had. And I kept presiding over solemn ceremonies wearing very precious *casulae*, or chasubles, kept in the Museum of the Duomo, as tradition requires. At the ordination of new priests, archbishops of Milan used to wear a ring with a splendid cameo which belonged to Cardinal Schuster. I did not give it up. I would feel ridiculous if I had to take on a style, meaning an external demeanor, which is not mine. What provokes me is the way of making a total gift of oneself, and the closeness to others that Francis witnesses to. I try to mold my personality and my pastoral ministry to that.

In the final years of your episcopal ministry in Milan, you performed various gestures like frequently visiting low-income communities and prisons, having meals with groups of refugees, and auctioning gifts to support the Family & Work Fund,[9] just to give some examples. Can we regard them as signs of a "conversion" to the Francis model?

To tell the truth, gestures of solidarity with the poor and the marginalized have been a constant of my ministry from the start. The true novelty, which no one noticed however, is that I always treated these people not as if they were in a separate category but as partners in dialogue like everyone else. In Grosseto, I used to visit AIDS patients when this disease still meant terrible suffering and certain death, and we would read a pastoral letter together, just like I did at parish meetings and with various organizations. I did the same at the women's prison in Venice. I daresay then that there is nothing new in the gestures you listed, except that they have been put in the spotlight of public opinion and emphasized a bit, for two reasons. The first is certainly their consonance with the teaching and action of Pope Francis. The second is the context in which I performed them because, especially in Milan, they have a relevance and a value, also symbolic, that they did not have in Grosseto, at the Lateran, and in Venice.

I must add something else in order to fully answer. In recent months, after I left my position as archbishop of Milan, I have been able to look back to my twenty-seven years as a bishop from enough distance to reflect about what I did and also about how I could have done things differently. As I already said, I have always been convinced that there is no more precious gift a bishop can give to his people than his magisterium. This does not mean undervaluing the importance of gestures. However, looking back, I must admit that the proportion between the time and energy I dedicated to the magisterium and that reserved for meeting and direct contacts perhaps was a bit out of balance because of the preponderant weight taken by the first aspect.

Pope Francis receives many praises and just as many criticisms. Do you agree with any of them?

If there is one thing that Pope Francis's many detractors and also many admirers share in common, it is an unbalanced judgment. Those who mistrust him and suspect him, or even openly accuse him, of promoting heretical positions are out of touch with reality. But also, those who exalt him as the pope who is trying to bring the Church back to live according to the Gospel, after pontificates marked by rigidity and triumphalism, do him a bad disservice. The former are angry because Francis does not say what they think. The latter feel content because allegedly Francis says what they have said and thought over the last fifty years, which saw the betrayal of the Second Vatican Council, which only now is being finally and fully implemented. This is not how things stand. I just expressed my thoughts about Pope Francis. I can add that I feel a special consonance with him on the insistence that the category of the encounter is decisive for a believer. "Being a Christian is not the result of an ethical choice or a lofty idea, but the encounter with an event, a person, which gives life a new horizon and a decisive direction." Francis quotes this sentence by Benedict XVI in one of the first paragraphs of the apostolic exhortation *Evangelii Gaudium*,[10] which is, to some extent, the manifesto of Francis's pontificate. And to stress its importance, he adds that he will never tire to repeat those words because they "take us to the very heart of the Gospel."

From this perspective, there is a close continuity, which instead many people deny, among Francis, Benedict XVI and St. John Paul II. The notion that Christianity is not primarily a doctrine or a morality, but a personal encounter with Christ, was Fr. Giussani's leitmotif, and his writings inspired the reflections of Cardinal Bergoglio, as he himself admitted more than once. Thus, because of my formation and my history, I cannot but find myself in deep and sincere consonance with Pope Francis. Then, sure, he experienced a personal encounter with Christ by assimilating the genius of St. Ignatius in the Spiritual Exercises. As a young man, I had the opportunity to know two great Lombard Jesuits, Fr. Giorgio Bettan and Fr. Luigi Rosa.[11] When I listen to the pope's speeches, I sometimes hear their style and their type of approach to problems once again. I also meet again, to be perfectly honest, the somewhat precept-heavy approach that popped up at the end of every homily during the Spiritual Exercises, the famous three points to be put into practice. I would rather like a stronger emphasis on the theme of freedom, which I consider fundamental for an education in faith.

Notes to Chapter 19

1. Walter Kasper (1933–) is a German theologian, bishop, and cardinal. From 2001 to 2010, he was president of the Pontifical Council for Promoting Christian Unity.

2. Mariano Rampolla del Tindaro (1843–1913) was an archbishop and cardinal. He was Leo XIII's secretary of state, and the favorite to succeed him in the conclave of 1903. After his election was nullified by the veto of the Austrian emperor, Cardinal Giuseppe Sarto (1835–1914) was elected and took the name

Pius X. One of Pius X's first decisions was to abolish the veto power that some Catholic powers had enjoyed. In 1954, he was canonized by Pius XII.

3. On January 17, 2007.

4. Instruction on Certain Aspects of the "Theology of liberation," *Libertatis Nuntio*, of August 6, 1984, and Instruction on Christian Freedom and Liberation, *Libertatis conscientia*, of March 22, 1986.

5. Johann Adam Möhler (1796–1838) was a German priest and theologian. An innovator in ecclesiology, he taught in Tübingen and Munich. Erich Przywara (1889–1972) was a Polish-German Jesuit philosopher and theologian. His thought, based on the notion of polar tension between opposites, exerted great influence on Balthasar; Gaston Fessard (1897–1978) was a French Jesuit philosopher and theologian. A friend of Raymond Aron's, he is regarded as one of the great political theorists of the twentieth century.

6. Miguel Ángel Fiorito (1916–2005) was an Argentinian Jesuit, and the dean of philosophy in the San Miguel Seminary attended by Jorge Bergoglio. Amelia Podetti (1928–1979) was a specialist in German philosophy and Peronist militant. Alberto Methol Ferré (1929–2009) was an Argentinian philosopher and political theorist. Juan Carlos Scannone (1931–2019) was an Argentinian Jesuit, a representative of the "theology of the people," and friend of Jorge Bergoglio.

7. "Polyhedron" is a term used by Pope Francis in his first apostolic exhortation, *Evangelii Gaudium* (November 24, 2013): 236.

8. Massimo Borghesi, *The Mind of Pope Francis: Jorge Mario Bergoglio's Intellectual Journey* (Collegeville, Minn.: Liturgical Press Academic, 2018).

9. The *Fondo Famiglia Lavoro* was instituted in 2008 by the archbishop of Milan, Cardinal Tettamanzi, to support families that suffered the consequences of the global economic crisis that started then. Cardinal Scola preserved and relaunched the initiative, adding professional development and microcredit components.

10. *Evangelii Gaudium*, 7.

11. Giorgio Bettan (1920–1994) was a Jesuit and homilist. He worked on the spiritual formation of seminarians and priests in the Archdiocese of Milan. Luigi Rosa (1920–1980) was a Jesuit, author, and expert on Catholic social doctrine.

CHAPTER 20

Free from the Outcome

Final Considerations

Pope Francis has put the Church in a state of perennial restlessness and constant mobilization. The Church is going forth. To where?

This expression, as is often the case with inspired and "viral" intuitions, sometimes risks being reduced to a vaguely activist slogan. However, for Francis, the Church that goes out is first of all "the community of missionary disciples,"[1] which sustains itself based on the personal experience of faith and is capable of facing all aspects of life. The direction is clearly set, as well as the destination. By accepting God's plan for each man's life, for the human family, for history and for the cosmos, we are going towards the Risen Christ. All of this is clearly spelled out by the pope, who likes to speak of enacting processes, but always from a Christocentric perspective.

However, what seems complicated is how to deal with the radical transformations we are going through, which have fragmented and weakened the person and society to such an extent that God's powerful and unitary design has been obscured. Conversely, we should take seriously the perspective of faith, showing all its cultural, social, and cosmological implications, as I already had the opportunity to explain during these conversations. This does not mean avoiding problems, contradictions and conflicts; rather, we are pushed to a decisive and courageous engagement, with the conviction that we are not alone but rather in communion with Christ, the Alpha and the Omega of the cosmos. Documenting and manifesting this bond—which is not an abstract principle, but a concrete experience of an encounter and a life together—means witnessing in full the Church that goes out towards the world.

The future of Christianity is intertwined with the question about the future of secularization. Will there still be room for the religious sense?

The religious sense will never disappear because the question about the meaning of life, which inexorably becomes a question about the mystery, cannot be eliminated from the heart of man. We can try to push it aside, like a bothersome thought, we can try to suffocate it, but sooner or later, in one way or another, it comes back. In the seventies, I lived for three months in Paris, not far from the Eiffel Tower, and when I went out, I always walked by what the French call a *terrain vague,* a lot covered with debris from a demolished building. One day, I was struck to see some tufts of grass sprouting here and there amid the piles of debris. Well, the religious sense is like those tufts of grass. It cannot be eradicated; it will always sprout again. This is true of everyone.

Then there is the religious sense as expressed in a religion. Theoretically, there could be as many religions as individuals, but normally a faith lives concretely in a social reality. It is precisely this link between religion and people that today seems to be in a crisis in Western society, especially in Europe, where Christianity keeps losing ground. I discussed this topic in one of my most recent works, dedicated to post-Christianity,[2] but with a question mark, because today there are still men and women who keep waiting for an Other to come and meet them. This waiting is what Christianity must enter into dialogue with. Our hopes for Europe, and more generally for the contemporary world, play out at this level.

If we look at numbers, the Church is destined to decline, except for the developing continents of Asia and Africa. Can we predict, in a not-too-distant future, a radical change of the social-cultural features of Christianity?

Just in terms of sociological analysis, the signals we are getting are somewhat mixed. By now we are used to saying that there has been a collapse of the Church in Europe, but Italy, Spain and Poland, for example, continue to display significant percentages of religious practice. In our country, Sunday Mass attendance is diminishing but is still above 20 percent. For sure, there are also countries like France where it is much lower. However, I recently read a small book by Jean-Luc Marion, *A Brief Apology for a Catholic Moment*,[3] in which he claims that the best aspects of the laïcité (secularity) that the French love so much is due to the influence of Catholicism, not to the radical secularists who exalt the laws of 1905.[4]

Regarding the center of gravity of the Catholic Church, which supposedly has now shifted to Latin America, also in this case things are not so simple. In the South American continent, we are witnessing a massive loss of Catholics due to the spread of evangelical sects. If we look at Africa and Asia, we see steady growth in the number of the baptized. But within the Asian continent there are conflicting phenomena: in South Korea, we have tens of thousands of adult catechumens every year, whereas in the Philippines, a traditionally Catholic country, Sunday Mass attendance is decreasing. So, it is hard to predict the future of Christianity in Europe and around the world. On the other hand, the history of the Church has been marked by ages of incredible expansion followed by long periods of marginalization and absence. Think for example of northern Africa, where between the end of the third century and the beginning of the fourth there were scores of monasteries, while today (and for a long time, by now) the Christian presence is barely symbolic, except for the Coptic Church in Egypt. Or, to give a more recent example, think of the Catholic associations in Italy, a strong and expansive network of structures which was decimated by the events of 1968.

This gives us great serenity looking toward the future. Ultimately, the destiny of the Church does not depend on us. Instead, it is we who must live depending on the event of Christ, which the power of the Spirit reproposes to us in everyday circumstances and relationships. What will remain of what we tried to build we do not know. But instead of causing us anguish, this makes us immensely free.

Free from what?

Free from the outcome of what we do. The outcome is never in our hands. This is true of the individual, true of a group, and true of the Church. This statement is not tantamount to indifference, because it does not take away the taste and passion for action. However, it dispenses us from playing the victim and from complaints about empty churches or young people who turn their backs on us, and so on. We are brought back to the origin of our initiative, what generated it, because the source of the energy that sustains our actions lies there, not in the outcome, which may or may not work out.

I must say that this reminder to be free from the outcome, which I emphasized throughout my episcopal ministry, was the most well received by the priests I met, in all the dioceses that were entrusted to me. I noticed that, in general, it provided them relief and peace of mind, and made their commitments more intense, regardless of what initiatives they fielded with varying success. As a rule, the initial attitude was the exact opposite. I remember an episode when I was bishop in Grosseto, where I used to urge priests to look for ways to dialogue with young people as informally and as openly as possible. When I insisted, a priest answered as follows: "Listen, I sent a letter to every young person in my parish inviting them to a meeting, and five showed up. Then I sent it again, but it did not have much of an effect. Enough, I did what I could." He had acted based on a plan, which had not worked, and therefore that was the end of it. But the task of educating young people in the faith cannot be reduced to one initiative, which then is quickly filed away. It is an impetus of life which the Christian, if he is truly such, carries inside, and which does not stop before a seemingly disastrous result. Being "free from the outcome" at its core means not to be prisoners of our own plans but to remain wide open to reality, which is always larger than our schemes. This seems to me precisely the direction that Pope Francis has chosen for the synod of bishops on young people which he has called for in October 2018.

Being curiously and boldly open to reality is the proper characteristic of youth. The pope already tackled the question head-on in the letter of preparation for the synod which he addressed to young people at the beginning of 2017. After citing God's words to Abraham, "Go forth from your country," he writes: "These words are now also addressed to you. They are words of a Father who invites you to 'go,' to set out towards a future which is unknown, but one which will surely lead to fulfillment, a future towards which He Himself accompanies you."[5] It is a fascinating description of what the word "vocation" means, which not coincidentally figures in the title of the synod, "Young People, the Faith and Vocational Discernment." Today, however, the "future which is unknown" scares us, and the biblical phrase "Go from your country" takes the meaning of prevarication, injustice, and war, the pope says. More generally, it is the very concept of vocation that needs to be relaunched, in my opinion, because today it looks more worn out and obsolete than ever. What has been lost is the awareness, sustained by faith, that life itself is a vocation, and thus the response to a call from Someone who knows the road and walks with us along the way.

In order to safeguard what you call "awareness sustained by faith," some people have proposed the so-called Benedict Option. It is an idea theorized by Scottish philosopher Alasdair MacIntyre and more recently by American journalist Rod Dreher.[6] It means small communities within which faith is preserved as the only form of resistance against general disintegration. What do you make of it?

I think that communities of this kind are providential if they stay connected with the existing ecclesial realities, particularly where they still have popular and vital roots. As a matter of fact, today, in many parts of the world, there are already small groups—but also large movements, with hundreds of thousands of followers—that witness to the beauty of the Christian faith and develop a counter-cultural style of personal and family life. We need to help graft these new scions on the old stock of the Church for a rebirth of Christianity.

Conversely, if the "Benedict Option" were conceived as a new model that must replace the current one, viewed as outdated and inadequate, then it would be a serious mistake. If this were the vision of its authors—that we should no longer concern ourselves with the Church in general as a large-scale organization, but rather build small communities to withstand the barbarism of our age—it would be a self-isolation project which contradicts the essence of Christianity.

Eminence, now you have a lot of time not only to rest, but also to study and pray. How are you living this time?

The "lot of time" part is not so obvious. When you get old, one thing becomes more and more evident—we live at the behest of an Other. There is no beating around the bush, this is the final stage of my life, the stage that borders on death and looks on to the beyond and thus, to a direct relationship with the Lord. I am experiencing the deep truth of what I used to say often to my priests but also to laypeople during the years of my episcopate. One is not mature in the faith until he feels pouring from his heart freely and spontaneously the cry of Psalm 27: "Your face, O Lord, I will seek. Do not hide your face from me." At the end of life, this invocation should become a constant entreaty. Unfortunately, I must admit that I am still very far from making it my own, every day, with humility. To get there, one must be able to look at death like St. Francis looked at it, calling it "sister." Because we do not expect something, we expect Somebody.

It is about a year now since you have left Milan and are an emeritus archbishop. As a retiree, so to speak, do you feel any nostalgia for the intense work and the all-out activity of the previous years?

Sincerely, I do not. On the contrary, I try to savor the good little things of my current situation. For example, something that makes me very happy is the possibility to enjoy some anonymity, after the very strong public exposure which I had to live with in Milan and already when I was in Venice, which at some moments really bothered me. It was so oppressive that during the last few years, I always spent my ten days of summer vacation in England, in particular in London where I could walk around, take the subway and drink a beer in a pub like anybody else. These small freedoms regenerated me, presumably much more than going to the mountains (which has always been a passion of mine) in some Italian locale where people would have recognized me.

To be clear, this does not mean that I am shirking my ecclesial responsibility, which has not ended because—and here allow me to correct your question—a bishop, like a priest, never retires. My priests always reminded me of that. From this point of view, I now have the opportunity to see the life of a pastoral community like Oggiono, where I have been welcomed with affection, from inside. I celebrate Mass in the parishes of the diocese that invite me, I hear confessions, I meet people who ask to speak with me; in short, I work as a priest. And I must say that working as a priest is very beautiful, and doing it again in a simple way, as much as I can, is a gratifying and joyful experience.

Furthermore, we must not forget that in the Catholic Church, cardinals have the task of supporting and accompanying the Holy Father. All the way to martyrdom if necessary, which is the meaning of the red vestments. Since 2003, the year of my appointment as cardinal, I have constantly been a member of various congregations and pontifical councils within the Roman curia—in particular the Congregation for the Doctrine of the Faith—which requires going to Rome. Working for the congregation requires a serious commitment, with regularly scheduled meetings which involve the study of a dossier on which one has to express his position in writing. I am also receiving a lot of invitations to give symposia, conferences, and lecture cycles in Italy and also in some universities in the United States and in Europe. However, in this first year when I have been settling down, I accepted only a few of them. Let us say that I am trying to get a sense of how much time and strength I have.

You mentioned that old age is a time for entreaty. If you allow me a very personal question, what is your prayer life like?

I often reflect about the fact that all the people who played an important role in my life—the popes I have known personally like St. John Paul II, Benedict XVI, and Francis, and my greatest teachers, like Fr. Giusssani and Balthasar—had the common trait of being men literally immersed in prayer. I always thought that, cutting through all the blather about the popes, one cannot carry the weight of such a responsibility without holding on to the Lord with all his strength. One needs this awareness in order to get up every morning at dawn and devote hours to prayer before starting the day, as Benedict XVI does and also, I am told, Pope Francis, or to stay awake all night as John Paul II used to do. I have seen this also in Balthasar and Fr. Giussani, especially in the final years of his life. In comparison, my prayer life is very poor. Besides the Mass and the breviary, I rely on reciting by heart the invocations and the traditional prayers during the day and the Holy Rosary at night. I also pray for my network of friends, living and deceased, by whom I feel sustained. And then there is adoration in front of the Eucharist in my little chapel, which however still struggles to become a real conversation with Jesus.

Once, you said that for you it is easier to pray to Our Lady. Why?

It is a complicated question. I hope I won't be misunderstood. You see, I always struggled, and I struggle still now, to have an affective relationship with Jesus, to say "you" to him. For many centuries, Christ has been treated in the Church as an asexual being, while we know that he became incarnate as a human being of the male sex. Thus, I strongly feel the need to turn to the Virgin Mary so that she can lead me to her Son. Praying to a feminine and maternal figure comes more natural to me. When I was little, I was struck by the image of Our Lady as a baby, what tradition calls the Child Mary, in a glass box on the dresser in my parents' bedroom. I retrieved it and now I keep it in my own bedroom. It is a sign that ties me simultaneously to Our Lady, to Jesus, and to my dead family, my parents and my brother.

Eminence, throughout our conversation I have noticed that friendship is a constant point of reference in your narrative and in your biography. Why are friends so important for you?

I have always been struck by that passage in the Gospel where Jesus, addressing his disciples, tells them, "I no longer call you servants..." To live is to share. I was a boy when I first heard this saying. This fundamental law of the Christian life has remained etched in my heart ever since. Who are true friends? Those who know each other, meaning that they know in depth the need and the truth of each other. In my life, a certain number of friends have been and continue to be very important, certain men and women, both married and consecrated. If they had not been there on many occasions to tell me—without deception, without adulation—"No, this is not going to work," and some of them also, "Try this direction, or try this other one," I don't know how I would have been able to stand.

I thank God for having had since my adolescence the gift of true and deep friendships, which have lasted over fifty years and are still fundamental for my daily life. Making a list of them would take too long. But I cannot avoid bringing up the friendship that has sustained my episcopal family, lived as a stable and nourishing dwelling place. I am referring above all to the consecrated people in *Memores*

Domini and the Fraternity of St. Joseph, who were joined, at different stages of my ministry, by Fr. Raffaele Muresu, Msgr. Gabriel Richi Alberti, and Msgr. Luciano Capra.[7] I am very grateful to these people, because they supported me all these years and continue to do so. They follow me and accompany me, taking care of me and guarding me. My episcopal family is in no way inferior to a family of flesh and blood. Many times over these years, I have stopped to think what it must have been like for Jesus to find rest in Bethany. The first answer that comes to my mind comes not in words, but in this experience. His experience must have been something like mine.

Notes to Chapter 20

1. Pope Francis, *Evangelii Gaudium* (November 24, 2013), 24: "The Church which 'goes forth' is a community of missionary disciples who take the first step, who are involved and supportive, who bear fruit and rejoice."

2. Angelo Scola, *Post-cristianesimo? Il malessere e le speranze dell'Occidente* (Milano: Marsilio, 2017).

3. Jean-Luc Marion, *Brève apologie pour un moment catholique* (Paris: Grasset, 2017).

4. On December 9, 1905, the French Chamber of Deputies passed a law on the separation of Church and State which established a strong form of secularity (*laïcité*).

5. Pope Francis, *Letter to Young People on the Occasion of the Presentation of the Preparatory Document of the 15th Ordinary General Assembly of the Synod of Bishops* (January 13, 2017).

6. Alasdair MacIntyre (1929–) is a Scottish philosopher. At the end of one of his best-known works, *After Virtue: A Study in Moral Theory* (Notre Dame, Ind.: University of Notre Dame Press, 1981), he famously advocated for "the construction of local forms of community within which civility and the intellectual and moral life can be sustained through the new dark ages which are already upon us." He added that this will require "another—doubtless very different—St. Benedict." Rod Dreher (1967–), an American journalist and author, developed MacIntyre's remark in one of his best-known books, *The Benedict*

Option: A Strategy for Christians in a Post-Christian Nation (Upper Saddle River, N.J.: Prentice Hall Press, 2018).

7. The Fraternity of St. Joseph is a lay association born within Communion and Liberation. It is formed by men and women who have decided to embrace consecrated virginity but, for various reasons, have not joined *Memores Domini*. Fr. Raffaele Muresu is currently the pastor of the Church of St. Felice in Venice; Msgr. Gabriel Richi Alberti directed the Oasis International Center from 2004 to 2008 and is now a professor in the School of Theology at St. Damasus University in Madrid; Fr. Luciano Capra was Cardinal Scola's personal secretary and is now in charge of the pastoral community of Cernusco, near Milan.

Published Works of Angelo Scola in English

Books

Test Everything: Hold Fast to What is Good: An Interview with Hans Urs von Balthasar by Angelo Scola. Translated by Maria Shrady. San Francisco: Ignatius Press, 1986.

Hans Urs von Balthasar: A Theological Style. Grand Rapids, Mich.: William B. Eerdmans Publishing Company, 1995.

The Nuptial Mystery. Grand Rapids, Mich.: William B. Eerdmans Publishing Company, 2005.

Let's Not Forget God: Freedom of Faith, Culture, and Politics. New York: Image Books, 2014.

Thou Shalt Not Kill: A Political and Theological Dialogue. In collaboration with Adriana Cavarero. Translated by Margaret Adams Groesbeck and Adam Sitze. New York: Fordham University Press, 2015.

Book Chapters

"Libertà, grazia, destino." In *Freedom in Contemporary Culture: Acts of the V World Congress of Christian Philosophy. Catholic University of Lublin 20–25 August 1996*, 127–44. Lublin: The University Press of the Catholic University of Lublin, 1998.

"The Integrity of Human Experience: Cultural Dimensions and Implications of the Encyclical *Fides et ratio.*" In *Restoring Faith in Reason*, edited by L. P. Hemming and S. F. Parsons, 256–76. London: SCM Press, 2002.

"A Style of Thought." In *A Generative Thought: An Introduction to the Works of Luigi Giussani*, edited by E. Buzzi, 3–33. Montreal: McGill-Queen's University Press, 2003.

"Freedom, Truth, and Salvation." In *The Uniqueness and Universality of Jesus Christ*, edited by M. Serretti, 1–5. Grand Rapids, Mich.: William B. Eerdmans Publishing Company, 2004.

"The Bishop and the Formation in Seminaries and Theological Institutes." In *Life and Ministry of the Bishop: Proceedings of the Seminar for the Bishops in the Mission Territories, Rome, September 8–21 2003*, edited by the Congregation for the Evangelization of Peoples, 215–28. Vatican City: Urbaniana University Press, 2005.

"Sexual Identity and Difference." In *Lexicon: Ambiguous and Debatable Terms regarding Family Life and Ethical Questions*, edited by the Pontifical Council for the Family, 907–14. Front Royal, Va.: Human Life International, 2006.

"The Marriage Between Faith and Culture." In *Ministering the Families,* edited by A. Chundelikkat, 10–39. Kottayam: Cana Publications, 2009.

"Christ, The Light of The Nations: The Church, His Spouse and Helpmate." In *Called to Holiness and Communion: Vatican II on the Church*, edited by Stephen Boguslawski OP and Robert Fastiggi, 17–47. Scranton: University of Scranton Press, 2009.

"The Whole Breadth of Reason: Facing the Challenge of European Political Identity." In *The Good Life in Common: Europe beyond the Crisis of Instrumental Reason,* edited by A. Pabst, 13–36. Venezia: Marcianum Press, 2011.

"The Good Reasons for a Broader Reason." In *The Whole Breadth of Reason: Rethinking Economics and Politics,* edited by S. Beretta and M. A. Maggioni, 25–31. Venezia: Marcianum Press, 2012.

"Taking in the Real: Human Beings and the Earth." In *Protecting Nature, Saving Creation,* edited by P. Gagliardi, A. M. Reijnen, and P. Valentini, 19–26. New York: Palgrave Macmillan, 2013.

Journal Articles and Contributions

"Nature and Grace in Hans Urs von Balthasar." *Communio: International Catholic Review* 18, no. 2 (1991): 207–26.

"The Nuptial Mystery: A Perspective for Systematic Theology?" *Communio: International Catholic Review* 30, no. 2 (Summer 2003): 209–34.

"Human Freedom and Truth according to the Encyclical *Fides et Ratio*." *Communio: International Catholic Review* 26, no. 3 (1999): 486–509.

"The Unity of Love and the Face of Man: An Invitation to Read *Deus caritas est*." *Communio: International Catholic Review* 33, no. 3 (2006): 316–45.

"Divine Law and Contemporary Culture." *International Journal for the Study of the Christian Church* 9, no. 2 (May 2009): 79–94.

"The Light of Moral Insight." *Journal of Law, Philosophy, and Culture* 3, no. 1 (2009): 71–85.

"The Garden of the Earth." *Second Spring: International Journal of Faith & Culture* 14 (2011): 10–16.

"The Good Reasons for a Broader Reason." *Rivista Internazionale di Scienze Sociali* 120, no. 3 (2012): 263–68.

"The Whole Breadth of Reason." *Humanitas: Christian Anthropological and Cultural Review* 1, no. 2 (2012): 46–49.

"Through Freedom to Truth." *The Tablet* (January 26, 2013): 11–13.

"The Nature and Scope of Religious Freedom in Our Contemporary Culture." *Communio: International Catholic Review* 40, no. 2–3 (2013): 317–33.

"Marriage and the Family between Anthropology and the Eucharist: Comments in View of the Extraordinary Assembly of the Synod of Bishops on the Family." *Communio: International Catholic Review* 41, no. 2 (2014): 208–25.

Index of Names

Mann, Thomas, 146

Manuel Paleologus, Emperor, 172

Manzoni, Alessandro, 83, 90n8, 139, 144n6

Marion, Jean-Luc, 3, 11n3, 71, 75n15, 169, 179, 232, 238n3

Maritain, Jacques, 1, 48, 83, 90n9, 96, 126

Martini, Card. Carlo Maria, 147, 152n2, 198–200, 210

Martini, Marco, 46

Maverna, H.E. Mons. Luigi, 36, 41n13

Mazzolari, Fr. Primo, 17, 22n7

Médina Estévez, Card. Jorge, 72, 76n18

Meisner, Card. Joachim, 135n8, 171

Melina, Mons. Livio, 95, 103n8, 127

Metalli, Alver, 71, 76n16

Methol Ferré, Alberto, 223, 228n6

Milani, Fr. Lorenzo, 17, 22n7

Mohammed, 162

Möhler, Johann Adam, 223, 228n5

Montagnana, Rita, 21n3

Montini, Giovanni Battista. *See* Paul VI

Moraglia, H.E. Mons. Francesco, 151, 153n8

Moro, Aldo, 17, 22n6, 92, 103n3

Mounier, Emmanuel, 48

Mozart, Wolfgang Amadeus, 66

Muresu, Fr. Raffaele, 238

Musil, Robert, 19

Negri, H.E. Mons. Luigi, 46–47, 54n4

Nelli, Mons. Roberto, 114

Newman, St. John Henry, 62n2, 122, 150, 153n6

Nicora, Card. Attilio, 25, 32n6, 49

Niero, Mons. Antonio, 138

O'Malley, Card. Sean, 205, 206n5

Onaiyekan, Card. John Olorun-femi, 205, 206n5

Ouellet, Card. Marc, 72, 76n18

Panebianco, Angelo, 116, 188n14

Pannunzio, Mario, 19, 23n13

Paul VI, Pope (Giovanni Battista Montini), 15, 18, 21n2, 23n9, 23n10, 33, 35–36, 69–70, 75n3, 92, 103n3, 111, 123, 182n8, 183n15

Pattaro, Fr. Germano, 138, 144n4

Péguy, Charles, 48, 113

Peretti, Fr. Mario, 46

Pfister, Oskar, 79

Philippe, Fr. Marie-Dominique, 63n7

Pius X, St. (Giuseppe Sarto), 221, 227n2

Pius XII, St. (Eugenio Pacelli), 36

Pizziol, H.E. Mons. Beniamino, 152, 153n9

Plato, 193,

Podetti, Amelia, 223, 228n6

Poma, Card. Antonio, 36, 41n13

Popper, Karl, 148

Przywara, Erich, 223, 228n5

Index of Words